# Lights Camei

## Ethiopia Through the Lens of a Community Film School

by
Robert David

ISBN-13: 978-1518765353

Design/Typesetting (Interior): Chris Moore www.fromprinttoebook.com

Dedicated to

Adanech, Wonde, Selam, Fikirte,
Habtamu, Sintayehu, Kebe, Misrak,
Wubit, Saba, Teddy, Shewaddy,
Mehbratie, Carmela and Andrew

# The Man in the Arena

It is not the critic who counts, not the man who points out how the strong man stumbles, or where the doer of deeds could have done them better. The credit belongs to the man who is actually in the arena, whose face is marred by dust and sweat and blood, who strives valiantly, who errs and comes short again and again, because there is not effort without error and shortcomings, but who does actually strive to do the deed, who knows the great enthusiasm, the great devotion, who spends himself in a worthy cause, who at the best knows in the triumph of high achievement, and who at the worst, if he fails, at least he fails by doing greatly. So that his place shall never be with those cold and timid souls who know neither victory or defeat.

*Theodore Roosevelt, 1920*

Many years later, after the events told in these pages took place, the film-makers of Gem TV received the Special Award at the One World Media Awards in London. Sponsored by Channel 4 and The Guardian newspaper, they are hailed as the Oscars of developing world filmmaking. The Special Award is reserved for *an outstanding project working on the ground in the developing world where media actively has made a real impact on peoples' lives.*

# About the Author

**R**obert David spent the first half of his career working as a copywriter for advertising agencies in London. Like many copywriters who wrote a lot of TV commercials he moved into directing and later was accepted to do the Single Camera Drama Directing course at the National Film and Television School. He set up his own TV production company and continued to make TV commercials as well as corporate films and documentaries. About this time he started making films for the Foreign & Commonwealth Office and also branched out to become a freelance travel journalist writing for The Times, the Guardian, The Observer and The Sunday Telegraph. A chance encounter at The Media Trust, which puts volunteers in touch with charities with communications needs, introduced him to Gem TV, a film school in Ethiopia that was training young people from disadvantaged backgrounds to become community film-makers. He initially went to Addis Ababa for a couple of months to help the Gem TV film-makers produce a campaign of TV commercials to fight the spread of HIV/AIDS, but ended up living and working in Ethiopia for seven years. As well as working at Gem TV he also worked as a communications consultant for many of the international NGOs based in Addis Ababa and filming assignments took him and the Gem TV film-makers all over the country. Robert David now lives in Brighton where he runs creative communications workshops, writes travel articles, makes films and continues to return to Ethiopia.

# CONTENTS

# Prologue

The faces of the children were pressed so tightly against the floor to ceiling windows that some of their features were ballooned flat against the glass. School children in distinctive red jumpers and blue shirts pushed and shoved at each other. The sound of their excited screams and laughter was muffled by the plate glass.

The wriggling throng was joined by a gang of shoeshine boys. There was half a dozen of them and not one of them looked older than ten. In stark contrast to the school children, whose parents had sent them out proud in their smart uniforms, the shoeshine boys wore ragged shorts and dirty t-shirts. I wondered if they had parents. Each one carried under his arm a plywood box that carried the tools of his trade, threadbare brushes and a tin of shoe polish. One in particular had managed to fight his way to the front. Not bad, I thought, for a scrawny six-year-old. By the look of him I guessed he had never set foot inside a school and for all I knew the chances were he never would.

Behind the kids there soon gathered a crowd of men and women who towered over the children and shaded their eyes from the bright sunlight that beat down from overhead. They craned their necks to try and get a glimpse of what we were doing, looking like a row of tall poppies swaying in the wind. A couple of the women carried babies slung in shawls across their backs. They wore grubby looking, hand-me-down dresses streaked with grime, and cheap, bright blue, plastic shoes that had begun to rip and were falling apart. They couldn't have looked more different to the other women who wore traditional white, cotton dresses embroidered with crucifixes of gold thread, and shawls that were trimmed with vibrant colours and designs.

Another passer-by who had stopped to see what was going on included an old man dressed in an ill fitting, ramshackle, pinstripe, three-piece suit that looked like it had done years on the commuter run from somewhere in Surrey to London Bridge station before it had ended up in a charity drop bin in somewhere like Egham or Cheam. He leant heavily on a long, wooden stick that was nearly as tall as he was and was topped off with a crucifix wrought from what could have been silver or base metal. The woman standing next to him bowed and kissed his hands as he mumbled a few words of a blessing.

Men in shiny suits and smart shirts and ties also joined the crowd. They looked like office workers and could have been employed by any one of the hundreds of international aid agencies that have their head-quarters in Addis Ababa.

Over their heads and across the busy road I glimpsed a young boy herding a flock of twenty or so scrawny sheep. He risked life and limb by driving them straight for us across four lanes of traffic. From time to time he vanished completely from view and I feared he had disappeared under the wheels of the heavy goods trucks that ground their way through the choking streets in the direction of the port at Djibouti a thousand miles to the north east, and landlocked Ethiopia's lifeline to the rest of the world. But miraculously he reappeared running hither and thither as he struggled to keep his flock bunched together, hurling curses at them as he cracked a rawhide leather whip over their rumps. Somehow he managed to arrive without losing a single animal.

Finally, one of the big, red and yellow city buses made an unscheduled stop right in front of us so that at least half the passengers crammed into one side of it could get a good look at what was going on.

A film crew will always attract a crowd, but in twenty years of filming I had never seen anything like this one. We were on location at a cafe next to a busy road in Addis Ababa where we were shooting a TV commercial. The set-up was a simple one, a guy and his girlfriend chatting over a coffee. The cafe was one of the smarter ones to be found in Addis Ababa. The black marble topped tables and matching chairs looked as if the cellophane wrapping had only come off a few minutes before we arrived. Waitresses wore bright lemon yellow uniforms with matching caps and lace aprons, and a long, glass counter took up most of one wall and was stuffed with cakes topped with thick swirls of whipped cream, chocolate and brightly coloured hundreds and thousands.

We were about to go for a take so I wrestled my attention away from the horde peering through the windows and back to the job in hand. The director, Adanech, was a young woman, and like the rest of the crew was barely out of her teens. But what made them even more remarkable was that each one of them came from an extremely disadvantaged background, and some of them had been living on the street.

They had been recruited to form Gem TV, Ethiopia's first community film school. I, on the other hand, had spent the best part of the last twenty years working in the advertising business in London making TV commercials, dining out at the most expensive West End restaurants and hanging out in places like the Groucho Club and other Soho dives frequented by assorted fashionistas, Brit Art wannabes and talentless reality TV stars.

We had been thrown together to make a campaign of TV commercials to fight the spread of HIV/AIDS in Ethiopia. The problem was I had never set foot in Africa before, let alone in one of its poorest countries. I didn't understand the issues we were supposed to be addressing. I couldn't understand the language, didn't have a clue about the culture, and couldn't even digest the food. And I was supposed to be training *them*.

While I had been distracted by the sea of faces outside, Adanech had been busy. She had arranged her extras in the background and had roped in a couple of the waitresses to walk through shot carrying trays of coffee cups. When they were told they were going to be in the commercial, the first thing they did was borrow a mobile phone and phoned their mothers telling them they were going to be movie stars. The excitement died down and a hush descended on the assembled cast and crew. Up until now Adanech had issued all her directions in Amharic, but when it came to the technical aspects of filmmaking she spoke in English.

"Turn over," she called out.

The tape started to roll inside the camera. The camera operator, another young woman in her early twenties, was bent over with her eyes glued to the viewfinder. After a few seconds, and without lifting her head, she said, "Speed."

The actors visibly tensed, the waitresses exchanged nervous glances as they prepared to make their grand entrances, and even the crowd outside pressed up against the window and went quiet as everyone waited for Adanech to say the magic word.

"And," Adanech let the expectation build for a few more seconds and then in a clear voice said, "Jemuru!"

There is no direct equivalent of "Action" in Amharic. Jemuru is the nearest equivalent and I was to learn it means "start" or "begin". But this was the first time I ever heard the word. If I had heard it in any other context it would have made no sense to me at all. I probably couldn't have told you where it began in a sentence or where it ended. But in the context of what we were doing it made perfect sense. I didn't need to have it translated because I knew exactly what it meant, and in that moment I realised two things. Although we came from backgrounds that couldn't have been more different, we had filmmaking in common. It bridged both our worlds and no matter how fleetingly those worlds touched, when they did we were no longer African and Westerner, but film-makers working together. It unified us and gave us common ground. It made us equals.

The other thing I realised was that I had arrived in Ethiopia with all the preconceived notions of a typical westerner brought up on images of Africa being mired in poverty, war, disease, hunger, lack of education and corruption. I had been in Ethiopia only a short time, but long enough to realise that the country had more than its fair share of developing world problems. But what I was witnessing didn't fit any of those stereotypes. Here was a group of young people, many of whom had not benefitted from formal education and had been surviving on the street for many years, who had mastered a complex technology, developed a creative voice, and were using it to help others. When I heard Adanech say "Jemuru" it was like a firework going off in my head, I suddenly realised that what these young filmmakers were doing was shining a ray of light into my preconceived Heart of Darkness image of Africa, and that working with Gem TV would be my passport to understanding this fascinating and ancient country. I may have been the teacher, but I was the one with the most to learn.

ONE
# Live Aid Remembered

**B**efore I went to Ethiopia I had spent my entire working life in the advertising business. I started out as a copywriter, ending up at one of London's biggest ad agencies, before branching out as a director of TV commercials. Like most people in the business, whenever I met someone at a dinner party and the conversation drifted round to what do you do, and I told them, the reaction was always the same – did you do any ads that I might have seen?

My claim to fame was that for ten years I wrote all the TV commercials for The Sun newspaper. Under its maverick and brilliant editor, Kelvin Mackenzie, these were the heydays of "the currant bun" as we insiders fondly referred to the paper. Kelvin's outstanding talent was that he knew unerringly exactly what large swathes of the British public thought about any issue of the day. And he combined his reporting of it with a biting wit that was part Carry On film and part naughty seaside postcard. At its best The Sun was funny, strident, campaigning, and liked nothing better than knocking the self-important off their perches, even if, as in the case of a few footballers and TV celebrities, it had given them a leg up onto the perch in the first place.

But beneath The Sun's sometimes comic exterior beat a ruthlessly commercial heart. The Sun was also a product, and it made its publisher, News International, a fortune. Winning the circulation war against the Daily Mirror was the key to success in the market, and to that end News International was prepared to spend heavily promoting The Sun.

For long periods we would be knocking out TV commercials at the rate of one a week. They regularly featured the hottest soap stars or TV celebrities, the sexiest super models or movie stars, or the headline grabbing sporting hero of the day, or whoever The Sun thought would help them sell more copies that week.

We shot them in their millionaire homes, at exotic locations and in lavish studio sets that were built in places like Elstree Studios where they normally shoot Hollywood movies. I remember shooting a Sun Bingo commercial in Elstree a couple of weeks after Steven Spielberg had wrapped after shooting scenes for *Raiders of The Lost Ark*. There's a famous moment in the movie when the hero, Indiana Jones, played by Harrison Ford, lands on to the floor of a tomb that is carpeted with hundreds of writhing snakes. This was in the days before computerised special effects were as big as they are now and they had shot it for real. We were all very excited about following in the footsteps of the great Hollywood Director until one of the stage hands who worked there told us that after they got the shot they counted up all the snakes and there were three missing, and that a couple of them had been seen sliding through the ventilation grills in the dressing rooms. You've never seen a more terrified bunch of hair and make-up girls in your life.

When we weren't filming celebrity "kiss and tells" or exposing their "sizzling behind the scenes secrets", we extolled the "sexy slimming" virtues of the latest fad diets, revealed the "hottest" new fashions, and showed readers how to "spice up" their love lives, and always with a bevy of "Page 3 Beauties". This often got us into hot water with the powers that be that govern what you can say in TV commercials, especially on what they deemed to be on the grounds of taste and decency. One classic battle, one of the few we sadly lost, was when The Sun's marketing genius, a tough talking Aussie, Graham King, came up with the idea of "Win a week's fishing on the River Piddle". (And a very pretty river it is too in rural Dorset.)

In fact, competitions were a big part of The Sun's promotions strategy. Our commercials created 30 seconds fantasy worlds where readers could win their "dream car", or "dream home" or "dream" holiday". In one commercial we made practically every Sun reader's wildest dream come true and gave away a pub. The commercials themselves were just like the paper – brash, cheap and "in yer face". The rest of the London ad agency scene looked down their noses at our efforts, but we didn't care. While they were winning awards crafting mini-movies at a million pounds a pop, we were having a laugh and cranking out TV ads that owed more to Carry On films than cinematic masterpieces. And very successful they were at selling the paper too. So, for a large part of my working life, if it had appeared in "your super-soaraway Sun", then chances were I had made a TV commercial about it.

Having written hundreds of newspaper commercials, and worked with a number of highly talented TV directors as a result, I then moved into directing. I cut my directing teeth on corporate videos and then started directing low cost TV commercials. My years working on The Sun had taught me how to turn around fast paced, hard sell TV commercials on a tight budget. About this time I also started to make half-hour documentary films for the Foreign & Commonwealth Office. They featured positive aspects of British life and were broadcast in numerous countries all over the world. And it was also about this time that I signed up to do the Single Camera Drama Directing Course at the National Film and Television School. Although there is no substitute for experience in the film business, I thought I owed it to my clients to make sure I knew all the things you were supposed to do when you were entrusted with lots of their money.

Life was sweet. I owned an open-plan rooftop flat in Crouch End, a trendy area of North London popular with media folk. I drove a BMW and later traded it in for a classic MGB. I ate at good restaurants and had money in the bank, and then just when I thought things couldn't get any better – they did. I was approached by a media buying company who wanted to set up their own creative agency, and they invited me to become a partner in the new venture and its Creative Director. To have your name on the door of your own agency was every creative adman's dream. I jumped at it. However, the new agency wouldn't be getting off the ground for a few months yet, which left me with a lot of time to kill.

Previously, I had heard about an organisation called the Media Trust. Their leaflet told me that they put volunteers in touch with charities with communications needs. Here was an opportunity, I thought, to give something back before I dedicated myself to becoming an even richer and more successful adman. So I gave them a ring.

"We're having an open evening, so why don't you come along," said the pleasant sounding man I spoke to on the phone. "It's just a cheese and wine affair. We do it once a year to thank our volunteers and meet new people from the charity world."

The Media Trust's offices were in a featureless, high-rise office block not far from Euston station. It was a miserable, wet February evening and a gusting wind whipped the rain into my face with stinging force as I trudged towards their door, bent almost at right angles against the force of the buffeting gales. Once inside their large, open-plan office, someone pushed a glass of warm Chardonnay into one hand and a cold samosa into the other and introduced himself as being from the Trust.

"So what branch of the media are you in?" he asked me.

"Advertising," I replied, "I make TV commercials."

"Christ," he spluttered, "we don't get many of your sort in here."

It transpired that most of the volunteers who worked for the Media Trust came from the ranks of journalism and TV documentaries – adland obviously not being that well known for its sense of altruism.

I wandered about for a while trying to make polite conversation. Most of the people were from small UK charities looking for help with fundraising. I noticed a TV monitor in a far corner of the room. The footage was like nothing I had ever seen before. The most striking faces looked out at me from the screen. They were obviously African but that was as much as I could tell. The images depicted a world of choking city streets in some far off, sun scorched land, and the language the people spoke was unlike any I had ever heard before, both guttural and melodic at the same time.

"Hello," said a smartly dressed woman who had materialised at my side, jolting me out of my reverie. Sharp, intelligent eyes peered up at me through large framed glasses. She was English but her accent was hard to place.

"Pretty amazing," I said nodding at the screen.

"Yes, it's an incredible country," she replied. "Have you been to Ethiopia?"

"No," I replied, before adding, "is that where you're from?"

"Yes, I've lived there for over twenty years," she said.

"So what's this footage all about?" I asked.

"I run a community film school in Ethiopia," she explained, "we took twelve young people from poor and disadvantaged families, including kids who had been living on the street, and we're training them to become filmmakers. The idea is to give them a start in life, but also to get them to make films that will help other people in the country."

She introduced herself as Dr Carmela Green-Abate and went on to give me the full story. The film school was called Gem TV, and it was part of a larger organisation she ran called the Ethiopian Gemini Trust. Carmela told me that Gem TV had been founded by a freelance TV producer, Andrew Coggins, who had been sent out to Ethiopia to make a documentary for the BBC. But it was now part of her larger organisation, the Ethiopian Gemini Trust, which looked after desperately poor families with twins in Addis Ababa. They relied on volunteers to do all the training, she explained, and over the years the Gem TV filmmakers had been trained by various television professionals from the UK who had been prepared to go to Ethiopia and pass on their skills.

"We've had cameramen, sound people, directors and editors who have come out," she said. At first, everyone we talked to, donors and people like that, said we were mad, it couldn't be done," she continued, "and they've nearly been proved right on more than one occasion. It's been a real struggle to get this far."

"So what sort of films do you make?" I asked.

"We've pretty much been concentrating on the training side of things up to now, but over the last year or so we've started making films for some of the NGOs in Addis."

"NGOs?" I enquired, revealing my ignorance of all things developing world.

"Non-government organisations," explained Carmela, "charities and aid agencies like Oxfam and Unicef."

"I didn't think people had televisions in Ethiopia," I said.

"It's not so much for television, more what we call "Videos on Wheels". We make films in remote parts of Ethiopia, using local people as actors. Then the films are driven to villages and shown with a generator on the back of a pick-up truck. It's not unusual for a whole village to stand under the shade of an acacia tree watching one of our films. Then a trained discussion leader will get the audience to discuss the issues raised in the film, sometimes separating the women from the men so they can talk more freely."

As I listened to Carmela I kept one eye on the screen as a montage of colourful images flickered past. I saw farmers ploughing with oxen against dramatic mountain backdrops, village markets thronging with people and village schools that were no more than one room shacks, and where the rapt attention on the faces of the children was plain to see. The people were obviously poor, but all of the faces I saw were strikingly handsome. I was intrigued.

"So what brings you here tonight?" asked Carmela.

"I'm just here to find out a bit more about them," I replied. "To be honest I don't seem to be the kind of person they're looking for. And you?"

"Well, I'm visiting my mother who lives in Primrose Hill. She's not been well. The Media Trust has helped us before with volunteers so I thought I may as well come along tonight on the off chance really."

"Well, good luck with it all," I said, as I made to move away.

"And what is it you do exactly?" she asked.

"Oh, I work in advertising. I make TV commercials."

"Really," she said with a hint of a smile, "well wouldn't you know it."

"I beg your pardon?"

"It just so happens we've been asked to make a series of TV commercials for Ethiopian television to promote condom use. It's part of a big effort to fight the spread of HIV/AIDS. The problem is we've never made a TV commercial before and I'm here on the off chance that I can find a volunteer to come out and show us how to do it." She let that sink in for a few moments, and then added, "Got any plans for the immediate future?"

The only image I had of Ethiopia was the one that had been defined by the TV footage of drought and famine that accompanied Michael Buerk's reports for the BBC at the time of the great famine of 1984. Night after night I watched people wasting away in front of my eyes. The images of the children teetering between life and death were the most affecting. Their eyes stared out at me from my television screen: empty, bewildered and questioning; framed by clusters of flies they didn't have the strength to brush away. Those images were so shocking they seared themselves into the consciousness of all who saw them.

Even so, normal life soon reclaimed us, compassion fatigue set in and the news agenda shifted to some other sad story in some other distant corner of the world. Ethiopia's starving were quickly forgotten. But some people did not forget, and two of those who didn't were Bob Geldof and Midge Ure. They were angry. But they were different. They turned their anger into action.

Saturday, 13th July, 1985 was a hot sunny day in Crouch End. But it began for me with a cracking hangover. The day before had been a total write-off. For weeks, Hugh, my producer and I had been churning out

Sun commercials at a rate of knots, one after the other. The last couple of months had flashed by in a blur of script meetings, castings, reccies, shoots and late-night edits that often ended in the early hours with discarded pizza boxes and empty beer cans littering the edit suite floor. It had been eight weeks of lots of pressure and little sleep, but it was fun, and we both thrived on it. Hugh was the consummate commercials producer. Always on the phone juggling schedules, camera crews, set builds, costume designers, agents and music composers, whatever the job threw at Hugh it disappeared into a bottomless pit of calmness and efficiency. When Kipling wrote, "If you can keep your head while all around are losing theirs and blaming it on you..." he must have had a Raj civil servant equivalent of Hugh in mind. Of course, the person who benefitted most from Hugh's unflappable talents was me. Whatever outlandish idea I came up with, if it was a hair's breadth this side of just about possible to organise in time, Hugh took it as a matter of professional pride never to fail to deliver. When The Sun launched a new cash prize game called "Crock of Gold", I came up with idea of a shot of piles of bank notes protected by a live Guard Croc with a gold chain round its neck. Hugh tracked down a crocodile, got a chain made and had a special studio set built for it in a couple of days.

If Hugh was the most "laid-back" man in the business, he met his opposite number in Tricia, a fiery Australian who worked for the TV ad watchdogs, and who was without doubt the most "up front" woman. Fortunately, it was a case of opposites attracting and they worked very well together. As the last six weeks had been particularly bruising with lots of negotiations over taste and decency and the like, Hugh and I had invited Tricia out to lunch. The restaurant was called Rue Saint Jacques in Charlotte Street, just across the road from the White Tower, which is where Rupert Murdoch held court whenever he was in town.

We met at 12.30 and emerged eight hours later having consumed some of the most expensive food served in London at the time, and copious bottles of heinously expensive wine. In a single lunch we managed to notch up a bill that was more than my secretary's monthly salary. Such was the advertising business in the eighties. So the next day, nursing a throbbing head, I met up with some friends for a barbecue and to watch Live Aid on TV.

The concerts were broadcast simultaneously from Wembley Stadium and Philadelphia. The Wembley concert began with an aerial shot of the stadium, packed to capacity with a crowd of over 70,000 young, happy music fans looking forward to one of the days of their lives. An announcer's voice rang out, "It's twelve noon in London, seven a.m. in Philadelphia, and around the world it's time for Live Aid." A huge cheer went up from the crowd and as the announcement faded away Princess Diana and Prince Charles emerged to take their seats. She wore a white and pale blue floaty number while Charles looked glaringly out of place in a dark, double-breasted suit. What made the heir to the throne look even more incongruous was that they were escorted to their seats by the man himself, Bob Geldof, who was more suitably attired for the biggest rock concert of all time in jeans and a denim jacket. The band of the Coldstream Guards commanded centre stage and announced the royal couple's arrival with a trumpet fanfare, which Geldof had the good grace to applaud.

Status Quo opened the concert with *Rocking All Over The World*. Francis Rossi and Rick Parfitt launched into the song with their trade mark guitar swinging stomp. As one, the audience exploded into a gyrating sea of bodies. No one at Wembley, or watching at home on TV, could have guessed how prophetic that choice of opening number would prove to be.

People knew about the famine in Ethiopia, but that wasn't really why they came. They had come to be part of the greatest rock concert of all time. It was the same for the couple of hundred million watching all over the world. Live Aid was our Woodstock. In the leafy North London suburb of Crouch End, as the steaks sizzled on the barbecue and the first cold beer began to work its "hair of the dog" magic.

The full impact of Live Aid took a while to sink in. First it had to build. Quo were followed by The Style Council, and then Bob Geldof and The Boomtown Rats. Headline bands followed one another like a rock factory production line as the warm afternoon stretched into early evening: Ultravox, Spandau Ballet, Elvis Costello, Sade, Sting, Phil Collins, Bryan Ferry, U2, Dire Straits and many more.

Then Queen came on stage. They were a controversial inclusion in the line up, having recently broken ranks with other rock bands and played concerts in apartheid dominated South Africa. Many of the bands thought they didn't deserve to play at Live Aid. If these concerns worried their flamboyant lead singer, Freddie Mercury, it didn't show as he strutted onto the stage dressed in virginal white jeans and a matching torso hugging vest. Bob Geldof later said it was when Queen hit the stage that he summed up the courage to ask how the donations were going. He didn't like the answer he was given and stormed off to the BBC's commentary box high above the Wembley arena. He was walking along the gantry when he looked out and saw 70,000 people clapping in unison along with Freddie Mercury to *Radio GaGa*. The sound of the crowd's short, sharp clapping – SHEE-SHEE – which accompanied the song would become the audio sound bite of Live Aid, and Freddie Mercury's performance that night would confer on him legendary rock icon status.

Geldof was momentarily transfixed as Freddie Mercury conducted 70,000 people effortlessly and the SHEE-SHEEs of the crowd's synchronised clapping became a rolling wall of thunder fuelling his anger. He later recalled that the moment was "extraordinary". Fired up, he stormed into the BBC's commentary box, interrupted a live interview with Billy Connolly, and took over. Speaking directly to camera he said, "You've got to get on the phone and take the money out of your pocket. Don't go to the pub tonight. Please stay in and give us the money. There are people dying now." He banged his fist on the table. "So give me the money. Here's the numbers."

He was about to read out the phone numbers when the presenter interrupted him and said they should read out the addresses first for people to send cheques. Bob was having none of it.

"Fuck the addresses, let's get the numbers," pleaded an impassioned Geldof.

Swigging our beers, we laughed out loud. I had never heard anyone say "fuck" on television before, and certainly not on the BBC. Even so, none of us thought to donate. After all, this was a rock concert, this was supposed to be entertainment.

Not long later David Bowie came on stage. He sang *Rebel Rebel, Modern Love* and finished his set with *Heroes*. As his voice faded with "We can be heroes, just for one day," little did we realise that the tipping point was about to be reached. Bowie grabbed the microphone on stage and said, "I'd like to introduce a video made by CBC television." He paused for a moment as if unsure what to say next. Then he said, "The subject speaks for itself." It remains one of the most moving and powerful pieces of television ever broadcast. It was a pop video, but like nothing we had ever seen before. The song was *Drive* by The Cars.

As the lyrics swelled, footage opened with daybreak on the desolate plains surrounding Korem in northern Ethiopia. We watched as a young boy woke up to face another day. He had matchstick limbs, his stomach was distended and he moved painfully slowly. His father sat behind him on the ground wrapped in a dirty blanket, looking on helplessly. Having seen the BBC reporter, Michael Buerk's, reports from famine hit Ethiopia some months before, we knew what to expect. Our guards were up. Or so we thought.

The video cut to a series of wide shots revealing that the little boy and his family were just one of thousands. The frame filled with people huddled in groups that stretched to the horizon. The video cut to close-ups of the faces of skeletal children lying listlessly in their mothers' arms. Breathing seemed to take all their strength.

The camera zoomed in on a very young child. It was impossible to tell if it was a boy or a girl. Famine had stripped those defining features away. What was left was a gaunt mask, pinched features etched in pain and misery. It was the face of a man of eighty on the body of an eight year old child in the last throes of survival. Then the moment happened. The child looked up and stared into the camera for a few seconds, straight at the millions watching all over the world. The effort proved too much and slowly, painfully, he lowered his head into his hands in a gesture of total despair. Young people, who only a few moments ago had been carefree concert-goers, stood in stunned disbelief. Faces crumbled. They broke down. They reached out and hugged total strangers. Later, many who were there said that moment changed their lives.

In the final shot a parent placed a bundle wrapped in dirty rags and tied with bits of string on the bare, cracked, sun baked earth. Slowly, the camera zoomed in to reveal it was the corpse of a child. As the image filled the frame, like millions of others all over the world I reached for the phone. As I pledged some money I didn't give the situation much more thought. After all, it was very simple. People were starving, they needed food and money was needed to buy and transport that food. So I gave some money. I had done my bit, my conscience was clear, and despite what Geldof had said earlier I still had enough to go down the pub that night.

But the whole issue of the famine and Live Aid wasn't that simple as it turned out, something I wasn't to learn until much later. Live Aid took place in a pre-hitech world. Mobile phones the size of a brick were the new must have accessory, and you carried them around with you with a battery that was only slightly smaller than the ones that powered your car. Not that there were that many other people with the things that you could phone up anyway. And as for text messaging are you having a laugh? Tweeting was something only birdies did, and only fans of Sci-Fi literature talked about the information super highway, which was how we referred to what became the internet. No, in 1985, the technologically advanced amongst us were boastful of our new-found mastery of the fax machine.

Yet, somehow, Live Aid managed to bring together one and a half billion people from across the world. Few were left untouched by the experience. Never before, or since, has the shared power of doing something good reached out to so many people across borders, faiths and cultures. The logistical achievement of staging and broadcasting Live Aid was simply colossal. Two live concerts were organised simultaneously in Wembley and Philadelphia. Over fifty of the most famous music bands and solo performers took part. TV stations around the world cleared their schedules and satellite hook-ups were established to cover the seventeen hours of live performance. It's been said that 98% of all the televisions in the world that day were hooked up to receive the broadcast, creating the largest ever community in the history of our planet.

After Phil Collins had performed his set at Wembley, he was rushed to Heathrow where he boarded Concorde to fly him at twice the speed of sound across the Atlantic so that he could also perform at the Philadelphia live gig. Even the space shuttle astronauts were put on standby to make an announcement. Little did we know it but Live Aid was the first hint that we stood on the brink of entering a globalized world, and that our first step was to help and do good, not make money. Live Aid didn't change the world, it did something much more important. It changed the way entire generations thought about the world and made us question ourselves about how we saw our responsibilities towards others. It also showed us how to express ourselves and demand action of those that hold the privileged positions of representing us.

To this day, debates about development continue to rumble around the marble halls of the World Bank and the UN, but now those arguments are carried by the echo of a guitar riff. Live Aid put the fight against poverty on the world agenda, changed lobbying and fundraising forever, and shifted the political world on its axis. Not bad for a bunch of rock and pop stars who showed us that if you wanted to change the world for the better, all you needed was a conscience and a guitar. Thinking about it I don't recall the international financiers, career politicians and diplomats getting off their backsides to do anything.

Live Aid certainly made memorable impressions on the people who went to the concerts, tuned in their radios or watched it all on TV. It had no less an effect on the people who appeared on stage too. Midge Ure from the band Ultravox, who together with Bob Geldof was the chief architect of Live Aid, recalled shooting an episode of *The Tube*, a rock TV show which also just happened to be presented by Geldof's then girl-friend, Paula Yates. Michael Buerk's famous BBC news item from the plain outside Korem which talked about the disaster as being like a "Biblical famine" had just been broadcast and everybody was talking about it. Midge knew immediately that he had to do something to help and had learnt a lot about the famine by the time he met up with Geldof. As he recalled later the only thing they felt they were capable of doing was putting a record together as a fundraiser. This became *Do They Know It's Christmas* which featured a host of rock stars under the name of Band Aid. The precedent had been set. The record was released on 25th November, 1984, and went straight to number one. It was the fastest-selling single of all time, and hit number one in 12 other countries.

Gary Kemp of Spandau Ballet remembers being in an antiques shop in the Kings Road the day after the BBC news broadcast. Geldof spotted him and came into the shop and as Kemp put it sucked the air out of the place. Kemp remembers Geldof being visibly moved and suggesting to him that they get a few people together like Duran Duran to make a record. Kemp said he was in and that was it.

Phil Collins was a little overawed by the whole Band Aid thing. He recalled turning up expecting to play something alongside George Michael, Sting, Bob Geldof and Midge Ure. What he encountered was a veritable Who's Who of contemporary rock royalty. He'd met Sting before and thought he was hip. Bono and Paul Weller seemed a bit unapproachable because they were cool and nothing like how Collins thought of himself.

But he remembers standing next to Bono at the recording and at the end of the song Bono was fantastic. They met many times afterwards over the years and were always happy to hark back to Band Aid. Not everyone was a fan of the idea at the time. Even Michael Buerk was sceptical. He had the stereotypical view of rock stars as being indulgent airheads lining their pockets and thought of them as creeps. Then he went back to Ethiopia a fortnight after Christmas and there stood eight Hercules transports packed with supplies standing on the tarmac. He was impressed.

The success of *Do They Know It's Christmas* had a galvanizing effect on Bob Geldof. He realised more needed to be done. He came up to Midge Ure with a drawing of the world looking like a plate with a knife and fork beside it, and the idea of putting on a concert. As Midge Ure remembers it this mad idea just grew and grew, and Geldof swiftly became something akin to a force of nature. Next to be roped in was the promoter, Harvey Goldsmith, who was a gorilla in the rock music business. An unperturbed Geldof steamed into his office and told him that together they were putting on a live concert for Ethiopia. Goldsmith simply wasn't given the chance to say no. Geldof, to his credit, knew no shame. He'd phone Elton John and tell him that Queen and Bowie were in when they weren't. Then when Elton John agreed to perform he'd phone up Queen and Bowie and tell them Elton John was in so they had better sign up as well. It was a high-risk bluffer's game. As Geldof confessed afterwards he was shitting himself because if no one turned up then 17 hours was one hell of a long time for his group the Boomtown Rats to fill on their own.

The day itself dawned bright and sunny but nobody really knew what to expect. For many life went on as normal, well almost. Noel Edmonds, the TV presenter who also happened to have a helicopter company as a sideline, had been roped in to ferry stars in and out of Wembley in his fleet of helicopters. The only place to put down close to Wembley Stadium was a cricket pitch about 400 yards away. Live Aid coincided with the climax of the local team's cricket competition and as anyone who knows the English can tell you, nothing stops for cricket. So the umpires were given whistles and every time a helicopter carrying an international rock star whopped-whopped-whopped into view the umpires blew their whistles and play was temporarily abandoned for a few minutes while the helicopter landed, disgorged its celebrity cargo and took off again. Whereupon play would resume as if nothing had happened.

Paula Yates had been charged with ordering a floral bouquet for Geldof's daughter, Fifi, to present to Princes Diana. Driving to Wembley that morning she realised she'd forgotten to order the blooms and had to stop on the way at a service station and buy a bunch of forecourt flowers. Fifi meanwhile wasn't too keen on the idea of having to present them to the Princess and had to be bribed with the promise of smoked salmon sandwiches. So when a smiling Fifi handed over the flowers, still bearing the price tag, Princess Diana was no doubt somewhat bemused when the little girl promptly asked her for more fish please.

Francis Rossi of Status Quo, who opened the Wembley concert, remembers worrying that you don't normally get a good vibe from such a large audience, but there was something totally unique about that day which he said he'd never felt since. Normally, people pay to turn up and see a show but this time he felt the crowd was actually part of it. Brian May of Queen was there from the start and was sitting in the Royal Box close to Charles and Diana when Status Quo launched into their opening number. He didn't envy them the responsibility of going on first but admitted that they rose to the occasion magnificently. A few hours later Bob Geldof came up to Francis Rossi and told him that apparently there were two billion watching. Rossi was grateful he hadn't known that when Status Quo walked on stage.

Phil Collins' big moment had arrived and after finishing his set he dashed to Heathrow where Concorde was waiting for him to whisk him over the Atlantic to the concert in Philadelphia. It was a normal, scheduled flight and as he collapsed into his seat he looked across the aisle only to see Cher sitting there. He'd never met the pop diva before so decided to go and introduce himself and tell her that *I Got You Babe* was one of the first records he'd bought. She asked what was going on and he told her about the Live Aid concerts being performed on both sides of the Atlantic. Cher's immediate reaction was to ask Collins if he could use his influence so she could sing a number or two at the concert in Philadelphia after they landed. He told her just to turn up.

The most poignant recollection of the concert surely belongs to Bob Geldof. It was only when he walked on stage with the Boomtown Rats that the enormity of what he and Midge Ure had done hit him. He'd simply been too busy throwing it all together to really think about it before. There was a moment when he pulled up short on *I Don't Like Mondays* after the line – *and the lesson today is how to die*. Geldof punched the air and recalls leaving his outstretched arm aloft for a long time as a hundred thousand people fell totally silent. He said that time seemed to become elastic, and as he gazed out over a sea of over a hundred thousand faces he said that it felt like he just stood there for hours.

At 5pm in the UK a transatlantic link hooked up the two concerts in Wembley and Philadelphia, and in that moment Bryan Adams became the first artist ever to perform simultaneously across two continents. His abiding memory is one of back stage chaos. As he walked up the stairs to the stage he was passed by Yoko Ono and then someone told him they'd found someone to announce him, Jack Nicholson. Tina Turner remembers stabbing Mick Jagger through the foot with one of her high heels during *It's Only Rock 'n' Roll*, and that they put the pair of them together on the cover of Life magazine. Phil Collins performed his Philadelphia set and by the time it ended it was like 5am for him so he left the show before the finale to go to his hotel and crash. But before he did he turned on the TV to catch the end of the concert. All the acts that appeared were packed on stage swaying to the music as they sang together *We Are The World*. Then someone familiar peering out from the back of the stage caught his eye. It was Cher singing her heart out. She'd just turned up.

Back in the UK people were making their weary ways home, and one of them was Midge Ure driving through the crowded streets surrounding Wembley Stadium. He remembers people throwing open their doors and inviting total strangers in for a party, something that simply didn't happen in London. But it did that day. Many years later when asked to comment on the legacy of Live Aid he told this story. A little girl who used to live next door to him told him that she had learned about Live Aid in a history lesson at school. She said she had been reading about it and that his name had come up. Midge Ure's take on Live Aid wasn't just the fact that there are people alive today in Ethiopia who wouldn't have been otherwise, but that young people's perspective of charity was changed forever. As he put it before Live Aid charity was something the Women's Institute did, but now all of a sudden our heroes are up there saying, 'I'm involved.

One person who didn't see Live Aid that eventful day was Michael Buerk who was reporting from South Africa where the townships were in flames. As Status Quo were getting everyone on their feet he was busy being tear-gassed by the police. But what he does remember is that even though the money raised helped save a million or more lives, Live Aid was to have a far more lasting effect forcing a change of policy in both the UK and the EU. Live Aid, according to Michael Buerk, mobilised public opinion and that was what counted.

But it wasn't just royalty, rock or otherwise, that were moved by Live Aid. The concerts had an equally impactful and sometimes life-changing effect on the people who turned up or simply tuned in.

One teenager set his alarm for 6.00am so he wouldn't miss a moment. He placed a cassette tape recorder next to his radio and recorded his favourite acts and continues to play them back to this day. For him, it was Bob Geldof managing to get the whole world to stop and listen that was the most amazing thing. That one man could pull the whole world together to make a difference became one of the most important lessons of his life.

A woman, who was sixteen at the time, was asked to list the three most important historic events that have occurred in her lifetime. She said they were seeing the space shuttle explode, the Berlin wall come down and Live Aid. Watching them all live on TV made her feel she was witnessing history.

A young mother recalled watching Live Aid on TV at a friend's barbecue. Her baby was just four months old and he was happy, healthy and loved. As she watched the harrowing footage from Ethiopia of starving mothers cradling emaciated children her heart went out to them. She and her partner had only a little money but sent a cheque for more than they could afford but, she felt, doing without for a week was a small price to pay.

For another teenager, 13 July 1985 marked another landmark occasion. It was the official date he left school. He and a friend celebrated by flying out to Hamburg on holiday. As they sat waiting to depart at Heathrow everyone had a radio on listening to Live Aid. When Status Quo came on nearly everyone in the terminal building got up and danced. Then when his flight took off the pilot flew over Wembley Stadium and banked so that everyone could get a good view of the concert, circled, and then flew off to Germany.

A couple from Newcastle were expecting their first baby and as Live Aid played on the television in the background were busy decorating the baby's room, a girl as it turned out. They kept stopping to watch. Nineteen years later their daughter returned from six months in Ethiopia where she had been teaching as part of her gap year.

Elvis Costello made a big impression on a woman in the USA. She remembers he strolled on stage with an acoustic guitar and announced that he was going to sing an old English folk song, and promptly launched into *All You Need Is Love*. She thought it was the greatest statement on a day that was about people taking real action to make a difference in the world.

The unsung heroes of Live Aid were the stage crews. Despite their best efforts the day didn't go without the occasional technical hitch though. One of the more embarrassing moments was Bob Geldof's microphone failing half way through *I Don't Like Mondays*. At the end of the UK show the crew were slumped on the stage gathering their strength before breaking the set when Bob Geldof walked by. One member of the crew, fearing a monumental bollocking from the great man, went over to shake Bob's hand and apologise. But before he got a chance to say anything Geldof grabbed him and hugged him like a brother and thanked him for everything. The crew member recalled it had been an extraordinary day and that he had been happy to have been a small part of a business that had done something useful for once. He summed up the feeling of many people who took part in Live Aid when he expressed the view that if Bob Geldof ever needed a hand again, he only had to say the word.

The lasting image for many people as they drove out of Wembley Stadium in packed coaches to all parts of the country was the sight of Bob Geldof dragging on a cigarette, leaning up against a wall too exhausted to stand up straight and with barely the strength to acknowledge the thousands of people shouting out his name.

So when Carmela asked me what I was doing for the next few months it was my own memories I had of Live Aid which came flooding back. It seemed another human tragedy was unfolding in Ethiopia, only this time I wasn't being asked to donate money, I was being invited to get involved; to use what skills and experience I had acquired since watching Live Aid to go and actually set foot in Ethiopia and try and make a difference myself, be it a very small one. I didn't really have to think about it. When life puts an opportunity like that in front of you, it's for a reason.

# TWO

# Early days

The ear-splitting roar of the low flying jet fighter made everyone on the street stop and crane their necks skywards. I assumed it was a MIG. Under the Derg, the military junta that ruled Ethiopia from 1974 to 1991, the Russians had bankrolled the military machine in Ethiopia. How much of the budget had been invested in pilot training was debatable though judging by this display. Each time the jet screamed in low the pilot tried to execute a victory roll, only to pull out of the manoeuvre halfway through.

I guessed the reason behind these attempted aeronautical sabre-rattlings had something to do with the news broadcast I had seen the night before on ETV, Ethiopia's state-owned television channel. The rhetoric it employed on reporting the war with Eritrea was always the same – well over the top: "Another crushing victory for the valiant forces of the Ethiopian motherland in their righteous struggle against the cowardly and evil Eritrean oppressors". The jet screamed in low a third time. This time the pilot got the wings to turn through an arc of almost 180 degrees before he thought better of going for the full 360. He straightened out, lifted the nose and headed for the relative safety of the wide blue yonder. If the Ethiopians were serious about concluding this war, I thought, all they had to do was get this guy to fly up to the Eritrean capital Asmara, and get him to perform a couple of loop-the-loops over the Presidential Palace. The Eritreans would be round the negotiating table faster than you could say "bi-partisan unilateral disarmament".

I had only been in Ethiopia a few days and I found myself in a country at war. Ethiopia and Eritrea had been fighting on and off for most of the last thirty years over a disputed scrap of semi-desert centred around a small town called Badme. The region was of no strategic or economic value whatsoever, so much so that the war had been described as "two bald men fighting over a comb". Over the last three years it had cost an estimated 75,000 lives and displaced a million people on both sides of the border. It was being fought with tanks, landmines and the sophisticated weaponry of modern warfare and at a cost of over a million dollars a day, and in a country where most of the people lived on less than one dollar a day.

As the drone of the jet receded into the distance Getachew appeared from the pharmacy where he had stopped to buy medicine for his wife. With a broad grin that showed his gold front tooth to perfection, he inclined his head and gestured for me to climb back into the four-wheel-drive. Getachew was my driver and had been assigned to pick me up from the guest house where I was staying and drive me to the Gem TV office. It was impossible to guess his age. He passed for what most Ethiopians would call middle aged, which wasn't bad in a country where the life expectancy for men was forty-four. Getachew was short, completely bald, and didn't speak a single word of English. The only other person I had met was my housekeeper, Ghidey. Gemini permanently rented a three-bedroom guest house in Addis Ababa for visiting volunteers. Ghidey cooked my meals, washed my clothes and kept the guesthouse clean and tidy. Every morning she was there preparing breakfast before I woke up, and every evening she was still there when I got home, putting the finishing touches to the evening meal.

I climbed into the passenger seat and Getachew edged the four-wheel-drive into the swirling current of early morning traffic. As we drove through the congested streets, a kaleidoscope of images turned within the frame of the cracked windscreen. Women at the side of the road hunkered down on blankets selling tomatoes, onions and bananas.

Other women washed clothes standing in plastic bowls, marching on the spot and squelching the wet clothes with their feet like winemakers, their grubby dresses rucked-up around their waists and their thin, pale brown legs stomping up and down on the spot. It was eight o'clock in the morning and the streets were alive with blue and white Toyota minibuses, which jostled each other for paying customers. *Wayallas*, young boy bus conductors, hung out the sides of the sliding doors drumming up trade shouting out their destinations: "*Bole! Guttera! Lancha! Arat Kilo!*" The gaps between their fingers were stuffed with *birr* notes of different denominations so that one arm always ended in a bulbous fist of currency that looked like a split boxing glove. White Land Cruisers, the bonnets and doors emblazoned with large, blue UN logos, glided through the traffic like elegant swans surrounded by ugly ducklings. As we flashed past side streets, I caught glimpses of shanty town shacks, their walls a hotchpotch of loose stones, the gaps between them stuffed with plastic shopping bags. Herds of donkeys stumbled under the weight of piles of hessian sacks of grain or mounds of firewood. Fruit stalls were piled high with mounds of pineapples, melons, mangoes and papaya. In the small butcher's shops, men in bloodstained coats hacked off lumps of meat from carcasses that hung on racks, their knives glinting in the early morning sunshine as they sliced through haunches of cow and sheep that buzzed with flies.

Getachew dropped me off outside a drab, grey building on a busy stretch of the Debre Zeit Road. I looked up and counted five floors. The downstairs was occupied by two showrooms displaying refrigerators and other white goods. What the women cleaning their clothes in the street would have given for one of the new washing machines, I wondered. Separating the showrooms was a door and a corridor that led into the building, guarded by an old soldier. At least I assumed he was an ex-military man as he was white haired, stooped and wore a faded, khaki uniform and a military cap. He leapt to his feet and saluted as I walked past him. Not trusting the lift, I walked up the stairs passing a travel agent's office, a catering school, a dentist's surgery, an import-export business, until, panting hard, I emerged from the narrow stairwell on to the top floor where I was faced by a pair of glass, double doors. It took me a couple of minutes to get my breath back. At well over 2,000 metres, Addis Ababa is the third highest capital city in the world, and even climbing a few flights of stairs seriously took it out of you when you weren't acclimatised.

I pushed open the doors and found myself in a dimly lit corridor. To my left came the rumble of voices talking quietly. Just as I turned towards it, the door at the other end flew open, flooding the corridor with a shaft of sunlight. A figure stood silhouetted in the doorway.

"Hello Bob, we've been expecting you. My name's Selam, welcome to Gem TV."

Selam turned and led me into a room which turned out to be her office. It had three battered desks and chairs, a computer of sorts, a printer cranked and whirred as it slowly pushed out a piece of paper. I'm sure mothers have given birth to offspring faster. And an office punch, a stapler, a couple of biros and a couple of bruised looking lever arch files completed the office equipment list. This was the nerve centre of Gem TV.

"I hope everything's okay at the guest house?" Selam enquired after inviting me to sit in the one decent chair in the office. This required no little agility as it only had three legs, the missing one having been replaced by a couple more stiffly packed lever arch files. I just hoped that no one was ever sitting there when Selam realised she needed a copy of an invoice from the receipts payable, because someone was going to take a flyer.

"Fine thanks," I replied.

"That's great, but if you have any problems you just tell me."

I warmed to Selam immediately. In her early twenties, like most Ethiopian women, she was strikingly handsome. Her hair was cut short and her eyes were large, almond-shaped, dark brown to be almost black and warm and expressive.

She had been managing Gem TV for three years, and I was to learn she ruled it with a mixture of efficiency, tenderness, warmth and an iron fist. Her word was law. She came from an educated, middle-class background and her English was faultless. She could easily have walked into a far better paid job at the United Nations in Addis Ababa or any one of the big international aid agencies, but she believed in Gem TV and what it was trying to do.

"So where are they?" I asked.

"They are having an English lesson," she said nodding towards the room at the other end of the corridor, from where I had heard the sound of voices earlier. "I thought when it is over you can meet them in there."

"Fine," I said.

While I waited for their lesson to finish I cast my mind back to a meeting I'd had a couple of weeks before I had come out. Before I had taken my leave of Carmela at the Media Trust, she had said there was one very important person I had to meet. His name was Andrew Coggins, and he was the man who had founded Gem TV.

I had met Andrew in the foyer of the Berners Hotel just north of Oxford Street in Central London. He lived in Fulham, and when I had spoken to him on the phone he said that the purpose of the meeting was to give me a briefing and a bit of background about Gem TV. Although I suspected it had just as much to do with him running his eye over me.

Andrew was a big, kindly bear of a man who oozed calm and reassurance. His eyes were kind, his handshake firm and his voice was mellow and was one, I suspected, he seldom had to raise. He had the natural air of a leader and I suspected would be the kind of man that would be an island of calm in a crisis. It may have been his meeting but I also had an agenda of my own. I wanted to know the Gem TV story from the very beginning.

"I was working as a freelance TV producer making documentaries," he told me, "when the BBC asked me to produce a documentary about Bob Geldof returning to Ethiopia ten years after Live Aid."

He went on to explain that he was particularly touched by the plight of the street children he came across in Addis Ababa, and when he returned to the UK was determined to do something about it. One of the ideas was to make a film about them that documented their lives.

"Then a very senior aid worker challenged me", he recalled, "and said don't speak for them – give them the tools to speak for themselves. It was a life-changing moment for me."

The idea of an Ethiopian community film school was born. Andrew then set about raising the finance for equipment, premises and everything else that was needed to get the idea off the ground. In Addis Ababa he heard about a British TV producer, Bill Locke, who was out there as the dependant spouse whose wife was working on a medical project. Bill teamed up with a local Ethiopian filmmaker, Alameyu, and together they interviewed an army of young hopefuls who all came from an Ethiopian NGO that looked after poor families with twins, the Ethiopian Gemini Trust run by Dr. Carmela Abate-Green. They chose six boys and six girls and immediately set about training them, the only problem was that not one of them spoke a word of English, so Bill would devise the training and Alameyu would do the translating. After nine months Bill's wife's contract ended and they had to return to the UK. Over the next few years Andrew was able to recruit various TV professionals including directors, producers, script writers, camera operators, sound recordists and editors to go out as volunteers and pass on their skills. I was the latest in a long line.

"If I may give you one piece of advice," said Andrew, referring to the immediate task at hand, "don't treat them as your crew while you're out there. Remember, you're not making your film, you're helping them to make theirs." He then went on to explain that the whole idea behind Gem TV had been to empower these young people to have their own view of the world, to express it their way in their films drawing on their own experience, and in doing so give a voice to other silent minorities in the country. In other words as filmmakers they had been brought up to be very independent. My job was not to take over and get them to make the commercials the way I thought they should be made, but to help them realise their vision of them.

Almost as if she had been reading my thoughts, Selam looked up and said, "You know Bob, actually we are very nervous about this. We have never had to work for a client before, and we are worried that we will look…" she paused as she searched for the right word, "unprofessional. We are not used to working with other people's ideas. Until now we have only ever made our own films. But this is a very important opportunity. We want to be an independent business and this is our first chance to prove that we can do that."

"I see," I said, obviously there was a lot riding on these commercials.

Then she brightened. "But we are so happy you will be working with us."

It seemed my challenge was to get a group of nervous, highly independent and opinionated young filmmakers, who had never had the discipline of working for a client before, or even made a commercial for that matter, to produce a TV campaign for national television.

"So maybe while we wait for them to finish their lesson you would like to read the scripts for the commercials." Without waiting for a reply, she added, "I have translated them into English for you."

I read them quickly, they were classic lifestyle ads featuring young, well-to-do Ethiopians. They couldn't have been further removed from what I thought life in Ethiopia was like. But I put that to the back of my mind, I had more pressing concerns. From our brief conversation it was clear to me that Selam's English was perfect, but what about the others.

"Selam," I said, looking up, "do they speak English as well as you do?"

"No," she replied, " they are a bit of a mixed group, some are better than others. A lot of it is confidence."

"Well in that event Selam, I want you to teach me some Ethiopian."

"Okay," a flicker of a smile appeared at the corners of her mouth, "what do you want to say?"

"When I meet everyone for the first time I want to be able to say in Ethiopian, "I look forward to working with you.""

"Ah, that's a great idea. I think they will appreciate that very much. But the language isn't Ethiopian Bob, it's Amharic, or that's what we speak here in Addis."

"Then I want you to teach me something in Amharic," I told her, before adding as an afterthought, "so what language do they speak out of Addis then?"

"Not just one language Bob, there are all together over eighty different languages spoken in Ethiopia. Amharic is the official one and here in Addis we are in the Amhara region."

"So do most people in Ethiopia speak Amharic?" I asked.

"No most people speak Orominia. The Oromo are the biggest group of people in Ethiopia, and they live mainly in the south."

"So these are the two most important languages in Ethiopia?"

"No, actually we have three, there is also Tigrinia. Tigrey is to the north and it is where the people who make up most of the government come from. Then there are many, many local languages all over the country."

"I see, but you speak Amharic because you're Amhara."

"No, actually Bob my family is Gurage." My head was beginning to spin.

"The Gurage people," she went on, "are very small, there are maybe a million of us, but we are all very good business people," she said with a hint of ill concealed pride. I was beginning to see why Selam was the boss. And I was also beginning to realise I was about to start working in a country, and in a diverse culture, I had absolutely no idea about.

"So what languages do the filmmakers speak," I said my voice betraying a rising sense of panic.

"Don't worry, they only speak two languages, Amharic and English, so you will have no problems. And what you say to them is: Kunanta gar messrat eh-fella-gallow."

Selam patiently took me through it a number of times, syllable by syllable, until she said I had it. I ran it silently through my head over and over again until the sound of the scraping of chairs announced that the English lesson was over.

"*Eshi*," said Selam, "let's go.'

"That's another thing, what's this *eshi*, Selam?" I had heard it a number of times already.

"In Ethiopia, *eshi* is the only word a *ferenji* needs to know.

"*Ferenji?*"

"Foreigner, and *eshi* means "Okay", but we use it all the time for all sorts of things. You'll soon get the hang of it. Shall we go?"

"*Eshi*, Selam," I replied.

I felt nervous walking into that room for the first time. I didn't expect them to greet yet another *ferenji* trainer with open arms and was prepared for them to be quite reserved, but what I wasn't expecting was naked hostility. As I followed Selam through the door the first thing I saw was a giant of a man who glared at me and held my eyes unblinking. Fortunately, he was a life-size drawing stuck on the wall opposite the door. An arc had been drawn from the top of his head to the soles of his feet and in neat felt pen someone had labelled it "Long shot". Another arc spanned from the top of his head to his waist and was similarly labelled with the words "Mid shot". And like the concentric rings of an onion smaller arcs had been drawn that segmented tighter framings of his body and were labelled with all the key shot sizes that are a major part of the film-maker's visual lexicon, from mid close-up all the way to extreme close-up. Not that I needed reminding because there was no mistaking I was in a film school.

The twelve young faces that looked up at me from the long central table registered expressions of mild curiosity rather than any malice.

They were six young men and six young women, and Selam introduced me to each one of them in turn. They had seen any number of *ferenji* trainers come and go by the time I had arrived. Some had stayed for a couple of weeks and some a lot longer. Some they had no doubt got on with well, and others perhaps not so well. I was just another do-gooder *ferenji* sent out from the UK so it was totally understandable that they should be reserved with me, not to say wary. As each one of them shook my hand, they also gave a little bow of their heads as they said their names. I didn't say anything as I wanted my first words to them to be in Amharic.

"So Bob," said Selam brightly after we had been round the table, "maybe now you could tell us a little about yourself and how to make TV commercials."

There was an expectant silence as all eyes swivelled in my direction. I took a deep breath.

"Kunanta gar messrat eh-fella-gallow," I said. Stunned silence. I had another go at it, more slowly this time, enunciating each syllable. "Ku-nan-ta gar mess-rat eh-fall-a-ga-low."

By now they were all wearing the same expression – total bewilderment. I shot a pleading look at Selam who was in an agony of self-control trying not to succumb to a fit of giggles. She gave me a quick encouraging nod to have another shot at it. This time I went for the confident, all in one go, rapid-fire delivery of the line, "Kunantagarmessratehfalagalow."

It was Sintayehu who caught on first. His features split into a huge grin and he burst out in a guffaw of laughter that made his shoulder length dreadlocks sway around his face, and which for a moment made him look like someone peering out through a bead curtain. The rest of them looked at him as if he had been bewitched by the new mad *ferenji*. Then he said something to them in Amharic and the whole room erupted as laughter bounced off the walls. Sintayehu repeated what it was he thought I had said, and each time he did so it was greeted with even louder hoots of laughter.

Meanwhile, Selam sat quietly at the back of the room beaming an encouraging smile at her new pupil, namely me. Finally, Sintayehu turned to me and in perfect English asked, "What were you trying to say?"

"What I wanted to say," I replied, "was I look forward to working with you."

"Ah, so you say it like this," whereupon Sintayehu slowly repeated the expression in Amharic, pausing over each syllable like you do when teaching a new word to a three year old. I repeated it back to him. He came at me with it again. I returned it with topspin. And we knocked it back and forth like this half a dozen times. This encouraged everyone else to get in on the act and I was soon getting pronunciation tips and advice from all quarters. Finally, I delivered the line to everyone's satisfaction and they burst into a spontaneous round of applause. I took a theatrical bow, spread my arms wide and said, "But heh, isn't that what I said the first time guys."

# THREE

# Turn Over

**D**awit drove a Mercedes that had clocked up so many miles the dial on the dashboard had clicked over to all zeroes. When he wasn't earning his living being a taxi driver, he helped Selam in the office. I say it was a Mercedes because from the outside it still looked like one. But lift the bonnet on any car in Addis Ababa and you'll find a complete hybrid of spare parts underneath – a bit of a Fiat here, a spattering of Toyota there. I viewed this as testament to Ethiopian ingenuity. If you don't have the proper spare parts, you make do. I witnessed it every day, from computers to construction. Adanech and Wondwossen, two of the film directors, and I were on our way to a pre-production meeting at Cactus, the advertising agency we would be working with. We would also be meeting the people from DKT, who were the clients.

Adanech, a young woman in her early twenties, sat quietly while Wonde, as everyone called him, talked non-stop and was keen to give me a quick introductory tour of Addis Ababa.

We headed off up the Debre Zeit Road in the direction of the city centre. It was mid morning and the temperature was nudging the high eighties. Dawit's Mercedes was built like a tank, but emerging into Meskel Square for the first time was like being inside a steel ball fired onto a pinball table. Meskel Square was a vast open arena into which most of the city's traffic poured. I counted ten lanes of traffic crossing in one direction, and another ten in the other. To my left stood a row of important looking office blocks, including the Ministry of Tourism. Next to it one wall of a high-rise was covered with an enormous poster for Ethiopian Airlines. To my right was a large open space where a dozen or so impromptu games of football were being played, and beyond them a series of terraced steps climbed up towards a wall of billboards bearing safe sex messages. Athletes, some of them wearing the red gold and green of Ethiopia, were in training jogging up and down the steps.

"Meskel means cross," Wonde told me. "And did you know that the true cross was found in Ethiopia?"

This was my first introduction to Ethiopian myth and legend. Much of Ethiopia's history is locked away in an African Dark Ages that lasted for thousands of years. In a culture where the oral tradition is strong, and where there are few official historical accounts, myth and legend plays a far more prominent role than you find in Europe or America. This is not to say these stories aren't true, however fanciful they may sound. To an Ethiopian they have all the historical validity of the Magna Carta or the Declaration of Independence.

As Dawit negotiated the streams of traffic Wonde told me the story in more detail. The True Cross on which Christ was crucified was found in Jerusalem by Helena, mother of the fourth century Roman Emperor, Constantine. She asked God to show her where it was to be found by lighting a fire and then following the smoke to where it lay. Hundreds of years later the True Cross was brought to Ethiopia by one of its kings. "We celebrate this," said Wonde as Dawit weaved the Mercedes through what was fast becoming a scary dodgem rink, "by burning fires. The people make a big fire with a big cross on the top. And when the cross falls the elders can tell what is going to happen in the next year. They know this by the way it points."

The last thing I expected to encounter in Ethiopia was a switched-on ad agency. Cactus's offices stood at the end of the Bole Road near the airport.

On first appearance their office was hardly what you might call inspiring, especially for a creative business. It stood behind a high, broken-glass topped concrete wall and had all the architectural design features of a bomb shelter. However, this atmosphere was dispelled as soon as I walked into their reception area. It was bright and leather sofas were arranged around a low table where a TV showed BBC World. This was more like it, I thought.

"We've been expecting you," said the receptionist, "I'll tell Selamawit you're here. Please take a seat."

The leather sofas made a soft whooshing noise as we collapsed into them, and while the others stared at the television I scanned the framed advertisements that lined the walls, examples of the agency's work. They were stylishly art-directed and included ads for Coca-Cola, Kodak and Mobil Oil. This was a client list any self-respecting ad agency on Madison Avenue would sell its mother for.

Moments later a young Ethiopian woman appeared wearing a dark, pinstripe, knee length skirt, with a simple but elegantly cut white blouse. Gold jewellery glinted discretely at her throat and wrist. She was slim and appraised me with kind and intelligent eyes. She oozed executive efficiency and when she extended her hand it was cool and firm. When she spoke, in faultless English I might add, her accent was mid Atlantic.

"I'm Selamawit," she said introducing herself, "everyone's waiting for us in the boardroom. If you'd like to follow me." With which she pirouetted elegantly and led us away along a corridor and into the agency's boardroom.

A long, wood, polished table dominated the centre of the room, surrounded by a dozen or more high-backed leather chairs. They weren't all empty. Selamawit, the consummate account executive, did the introductions.

"This is Baroo, he's one of our art directors," Baroo nodded a large, domed head. Next to him sat a young blonde English woman in her mid twenties. "This is Karen," said Selamawit, "she's working for us as a consultant." It transpired she used to work for a sales promotion company in the UK and was in Ethiopia because her husband was setting up a Guinness brewery somewhere in the north of the country. Then Selamawit introduced the two clients. They worked for an NGO called DKT, which specialised in what they called "social marketing". They were both Ethiopian and couldn't have been more different. Reyhil was a slight built young woman, and next to her sat her assistant, Joki, a man who was probably about the same age but whose physical build would have got him into the scrum of the Barbarians first fifteen.

The night before Selam had given me some homework to do. She had packed me off back to the guest house with a bunch of reports from various NGOs about the HIV/AIDS pandemic in Ethiopia. The big picture went something like this.

The first case of HIV was recorded in Ethiopia in 1987. That much they seemed to know. How many people have died of AIDS related deaths since then, or were living with the virus, it was difficult to say. Lack of infrastructure makes it difficult to gather accurate information. Many NGOs and government ministries had been forced to resort to educated guesswork, and the true figures were generally thought to be higher than the official ones. What was undeniable though was that HIV/AIDS was a devastating problem.

For many developing world countries the model is practically the same. HIV/AIDS attacks the adult generation because they are the more sexually active. They are also the economic backbone of a country making up the workers, the farmers, the teachers, the mothers, the carers. If they can't work because they're sick, or dying, then their families don't eat. There are knock-on consequences. As the adults, who are often parents of large families, continue to die so their children step into the breach, leaving school to look after younger siblings.

The level of education in the country takes a direct hit. The old are affected too. Without a welfare state to look after them, the elderly rely on their adult children to care for them in their old age. HIV/AIDS is wiping out that vital support. The young are another high-risk group. I read that in Ethiopia it was estimated that ten percent of all adolescents were infected. Girls in the countryside are particularly vulnerable because they are often the helpless victims of early marriage, which sees them being married off by their parents in their early teens, or even younger, to men many years older. Another cultural practice that contributes to the spread of the virus is Female Genital Mutilation (FGM). Described as a scream so loud it would shake the world, FGM is an unavoidable right of passage for millions of girls and young women. The "procedure" is usually performed with a razor blade or knife, which goes from girl to girl without being sterilized. Prostitution also spreads the virus, especially in the towns and cities, and in areas that saw large concentrations of the military. Often the women lack the negotiating skills to make men wear condoms.

Many people are malnourished and their weakened systems mean their resistance to the virus is severely compromised. As the AIDS pandemic tightens its grip and more people die the resulting loss in productivity hits the national economy. This places an even greater strain on Ethiopia's rudimentary health care resources. The Ethiopian government simply didn't have enough resources to put behind a programme of prevention and education or pay for anti-retroviral drugs. At the time it cost the National Health Service in the UK £15,000 a year to treat an HIV/AIDS patient. In Ethiopia the vast majority of people lived and raised large families on less than £250 a year. Being told you were HIV positive must have been like having your death sentence read out.

Aid agencies and NGOs were doing what they could and HIV/AIDS was top of most of their agendas. This in turn created a whole new set of problems. As more resources were diverted into fighting the spread of HIV, so they were diverted from other diseases, and malaria and tuberculosis and other killers were staging a comeback. It was a vicious circle. Having survived one of the world's most terrible famines, and the longest civil war ever fought in Africa, Ethiopia was reeling under yet another devastating body blow.

The aid agencies and NGOs were doing their best, establishing health care centres for testing, and spreading health education and safe sex messages at both community and national levels, and one of them was DKT. They imported, branded and distributed condoms and contraceptive products in the territories where they worked. In Ethiopia, DKT had created a brand of condom called Hiwot Trust. They had employed Cactus as their advertising agency and Cactus had written scripts for four TV commercials to be broadcast on ETV, the Ethiopian national television channel. Cactus had invited Gem TV to produce the TV commercials, and Gem TV, or rather Carmela, had invited me to help them do it. All of us were gathered around the boardroom table at Cactus to discuss how we were going to work together to produce the first two commercials and get the campaign on air. And, despite the fact that I had only newly arrived in Ethiopia, I soon began to realise that they expected me to have all the answers.

The first commercial featured a young, successful businessman. The action called for him to be seen in a business meeting, smartly dressed in a suit. Then we see him leaving a restaurant with his drop dead gorgeous girlfriend. Finally, we see him enjoying a night out with a group of male friends at a bowling alley. Similarly, the second script featured a stylish, young woman, say a flight attendant on Ethiopian Airlines, who we saw enjoying an equally aspirational lifestyle around Addis Ababa. The action started with her graduating from university, then we see her at a cafe with her boyfriend, and finally with a group of other young women working out at a gym.

The only contrivance in each of the scripts was that at certain points in the action, the guy and girl would somehow manage to "accidentally" drop a packet of Hiwot Trust condoms into the action. The underlying message in each commercial was the same. HIV/AIDS affects everyone, not just the poor, but that for modern, educated young Ethiopians there was no shame in condoms being a part of your everyday lifestyle. Both scripts ended with a pack shot of the Hiwot Trust condoms and the slogan – "Superior Protection. Value Your Life."

"It is very important," said Reyhill kicking off the meeting, "that the actors look smart and stylish."

In a career spanning nearly twenty years of making TV commercials, I have always found casting to be the most nerve wracking part of the entire process. So much depends on it. Props, set design, wardrobe, they're all important but if one of them isn't quite right with a bit of luck you can generally get round the problems. However, if your casting isn't absolutely spot on, you're stuffed. The other crucial thing about casting is the relationship between the actor and the director. It's the director's responsibility to get the performance out of the actor, so the director should have the final say about who gets the part. Many times before in my advertising career I have seen clients overrule directors in casting sessions, insisting this or that actor gets the part simply because of how they look when they can't act to save their lives. This has always led to fractious shoots, lousy ads and disappointed clients. So my first concern was how on earth were a bunch of ex-street kids going to know where to find contenders to be the next Mr And Miss Ethiopia. I was mid gulp when Selamawit chipped in. "We've worked with many of the top actors and models in Ethiopia for our Coca-Cola and Kodak shoots, so perhaps we can put together a candidate list for a casting session."

All the assembled heads swivelled in my direction. This seemed like a good idea to me but I was very conscious of the fact that this was really Wonde's and Adanech's call. The last thing I wanted was for them to go back to Gem TV and tell the others that I had just followed the client's lead and not stood up for the directors. I needn't have worried. Before I could stumble out an answer, Selam added, "Of course, the final choice should be down to the directors." I could have hugged her.

I looked across at Wonde and Adanech. "Does that work for you?" They nodded their agreement.

The discussion started off in English for my benefit, but soon lapsed into Amharic the more enthusiastic everyone became as they discussed the individual aspects of the commercials: the look of the actors, the dialogue, the locations, wardrobe and all the other small details that make shooting a TV commercial very similar to making a little movie. I leaned back in my high back chair and tried to look professorial as the quick fire Amharic rat-a-tatted across the table. Wonde and Adanech I noticed could not have been more different. Wonde was all passion and excitement and enthusiasm as he outlined his vision for his commercial, whereas Adanech was more thoughtful and reserved. But from what I could see they both possessed the director's passion for storytelling, and how to do it visually.

Just as we were about to break up the meeting, Selamawit leaned across to me and said, "Can our Managing Director have a few minutes with you."

Omar Bagersh epitomised a modern, international businessman. He wore a dark blue suit, a white shirt and pale blue silk tie. He came from a large Muslim family of brothers who managed a wide portfolio of business, including coffee growing, newspaper and magazine publishing, satellite television, restaurants, retailing and tourism. Omar seemed to have a hand in running most of them. His office was functional rather than flash and his desk was uncluttered and well ordered. When he spoke it was in faultless English and in the language of the Harvard MBA. Omar never had to raise his voice because people always wanted to hear whatever he had to say.

"I am very pleased to meet you," he said, getting up from behind his desk and extending his hand in a firm handshake, "we are very happy to be working with you. I'm sure we will learn a great deal from the experience."

It was becoming obvious to me that if there was any learning to be done, it would be me who would be doing it.

Back at Gem TV I suggested to Wonde and Adanech that we sit down and tell Selam what had been discussed at the meeting. That way, I thought, I might be able to find out what had been agreed.

I liked Wonde immediately. It simply wasn't possible for him to talk about a film without betraying bubbling, pent-up enthusiasm.

"We talked a lot about the actors," said Wonde, "how they should be young, not old, what clothes they wear, this sort of thing."

I turned to Adanech. "And what did they say about the locations?" I asked.

"They said that the action should take place in nice places, not poor ones," she replied.

"So how we do we go about finding the locations?" I asked.

"*Chigre yelem*," she replied. "No problem," Selam explained for my benefit.

"Okay, it's your city not mine, so I guess the locations are down to you guys, any ideas?"

For Wonde's businessman commercial we needed a boardroom, a bowling alley and a cafe. The action in Adanech's commercial called for a university graduation ceremony, another cafe and a gymnasium. The three of them put their heads together and a few minutes later Selam turned to me.

"For Adanech's commercials there are a couple of gymnasiums in hotels here in Addis. They'll also have meeting rooms which we can use as the boardroom in Wonde's commercial. The graduation ceremony we can shoot in the gardens of the Ghion hotel, which is where all the university graduations take place. And if we can find the right cafe, we can make it look different and use it for both commercials."

"Great," I said, "but what about the bowling alley?"

"Oh, that's easy," said Selam, "we only have one of those in Addis."

~

With Selamawit at Cactus and Selam at Gem TV co-ordinating everything between them seamlessly, the shoots went mostly according to plan. Even their best efforts were only occasionally thwarted by the Addis Ababa city authority. We would arrive on location, set up the camera and the lights, rehearse the actors and then just as Wonde or Adanech was about to shout "Jemuru!", there would be a power cut. The first time this happened, Selam explained the problem.

"It's the lake," she said, "the level is now very low."

All the electricity in Ethiopia was supplied by hydro electric power. Addis Ababa was fed from a large hydro electric power plant located at one of the rift valley lakes. We were shooting at the start of the rainy season, which meant that the water in the lakes was at its lowest level of the year. In three months time when the rainy season ended, the water level in the lake would be topped up again, but until then Addis Ababa was on electricity rationing. I had this image of the lake being like a colossal battery that was now running on empty and desperately needed re-charging.

The trick was to plan the shooting schedule around which areas of the city had power at any given time. Sometimes power cuts were announced, but more often than not entire areas of the city would be blacked out at the flick of a switch. These blackouts could last for days.

Power cuts aside, the only slight hiccup Adanech had to contend with was when we pitched up at the gymnasium we had found. It was on a busy stretch of the Debre Zeit Road about a five minutes walk from the Gem TV office, close to shops and government ministries. We arrived at lunchtime when it was packed with men from the local offices working out during their lunch breaks. As well as our featured young woman, the scene also called for her to be with a couple of her girlfriends.

The arrival of three attractive women had a galvanizing effect on the clientele. The men threw themselves into a frenzy of pumping iron.

Adanech sent the girls off to get changed into their gym gear and started briefing her crew about her set-ups. Five minutes later the girls returned in figure hugging gym outfits. This resulted in a blur of even greater activity from the men. Like men the world over, they believed their mastery of things mechanical was sure to impress. The girls knew the game and played it to the hilt. Whenever one of them got onto a piece of exercise equipment, she would crook a finger and half a dozen would be bowled over in the stampede to help her adjust it. By the time we had set up the camera and lit the scene, it was impossible to see the girls because they were obscured by hordes of men pushing buttons, adjusting weights and lowering the heights of seats. When she was ready to go for a take, Adanech waded in barking orders like a sledge driver trying to separate a pack of snarling huskies. Eventually, she managed to clear the shot. But every time she shouted "Cut!" the pantomime would start all over again.

The shooting of Wonde's commercial went smoothly and the most interesting location was the bowling alley. The interior looked like the kind of bowling alley you would find in a shopping mall in America, just a bit more run down. But beneath the veneer it worked very differently. Instead of a machine automatically placing the pins at the end of the lane, a little man hung in a hammock above them, out of sight, and did the job by hand. Each time our man rolled a bowl down the lane and knocked over a few pins, a little arm would appear and lift them out. Then he would arrange all ten pins in a perfect pyramid for the next player. It was like watching something out of the Flintstones.

Both shoots had gone well and Karen asked me if I'd like to go to a party on Saturday night.

"One of the girls from the American embassy is throwing it," she said before adding, "actually she's quite high up. Anyway, Chris Purdy will be there and it'll be a good opportunity for you to meet him." I had heard a lot about Chris Purdy, he ran DKT in Ethiopia.

I agreed to meet Karen and her husband, another Chris, at Stanley's bar in the Sheraton for a drink first. "This is Sheraton," my taxi driver told me proudly as we emerged from a side street to be greeted by a high, forbidding looking brick wall. I busied myself to pay the man but I needn't have bothered, it was a further five minutes drive before we got to the entrance. The Sheraton sits in the middle of Addis Ababa like the Forbidden City in Beijing. As we drove along its perimeter wall I looked up and saw satellite dishes pointing skywards and searchlight beams criss-crossed the night sky. At the main gate two flunkies in heavily brocaded velvet capes waved my little blue and white Addis Ababa taxi to a halt and eyed it suspiciously. But not as suspiciously as the two armed guards who stood behind them with very serious looking Kalashnikovs slung over their shoulders. They were more used to waving through four-wheel-drives with UN logos emblazoned on their bonnets and doors, or gleaming BMWs with diplomatic plates. They barked a few words of Amharic at my taxi driver who nervously pointed at me in reply, repeating, "*Ferenji! Ferenji!*". However, we still weren't allowed through until the driver had opened up the boot for their inspection and one of the armed guards had checked for explosive devices under the car with a shaving mirror tied to a long stick.

We drove into the Sheraton down a long tarmac driveway, the only stretch of un-pockmarked road I had come across in Addis Ababa. We drove past a fountain that suddenly erupted in choreographed explosions of water, which shot up into the air in sync with a display of changing coloured lights. It played music too. Burning braziers threw out a golden glow rendering the features of the facade in a flattering, soft light. A grand portico jutted out from the building and a red carpet led through twelve feet high doors into the main reception area. Flunkies tripped over themselves in their haste to be the one to open my car door. A spotlessly clean, white, gloved hand wrestled with the handle for a few moments and wrenched open the door for me. Only momentarily did his expression slip when he betrayed himself with a look that seemed to say, how on earth did *that* get in here.

If the Sheraton was plucked from Addis Ababa and dropped somewhere on the Las Vegas strip, it wouldn't look out of place. So what was it doing in the middle of one of Africa's poorest countries, I wondered. Like many people new to Ethiopia my first impression of the Sheraton was all wrong. Many NGO and aid workers hated the place, finding its swaggering opulence an affront. This was an easy impression to have, especially when you realised that yards from the perimeter walls the shanty town began. But they didn't get it. It wasn't the Sheraton that was the eyesore, it was the hovels that surrounded it. If you talked to an Ethiopian about the Sheraton you got a very different picture. They were very proud of the place. It showed the rest of the world that Ethiopians could run a first class, international facility, one that boasted the highest standards of quality and service in a highly competitive industry. For four years running, the Sheraton had won the award for being the "Most Luxurious Hotel in Africa". It was a model employer and helped to set standards of employment for other businesses in Addis Ababa. Getting a job there was like winning the lottery. And it spawned a lot of other businesses servicing its needs: laundries, and farms outside the city that grew only organic produce for its kitchens. I thought what Ethiopia needed was more places like the Sheraton, not fewer.

Inside the floor was like an ice rink of polished pink marble. Liveried attendants glided to and fro, or sat behind antique desks helping guests with directions. I spotted Selamawit sitting with a group of friends. She caught my eye and beckoned me over. Rising to greet me she introduced me to her fiancé, a tall, aristocratic looking Ethiopian who worked for the French news service Agence France Presse. Friday nights at the Sheraton was where the Ethiopian professional elite hung out.

Stanley's bar was all rich brown mahogany, ankle deep carpets and crystal chandeliers. I managed to climb onto one of the tall, wooden barstools without having to ask a passing waiter for a leg up. I ordered a cold beer, which moments later arrived in a cut-glass tumbler that made a satisfying thud as it was placed on the bar in front of me. A few minutes later Karen and her husband, Chris, arrived. They would be leaving soon, the Guinness brewery was nearly complete. "As soon as the first bottles of Guinness roll off the production line," he told me, raising his glass in a toast, "we're off to Tanzania."

It was a short drive to Sheri's party. Shiny, new four-wheel-drives lined one side of her street outside her house and loud music thudded from behind a high wall. Inside the compound the house was spectacular. It had three floors and a large central courtyard. We walked in and the ground floor was open plan and spacious. A couple of American guys in t-shirts, baggy shorts and baseball caps were slouched on sofas watching an NBA basketball game on television. They raised their hands in lazy waves as we walked past and pointed up the stairs. We emerged onto a roof terrace the size of a small tennis court. The whole of Addis Ababa twinkled below us. In one corner a DJ stood behind a record deck and in another stood a large bin filled with ice and bottles of Budweiser. Between the two a small knot of people danced to a Bee Gees disco hit.

Some years before I had made a series of documentary films for the Foreign and Commonwealth Office, which often entailed hauling a film crew around some of the more far flung outposts of Her Majesty's diplomatic service. One time we made a series of films in New Delhi. The diplomatic community in India was a very enclosed one. Most embassies were clustered in one area of the city covering several square miles, and most of the westerners who worked at the embassies lived on-site in vast compounds. The embassies catered for every need. At the British High Commission, the top officials lived in beautiful houses and bungalows in well-groomed, landscaped grounds, which were attended to by a team of Indian gardeners. Lower down the employment scale, people lived in well-maintained apartment blocks. There were shops on site selling imported British essentials that life in India would simply have been intolerable without Ty-Phoo tea bags and jars of Marmite and the like.

The recreational facilities included tennis courts, a swimming pool, cafes, restaurants and, of course, a bar or two. There was even a small hospital on site. The place was so self-contained, and catered for every imaginable need, it was perfectly possible to live entirely on site through-out your three years posting without ever once having to venture out into the real India that was right on your doorstep. I met one diplomat who decided to do just that. Shortly after he arrived in India he took one look at Delhi, decided he didn't like it, and never ventured off compound again. He spent his entire three years there living in a triangle of going to the office, decamping to the bar and then the restaurant, and then retiring home to bed. The only exception to this well ordered routine was when he went on holiday, and had to take a taxi to the airport to catch a flight home to the UK.

The entire diplomatic community took on the feel of a street in a TV soap opera. Everybody was everybody else's neighbour and socially, at least, everyone was always popping in and out of everybody else's place. Thursday evenings the Brits hosted an all comers darts match, and every Friday night it was all round to the Australians for a barbecue. But at the American embassy it was open house every night.

The Americans were definitely the richest people in "the street". They always had the freshest steaks and the latest videos flown in, and when the other missions ran out of beer, the Americans never did. They had the best of everything and they were incredibly generous with it all. You didn't even need to be invited. On any number of evenings, having enjoyed a beer or two, if we fancied a decent hamburger or pizza we would simply flash our IDs at the gate of the American embassy and stroll into their canteen as if we owned the place. There we would meet groups of assorted French, Italians, Germans and Russians, all tucking into quarter-pounders with fries and washing them down with ice-cold

Buds. I don't think I ever saw an American in there. Of course, 9/11 put paid to all that, but this party had the same laid back feel.

A few minutes later Chris Purdy arrived. At well over six feet tall, with finely chiselled features and a cultured Manhattan accent, Chris looked like Liam Neeson's younger brother. You could almost hear the 'whoosh' as half the girls on the dance floor deserted their posts and surrounded him. Spotting Chris and Karen he managed to disentangle himself and made his way over to us.

"Bob, heard a lot about you," he said shaking my hand, "Karen tells me you guys are doing a fine job with these commercials."

"Well, it's early days, but so far I'm feeling very encouraged."

"That's great, but heh listen, if you have any problems about anything at all, you just give me a call, Okay."

"That I will, thanks," I replied. I liked Chris immediately.

Just then he was hauled onto the dance floor by an attractive blonde. The rest of the night was spent grabbing snippets of conversation with him between various young women dragging him back onto the dance floor. He told me that he was New York born and bred and that he had worked for DKT for many years in various parts of the world and had been in Indonesia before he was posted to Addis Ababa. Most of the programmes he had worked on were to do with HIV/AIDS in one way or another.

"I'm the condom salesman to the world," he told me with a grin, "before adding, "Heh, do you play poker?"

"It's been a while Chris, but I think I still remember the basics. Which is higher, a run or a flush?" I added as an afterthought.

"Look, a few of the guys get together one a week for a game. It's nothing serious and nobody wins or loses more than a hundred birr, why don't you come over next time."

"Sure, I'd like to," I said.

"No problem, I'll be in touch when I know who's hosting the next game."

And with that Donna Summer gave way to Michael Jackson, and Chris was dragged back on to the dance floor. The last I saw of him was his head bobbing up and down amidst a sea of gyrating women.

I had been at Gem TV a few weeks when I decided to dispense with Getachew's lift to work in the mornings, and walk to the office instead. When Selam explained this to him he fixed me with a look that suggested I had been out in the sun too much without a hat. What really irked him was that it meant he would miss his cup of coffee and catch-up chat with Ghidey every morning.

Instead of walking up the Debre Zeit Road I headed off into the back-streets and let myself be guided by my sense of direction. Away from the main roads, the whole of Addis Ababa was made up of a huge, sprawling, intricate warren of these streets. Not one of them had a name. I wrestled open the wrought iron door set into the larger double doors that shielded the compound of the guesthouse from the outside world, and stepped out into a narrow alleyway pitted with potholes and jagged lumps of stone that stuck up through the red, hard baked clay like little rocky icebergs. At eight o'clock in the morning the air was pleasantly cool, but the sun was well into its upward arc and the heat was steadily building. The street was only a few feet wide, and an open sewer ran down one side of it, clashing with the perfume of fragrant flowers that tumbled over the walls of the other compounds.

I turned left and had only walked a few yards when I was greeted with a cheery "Allo". A man with a wonky eye and a broad smile waved at me from a small hatch that looked out onto the alleyway. He beckoned me over. As I approached he stepped back so that I could peer into the small room beyond. It was a shop, but from the outside there was nothing to tell you. A wooden shutter covered a hole that had been hacked into the bare brick wall. In stark contrast to the bright sunlight outside, the small room was in deep shadow. I peered in and it took me a few moments for my eyes to become accustomed to the gloom. I saw bare concrete walls lined with shelves of rough wood, stocked with baskets of fruit and vegetables, together with tins of sardines and corned beef, rudimentary household items, soap, rolls of toilet paper, a few beauty products, soft drinks and bottles of beer. He did a lot of business hiring out a battered telephone that stood on the window sill, charging customers by the minute. Ghidey, generally with a house full of *ferenjis* to look after, was one of his biggest customers. In the weeks that followed his bright and breezy "Allo" on my walk to the office every morning became something of a ritual, and quite often I'd have to stop off to return empty beer bottles. There was a fifty cents refund on each one.

After about fifty yards the alleyway ran into a larger road which cut it at right angles. It too was bare earth, rock and rubble but it was wider and the compounds that lined both sides of it were more well-to-do. Just before the alleyway met the road I noticed in the shade of a high wall a mound of sticks and stones that had been fashioned into a makeshift igloo. Outside it a mangy mongrel nibbled at its coat hunting for fleas. It raised its head and eyed me suspiciously as I walked past. I turned the corner and came face to face with its owner. Two blazing eyes stared at me from a dirt smeared face that was shrouded in a tangle of dirty, matted hair. His clothes were black, ill-fitting and obviously cast-offs. His trousers were held up around his scrawny waist by a length of string, and he wore a self-styled hat made from a ripped up cardboard box. He looked like an Ethiopian version of an Indian *sadhu*, except that *sadhus* chose to adopt lives of poverty for religious reasons, this man was just desperately poor. I took this all in during the second or two we stood facing each other. If I was startled by this wild apparition it was nothing compared to the effect I had on him. With a strangled, high-pitched wail, he leapt a couple of feet into the air and scuttled past me in a hunched over stumbling run.

His was a sad story. I later learnt he had once been a student at Addis Ababa University. Then he was struck down by mental illness. Now he spent his days wandering the streets of the neighbourhood, constantly talking to himself from dawn till nightfall, picking up stones with which he constantly and compulsively rebuilt his house. Local people left parcels of food outside it for him, and the only friend he had in the world was the dog, who guarded his little hovel while he was out collecting rocks. The sight of me walking to work every morning became a regular occurrence, and he became a little more accepting of the strange *ferenji*. If he was sitting outside his stone igloo as I walked past, or foraging in the street, he would stop what he was doing and fix me with a stare. It was never hostile, just curiosity, and I always acknowledged him in return with a slight nod of my head.

Months later, I had been out of Addis Ababa for a few days, and on my first day back I was walking into the Gem TV office as normal. But when I turned the corner the stone igloo was gone, a scorched patch of black earth was all that remained where it had stood. My first thought was the city authorities had moved him on. But later I learnt what happened. Every night, when he retired into his igloo, he lit a home-made lamp he had fashioned from a tin can which he filled with kerosene. This gave him a small, naked flame. The rags, old newspapers and bits of wood that were stuffed between the stones of his home were like kindling and they caught fire. How he died I never found out. I hoped that the stones had fallen in on him knocking him unconscious before the flames engulfed his body. The dark patch of earth eventually grew over with grass. I never saw the dog again.

Continuing my walk into the Gem TV office that first time I soon entered backstreets where the houses were grander. They stood behind high walls topped with spikes or jagged pieces of broken glass embedded in concrete. I noticed that most of the houses boasted vast TV satellite dishes. Outside the houses, gardeners worked trying to tame the patches of wild grass that grew up against the walls. Short wooden stakes had been driven into the ground and strung with barbed wire to make fences. But this didn't deter the sheep that cropped at the grass behind them.

Sitting by the side of the road was a group of three women, their hands outstretched to passers-by. As I approached them a little girl shot out from behind her mother and came running straight at me. Her mother wore a faded and grubby print dress but her daughter was turned out in a spotlessly clean white dress with frills and matching white ribbons in her hair. She looked as pretty as a bridesmaid. Her mother turned her head to follow her but her eyes were coated with the milky film of trachoma. I could only guess how hard this woman's life must be, but to her little girl it was still a game. "You! You!" she called as she approached with her hand outstretched. I fished into my pocket and dropped a few coins into her palm. Podgy brown fingers closed over them and with a flash of her smile she turned tail and dashed back to her mother with her prize, as happy as a puppy with a slipper.

Every day she waited to pounce on me as I walked by. She had a totally uncomplicated view of the world. "Look, it's very simple," her look said, "you have lots of money, we don't, so you have to give us some. That's only fair." It was difficult to argue. I never left the guest house in the morning without some small change to give her. And I would always pass a few birr notes to her mother, who would bow her head and mumble a blessing in Amharic.

Leaving the little girl and her blind mother behind, I turned into another side street which in turn led to another and another after that. The distant hum of the heavy traffic on the Debre Zeit Road away to my left told me I was heading in the right direction. At one point I had to flatten myself up against a stone wall as a street urchin herded a flock of sheep down the narrow road in the opposite direction. He twirled a long rawhide whip around his head and flicked it at their rumps to keep them moving. I had never seen sheep like them before. They looked more like goats and their fleeces were matted and patchy. More colourful were the men I encountered selling household goods from door to door. I heard them before I saw them. They called out their wares in low, sonorous tones that briefly echoed along the deserted backstreets. When one turned a corner and came into view he was a spectacular sight. He was selling plastic washing bowls and he carried dozens of them in all shapes and sizes. They completely obscured him so that all I could see was a pair of thin legs under a canopy of interlocking, multi-coloured plastic. He looked like a psychedelic tortoise that had got lost.

The further I went into the backstreets, the poorer the houses became. The streets continued to be divided up into compounds, and inside them one and two room dwellings huddled together cheek by jowl. Each one was home to an entire family, with all of the families sharing one stand-pipe of water for drinking, cooking, cleaning and washing. I may have been only a few hundred yards from the main road with its shops, bars and restaurants but I felt I was in another country. Young children stared at me in fascination or screamed and ran to hide behind an elder sister. Some of the women had vegetables to sell – tomatoes, chillies and onions – which they had placed on blankets on the ground. Others sat over small wood burning stoves roasting corn on the cob, the sweet aroma of burning eucalyptus twigs filling the air. In the distance I thought I saw a sea of cockroaches writhing on the ground, but as I got closer I saw it was a pile of copper coloured leaves that had been smoothed out to dry under the sun. They were deep red-rust and gold in colour and as the breeze gently turned them they glinted in the sunlight which gave them the sense of movement. They would be used for making *berberi*, Ethiopian pepper.

Eventually, I made my way back to the main road close to the Gem TV office. Lorries and cars, and buses and taxis, and the ubiquitous blue and white Toyota minibuses weaved in and out and around each other. Their drivers were more inclined to push their horns than hit the brakes when a collision loomed, which was often. People stood in little groups at the side of the street flagging down buses. I walked past big, imposing office buildings. The signs outside them announced them to be banks, insurance companies and there was even one corporate name I recognised, Unilever, the fish fingers to soap powders conglomerate. Men sat on upturned crates picking green shoots from bunches of *khat*, popping them into their mouths and chewing on them. While small boys ran out of cafes carrying trays of steaming coffee in small handle-less cups and disappeared into the nearby office buildings with them. They kept up this steady stream of delivering coffee to office workers all day long.

# FOUR

# That's a Wrap

**"I** don't like that one," snapped Misrak. The actor, a handsome young man, had just left the room. He had read his lines well, looked the part and been courteous throughout, which was more than could be said for the director. He was the last out of six actors that Cactus had lined up for Misrak to see. Together with Misrak in the Cactus boardroom, where the casting session was being held, there was myself, Selamawit, Reyhill and Joki. Earlier Wubit's casting session had gone well. Misrak's was a very different story.

Everyone looked at me, except Misrak who stared out the window. Although the casting session had been held in Amharic I would have had no problem using at least three of the actors out of the six we had seen. Clearly, Misrak had other ideas.

"What was wrong with the last one?" Reyhill said turning to Misrak, who mumbled something back in Amharic forcing Selamawit to translate what she had said for my benefit, which was along the lines of, "I didn't think he was any good." Selamawit looked down at the notes she had made.

"We all liked the second one. You said he looked the part best of all."

"I don't think he can act," said Misrak still staring out the window.

Beside me, the six foot plus frame of Joki was beginning to tremble like a volcano about to lose its stack. All the people in the room were highly educated Amharas, who prided themselves on their professionalism above all else. That they were having to *kow-tow* to a slip of an ex-street girl was not something they were used to.

I tried to appear calm but inwardly I was squirming. Misrak had put me in the jaws of a dilemma. First of all, I didn't know her anything like well enough to know if she was being genuine with her criticisms. If I sided with Misrak I lost face in front of the clients, who would probably think that I couldn't control Gem TV. After all, I was supposed to be in charge. On the other hand, if I sided with the clients and forced Misrak to accept one of the actors, I would have broken one of the unwritten rules of filmmaking and would instantly lose any respect Gem TV may have had for me. I recalled a quote I had heard once from a Hollywood producer, who when asked to describe his job said, "I arrive at the office every morning, zip myself into my rhinoceros hide suit, and just get on with it." I was beginning to understand what he meant. All eyes – even Misrak's – were now looking at me.

"These commercials are very important," I began. "We're not selling products, we're trying to save lives. I think we owe it to ourselves, and all the people out there, that we make every effort to work together to make the most effective commercials possible." There were nods of agreement around the table, with one noticeable exception. It was late on a Friday afternoon so I used this as an excuse and suggested that we leave it here for the moment and think about it over the weekend. I needed to get Misrak out of there before she could do any further damage. Normally, my tactic would have been to get back to Gem TV and hand the whole Misrak problem over to Selam to sort out. Only problem was Selam was away for a couple of weeks, as was Carmela. I was on my own.

As Dawit drove us back into town along the Bole Road, he drove the big Mercedes in and around taxis, beaten up old cars and herds of sheep and goats like an Olympics slalom skier, while I tried to fathom out the two young women directors I was now working with.

Nothing ever seemed to bother Wubit. She was always calm and relaxed about everything in a "mumsy" sort of way. Whatever the world threw at her, Wubit treated it with a shy smile and a shrug of the shoulders. "That's life, nothing surprises me any more," was her attitude.

Wubit always seemed to be able to take everything in her stride. Misrak, on the other hand, was a tightly drawn bundle of nervous energy on a short fuse. She was the youngest in the group, slender and had long, straight hair that she wore scraped back off her face and tied in a tight bun, which gave her a pinched expression. She dressed as a tomboy and wore a threadbare anorak with the sleeves rolled up to the elbows as if she was always on the lookout for a fight. However, if something made her smile the transformation was total. This beautiful, young woman would appear, and then just as quickly the clouds would roll back over her features, lightning would flash in her eyes, her mouth would retract into a thin-lipped, straight line and the temperature in the room would drop by a couple of degrees. It was Misrak more than anyone else who made me realise that before they joined Gem TV these young people had experienced incredibly difficult lives, which had been shaped by circumstances and cruelties I couldn't possibly imagine. It was bound to have an effect. I consoled myself with the thought that it was probably best that I had given Misrak the benefit of the doubt, which just goes to show that the easiest person to convince is yourself.

At the next casting session Misrak was even worse, taking no point of view herself and agreeing to every suggestion in a patronising manner. She made little effort to hide that she didn't care who was cast to appear in the commercial. Eventually, committee decisions were reached and we had a cast.

Both commercials were to be shot in the same location, a smart house in a compound that belonged to one of the senior people working at Cactus. Wubit's commercial, which took place inside, featured a couple and their children visiting another family. Over preparing coffee, the two women get to talking about family planning, and the script ends with a pack shot of a range of DKT family planning products. Misrak's commercial was set in the garden and featured a pharmacist relaxing after a hard day's work. He is paid a surprise visit by his brother and they too get to talking about various methods of contraception. Not, on the face of it, the most exciting of scripts, but they showed key people types talking openly amongst themselves about a subject which was normally taboo. I imagined that just to get people talking about HIV/AIDS on television beamed into people's homes was probably a big step forward.

The challenge with Wubit's and Misrak's scripts was that they were wall to wall dialogue, which technically made them far more difficult to shoot than Wonde's and Adanech's commercials had been. The two girls had drawn the short straws. It meant that as every shot had a character speaking in it the timing of each shot had to be absolutely precise. And when all the shots were cut together in the edit they had to be no longer than 60 seconds. It was a tough call even for an experienced drama director, let alone two students still in film school doing their first commercials for national television. To make matters worse by my reading of the scripts they were too long, more like 75 seconds.

This is where I made my first big mistake. Well, I thought, if the scripts are too long it will give them a problem to solve which will be a good experience for them. All I succeeded in doing was putting more unfair pressure on them. I had completely forgotten how nerve shredding it is to be a start out director. If I had been more sensitive I would have recognised that they were probably already petrified. What's more, to be fair to both of them, instead of complaining about the problem they rolled their sleeves up, pitched in and did their level best to try and make the unworkable workable. And to make the matters worse, the smart-arse, know it all *ferenji*, whose job it was to make things easier for them was only adding to their problems. I had been entrusted with their fragile self-confidence as directors and had completely failed to protect and develop it. Worse, I had probably shattered it into a thousand pieces.

The silence dragged on and on and on. Crammed into the small room that was Gem TV's edit suite with me were Misrak, Wubit, the editors

Mehbratie and Sintayehu, Selamawit from Cactus and Reyhill and Joki from DKT. We had just shown them the rough cuts of Wubit's and Misrak's commercials. No one wanted to speak first. Sintayehu fidgeted with the buttons on his keyboard, and Wubit and Misrak continued to stare at the empty, black screen of the monitor, where the commercials had just played, as if something was still being shown on it. Selamawit seemed intent on studying her shoes, and Reyhill and Joki exchanged nervous glances. It was obvious to everyone, the commercials didn't work. What made matters worse, was that earlier we had shown them Wonde's and Adanech's commercials which were very good.

"I think there are things we can do," I said. I don't know if it was politeness or a misplaced sense of belief in my abilities, but Reyhill and Joki allowed me to rattle off a list of thoughts and ideas about how to re-edit the results, but even I could tell they knew my heart wasn't in it. I tried to shift the emphasis away from Gem TV.

"I think by cutting the dialogue in a few places and shooting a few pick up shots we can fix things."

"So, Misrak, what do you think?" Reyhill asked.

"What did you expect" snapped Misrak at Reyhill, "this is what was in the scripts." Misrak was right but I had been the problem not Reyhill. I should have spotted this earlier and brought it to everyone's attention before the shoot so we could have changed the scriots before we turned over. I sensed that Reyhill was nervous about going back to Chris Purdy with bad news. In the meantime I made a mental note that Misrak's client handling skills needed work.

"Can I make a suggestion," I said, "leave it with me to think about for a while and please don't decide anything yet."

Fortunately, they agreed. I was responsible for the problem so it was up to me to find the solution.

I learnt early in my advertising career that if you ever had to go back to a client with bad news, you had better make damn sure you had some good news to go with it. I knew the commercials weren't saveable. I also realised that if we re-shot them we would meet many of the problems we had encountered the first time round. And DKT would not be best pleased at having to pay twice for commercials they should only have had to pay for once. The answer I came up with was to give them two completely different commercials. Two new commercials that were so much better they would forget about the old ones, I hoped. This also meant I could write scripts that worked comfortably within the time, and were easier for Wubit and Misrak to direct. I put my thinking cap on. Fortunately, having been brought up writing fast turnaround TV commercials for newspapers, by the following morning I had a couple of scripts that I felt confident would make better commercials, and which Wubit and Misrak would feel a lot more confident about directing.

Both commercials were similar in structure. First of all I managed to tell the stories in thirty seconds, not sixty. The other major difference was they were both presenter commercials, which would make them much easier to shoot. Wubit's commercial featured a doctor. We open on him in his clinic where he is treating a young woman and her baby. He looks up to camera and tells about how easy family planning is, and that contraceptive injections can last up to three months. Then we cut to him in close-up as he tells us that as well as being a doctor, he's also a husband and father, at which point we cut to find him now magically at home him with his "small" family of wife and two kids, so the audience sees that he practices what he preaches. The "trick" of the commercial which transports the doctor from his surgery to his living room in a fraction of a second is a simple editing device. At the end of the sequence in the surgery you cut to an extreme close-up of the doctor. But this extreme close up is actually shot in his living room and you pull out from it to reveal the doctor suddenly magically transported from one location to another, and all in the blink of an eye.

Misrak's commercial used the same technique only it featured a young woman teacher. We see her surrounded by children in a school playground. She looks to camera and tells us that she loves kids and that's why she's a teacher. And then she tells us that she is also a mother and we use the same editing device to magically transport her to her home as well where she is surrounded by her husband and two adoring kids. The underlying message in both commercials is that because both sets of parents love their children they have decided to have small families so they can give them more attention, and that family planning is the key to this lifestyle. But before I tried to sell them to Cactus and DKT, first I first had to get Wubit and Misrak on board with them.

"Here you go," I said, trying to sound positive and upbeat as I handed over the scripts. I had called them into Selam's office which I was temporarily occupying while she was away in the UK. I took them through the scripts shot by shot showing them how straightforward they were to shoot. When it came to the tricks editing device they were a bit confused at first and I could sense hackles beginning to rise. So we role played it a few times with me framing the size of the shots with my hands for the extreme close-ups and my outstretched arms for the wide shots. Being the smart directors they were they quickly grasped the idea.

"This is good," said Wubit as relaxed as ever. Misrak didn't say anything.

"Are you happy for me to talk to Cactus and DKT about them?" I asked. They both nodded.

Brilliant, I thought, and when DKT told me they liked the scripts I thought I was home free. It was Selamawit at Cactus who broke the bad news.

"Reyhill is happy to go ahead," Selamawit told me over the phone the next day, "but there's one condition. They don't want Misrak to direct the commercial." I couldn't blame Reyhill really.

I called Misrak into the office to tell her the bad news. Ten minutes later she was back, only this time she wasn't alone. She had brought the rest of Gem TV with her.

"We're not making the commercials," said Misrak, giving me back the scripts. "And we're not working for DKT client anymore."

"Does that go for you too?" I asked Wubit, who nodded her assent before handing me back her script as well. Before I had a chance to protest, everyone started speaking at once.

"We should not have to work for clients... "

"We should only make our own films..."

"We never wanted to make these commercials..."

I quickly realised what lay behind this outburst was a sense of pride in their work. They were terrified of putting anything sub-standard out there, of being seen to produce work that was "not professional". It also began to dawn on me that perhaps the last few weeks making these commercials had not been a good experience for them. This was the first time they had worked for a client and to a client's brief. Previously, all the films they had made were for themselves. They certainly hadn't been shown to a nationwide audience. And they were still learning their craft. I had forgotten how nerve wracking it is the first time you put your creativity on the line and hold it up for all to see. I was used to it, but it had taken me years to build up my confidence. It's a process that tends to put even the most seasoned professionals on edge.

To their credit they were all highly quality conscious. I couldn't blame them for that, it showed they cared. To that extent I had to admire them. And I think this was exactly the kind of situation Andrew Coggins could foresee and had tried to warn me about when I first met him at the hotel in London. But another part of me wanted to scream. What's more important, I wanted to shout at them, your sense of professional pride, or that fact that thousands of people are dying out there every day – your people – and you're in a position to do something about it, even if it does mean compromising a precious filmmaking principle or two.

But I didn't. It was late Friday afternoon. We had all had a long and stressful few weeks. And there was something else I had been slow to realise. They had been through a lot together. They were fighters by nature, some of them had survived living on the street. They had had to learn a new language, a complex technology and work in an alien culture, and most of them at best had not even completed a standard education. They knew that when Andrew started Gem TV, many people said he was mad, that you couldn't turn ex-street kids into film-makers. They knew the spotlight was on them. They may have argued with each other and fought like cats and dogs, but if an outsider criticised one of them the rest rallied round and there was hell to pay. Misrak might be a monumental pain in the arse to all concerned, including more often than not her own Gem TV colleagues, but as far as they were concerned she was *their* monumental pain in the arse, and you picked on her at your peril.

"Please let's not make any decisions about this now," I said. I know how you feel, believe me, I've been there myself. Selam will be back on Monday. Let's talk about it then."

If anyone could sort out this mess it was Selam. And if she couldn't I was dreading the phone calls I was going to have to make to Andrew and Carmela. How was I going to explain to them that the film school they had dedicated years of their lives to building up, I had managed to destroy in just a few weeks.

"Hi, Bob, how's everything," Selam was all smiles as usual. I had got in early to give her my version of events before everyone else arrived.

"Great, Selam," I lied. "Good to have you back." It was. Then I gave her chapter and verse.

"Actually Bob, this is not the first time I have had this type of complaint about Misrak," she said. "Some of the trainers who have come out here before have had similar kinds of problems with her. It's very bad, especially as this is the first time Gem TV has had the chance to do a professional job for a client." Then after a pause she added, "If you don't mind, perhaps it's better if I talk to them on my own."

"Fine by me," I said, relieved to be able to let Selam sort out the mess. I took the opportunity to go to an internet cafe and check my emails. Selam was not happy, and I had been around Gem TV long enough to know that when Selam wasn't happy then the best place to be was somewhere else. Managing Gem TV wasn't easy, as Selam often said to me, and she performed the almost impossible task exceptionally well. At different times she had to be mother, friend and boss to them all. It was a very difficult juggling act to pull off, but somehow Selam always managed to get the balance absolutely right. She had unerring judgement. Of course, the hard part was when she had to be the boss, and not once did I ever see her shy away from taking that responsibility. I had only witnessed her lose it with them a few times, and it was generally Mehbratie who more than anyone else had the knack of winding her up to eruption point. On these occasions Selam would harangue him with a sustained, high volume, machine gun burst of high velocity Amharic, which went on for minutes on end. How she managed to draw breath I'll never know. Every time it happened I would go and hide in one of the edit suites and tell the others that "Selam was breathing through her ears". They knew exactly what I meant. As I left I noticed that I had never seen Selam looking less happy.

When I got back to the office a couple of hours later there was an eerie and unmistakable atmosphere of calm and authority. There was no doubting the Selam effect. Order had been restored. Selam looked up from her desk as I tip-toed into the office.

"Ah, there you are, how is everything in the UK?"

"Fine thanks, but what about here?" Selam may have appeared relaxed but I wasn't.

"You know, it was amazing. I have never seen this before. I explained to them that if Gem TV is ever going to be a business then we have to learn to work for clients. They all understood and for the first time they didn't let Misrak get away with it."

"They didn't?" I said, my voice rising an octave or two as my sense of incredulity kicked in. Thank God for peer pressure I thought

"No, I explained to them that in the future if no client wants to work with us then there will be no more Gem TV. Then I told Misrak that if she doesn't improve her behaviour it will be very difficult for her to work here."

"And how did she take it?" I asked.

"You know Misrak, she just said that maybe she didn't want to work here."

"Do you think she meant it?" I asked with rising panic. I suddenly had visions of returning to London and trying to explain to Andrew how I had managed to lose one of Gem TV's directors.

"No, don't worry. An hour later she was here in my office crying. She said she is very sorry and wants to apologise to you, and everyone."

"Well, that's a start I suppose," I said.

"So," said Selam, flicking her winning smile onto full beam, "I have a favour to ask you Bob."

"Yeeeeeeeeeessssssssss?"

"Can you ask Reyhill to have Misrak put back on the commercial. I can ask them but I think it would be a lot better coming from you." And with that she ratcheted up her smile a couple more notches and I knew it was useless to try and refuse her.

I hung around the office and tried to make myself look busy while waiting for Selam to leave on some errand or other. When she did I grabbed the phone and did what any man in my position would do, I called Selamawit at Cactus and passed the problem over to her.

"Honestly Selamawit, Misrak's a changed woman," I chirruped. "If you had been here and seen her for yourself in floods of tears you wouldn't have thought it was the same girl. Please, if you could just have a quiet word with Reyhill and Joki, because you know … I think it would be a lot better coming from you." I was learning fast from Selam.

"Leave it with me," Selamawit, ever the consummate professional replied, although this time there was a distinct hint of resignation in her voice, "and I'll get back to you."

She phoned the next morning.

"DKT will give her one more chance," she told me, "but there is one condition. They want someone else to be on hand to take over in case there is a problem with Misrak again. In fact, they insist that it's you."

Not every child went to school in Addis Ababa, for those that did it was obviously a source of great pride to their parents, who dressed their children in smart, dark red and blue school uniforms. Often the school children were far better dressed than the parents dropping them off at the school gates.

Selamawit had found us a primary school half way along the Bole Road where we could film. Misrak had been sweetness and light in the casting session and had selected a charming young actress to play the teacher. The school was one of the better ones in Addis Ababa. Three sets of low breeze block buildings, which had all the appearance of army barracks, were centred round a dusty courtyard that doubled as a playground, and which was dominated by a large acacia tree that threw out a welcome canopy of shade.

It was early morning and the courtyard was milling with children running, shouting and wrestling as they waited for lessons to begin. A large bell hung on a chain from a branch of the tree and suddenly it rang out stridently as one of the teachers hit it with a stick. Immediately, the bedlam was quelled and the children walked off to their respective classrooms, like well marshalled soldiers, leaving the school yard eerily quiet.

We met with the headmaster, who was very helpful. He told us that we could have the children for the one half hour they were allowed during their playground break, but no more. Nothing interrupts education in Ethiopia, not even a film crew.

DKT's offices were only round the corner from the school, so a few minutes later Chris Purdy pitched up to see how we were spending his money.

"How's it going?" he asked me.

"So far so good, Chris," I said, which was perfectly true because we hadn't actually shot anything yet.

Misrak had about thirty children under her command. They were very nervous at first but the actress playing the teacher was brilliant with them. I don't know if she was using "the method", but she managed to convince the children she was the real thing. They jumped to her every command. Once Misrak was happy with the rehearsals, Reyhill took the teacher aside and went through the script with her a couple of times pointing out how she thought the lines should be performed. I shot a nervous glance over at Misrak as dealing with the actors is strictly the director's territory. But if Misrak noticed she didn't let on. Then Reyhill walked over to where Misrak was standing with the children and greeted her in the traditional Ethiopian manner by touching her on the cheek. At this point I was fully expecting for Misrak to haul off and land Reyhill a right-hander, but instead she treated her to a shy smile. Meanwhile, Chris wandered about taking photographs for the DKT scrapbook, high-fiving the kids and making them laugh with his heavily Manhattan accented Amharic.

Misrak had set up the camera angle and Kebe and Fikirte were ready on sound, so Misrak told everyone that she was going for a take. The actress promptly slipped into teacher mode and brought the children to order. Misrak arranged a few of the children to be playing in the foreground and then cued the teacher to walk into shot and sit amongst the kids on some steps in front of one of the classrooms and then deliver her opening line to camera. Once she had the first take in the can,

Misrak repeated it a couple more times from alternative angles, and then moved on to the next set-up. It was working like clockwork.

Half an hour later the headmaster appeared. "Please, the children have to return to their class now."

Misrak gave him her most winning smile and promptly ignored him as she went for another take. With a good one in the can she shouted, "Cut!"

Whereupon the headmaster stepped forward tapping his watch insistently. Once again, Misrak fixed him with another one of her dazzling smiles and immediately started setting up for an alternative angle, marshalling the children like a general on a battlefield, who all thought that this was a lot more fun than sitting in a classroom. By now the headmaster was getting increasingly frustrated. Teachers in Ethiopia are highly respected members of the community and headmasters simply weren't used to being completely ignored, especially by a young woman. For once I was all for her. There isn't a decent film-maker born who won't sell their own mother for a chance of a better take. But watching a respected member of the teaching profession go quietly insane was turning into something of an embarrassment. I didn't know where to put myself. Actually, I did. I grabbed Chris and pulled him out of sight with me behind the acacia tree.

"Heh Bob," said Chris, "shouldn't you be out there smoothing things over?"

"Normally I would, Chris," I said, "but what you've got to remember is that's Misrak we're talking about out there.

"Yeah," he said, and then after a few moments added, "she's kinda scary, isn't she?"

I peeped out from around the tree again to see the headmaster pacing up and down behind the camera muttering away to himself. Meanwhile, Misrak was busy marshalling the kids for another set-up. I ducked back.

"Well, look on the bright side, Chris," I said, "it'll make a better commercial."

This was true and it was one of the things I was beginning to admire about Misrak as a director. She was very strong, very determined. This could be a nightmare when she was on the wrong track as I had seen, but when she was on the right one it was a positive asset. Misrak possessed the most essential quality all good directors must have by the bucket load, you don't stop until you've got the shot. My respect for Misrak rocketed.

"Cut," I heard her call out, which was followed by a few words in Amharic and a general groaning from the kids. The headmaster herded the children back into class, and Chris and I emerged from our hiding place trying to look nonchalant. The afternoon shoot in the teacher's home went off without a hitch, and when we looked at the rushes back at Gem TV I knew Misrak had a very good commercial on her hands.

Wubit's commercial, featuring the doctor, had been shot without incident, and a week later Selamawit, Chris, Reyhill, Joki, Adanech, Wonde, Wubit, Misrak and I, together with Sintayehu who sat at the editing console, crammed ourselves back into the edit suite and watched all the commercials together for the first time. There wasn't room for anyone else so Selam and the rest of Gem TV huddled outside in the corridor and peered in through the doorway. Sintayehu hit the play button and months of hard work flashed by in a couple of minutes.

My first reaction on seeing the four commercials together for the first time was that they were amongst the best home produced commercials I had seen in Ethiopia. Admittedly, at times this wasn't particularly difficult. TV was still a novelty in Ethiopia and having seen some of their commercials I was convinced you could put a picture of a business card up on the screen for thirty seconds and it would have customers beating a path to your door. Cactus's work was the exception.

As for the rest, the high water mark of the Ethiopian adman's art was without doubt the TV commercials for dental surgeries. They were always at least two minutes long. Most of the screen time was dedicated to showing close-ups of hideously deformed teeth, which were followed by shots of trays of dental pliers, drills and clamps. If Doctor Mengele had ever contemplated making home movies, they would have looked like these ads.

When the last one ended Chris turned to everyone and said, "They're great." Reyhill and Joki smiled, the Gem TV directors beamed, Selamawit let out a small sigh of relief, and everyone else cheered. Then Chris went round everyone thanking them personally. Working together, Cactus and Gem TV had made four very professional looking TV commercials.

Everyone had played a key role in getting them made, and as it turned out no one made a bigger personal sacrifice than Teddy. The two condoms commercials ended with a pack shot. We shot this in a corner of the Gem TV office on a piece of red velvet. A lot of manhandling of the product went into the setting up and shooting of the pack shot, and as a result we got through quite a few packets of condoms. Whenever we needed a few more packs, Teddy volunteered to go to the pharmacy across the street to buy some more. He fancied the girl who served behind the counter and was desperate for any excuse to talk to her. The third time he went over there he asked her out.

"She looked at me and said do you think I would go with a man who has more condoms than a hyena has fleas?"

"No, it's okay, I'm a cameraman," I told her, "and we're making a TV commercial about condoms. And then she said that she was the long-lost daughter of Haile Selassie and to get out of my shop and not come back."

# FIVE
# **Expat Addis**

The sun was well past its zenith and was descending slowly in an azure blue, cloudless sky. The earlier heat of the day had given way to a gentler, more caressing, airy kiss, that didn't burn the skin but made it tingle. I had managed to find somewhere high up in the cool of the shade, and from my lofty perch I looked out across the rooftops to the encircling Entoto mountains that completely ringed the city, gripping Addis Ababa like a jewel set in a rocky clasp. Just then a familiar movement caught my eye. I looked up again and they were still there, two vultures riding the late afternoon thermals, soaring majestically in the warm currents of rising air. I watched them effortlessly circling on extended wings for a couple of minutes. Unfortunately, for the last hour they had taken up permanent station above our back four. Typical, I thought, and returned my attention back to the game.

It was a typical Buna performance. We had enjoyed the majority of the possession. Our passing game had been controlled and we had moved the ball to feet rather than hoofing it up the pitch at every opportunity to a big, burly centre-forward, which was how most football teams in Ethiopia played. Yet despite this we hadn't been able to find the all-important finishing touch in front of goal, and in our zeal to play open, attacking football, we had left ourselves open at the back a couple of times, and with half an hour to go we were two nil down.

Just then, Yiordanos, our highly skilful playmaker, picked up the ball deep in his own half. He glided past a couple of clumsy tackles and accelerated smoothly into the space that opened up for him. He drew the central defender, sent him one way with a step-over and drop of his right shoulder and waltzed past him leaving him standing. Sensing the danger, their right back had cut inside to take him out, but Yiordanos had anticipated this. He dummied to cut inside the player and then flicked the ball wide with the outside of his left foot.

In desperation the defender launched into a sliding, two footed tackle, but Yiordanos was too quick for him, riding the scything challenge like a hurdler. But the manoeuvre had cost him vital space and time. Now he had only the goalkeeper to beat. But avoiding the last tackle had pushed him out wide, and he found himself on the far corner of the penalty area. The goalkeeper came off his line like a cheetah, hurling himself at Yiordanos to narrow the angle and give the Buna player nothing to shoot at. As the goalkeeper leapt at him, Yiordanos unleashed a curling shot with the inside of his right foot, imparting a wicked spin on the ball. It flew wide of the goalkeeper's despairing outstretched arm, but on a trajectory that took it wide of the goal. Then the spin that had been imparted began to take effect, curving the flight of the ball back on target. The goalkeeper knew he was beaten.

A hush descended on the crowd of ten thousand Ethiopians – and one *ferenji* – packed into the Addis Ababa stadium. Time stood still as everything happened in slow motion. Like a guided missile, the ball flew past the goalkeeper's despairing dive and was zeroing in on the top corner of the net when it … cannoned off the crossbar. It looked like it wasn't going to be our day.

Football fans are a rare breed of masochist, and the Sunday afternoons I spent at the Addis Ababa Stadium only served to prove to me that under the skin we're the same the world over, hopeless optimists. One team dominated in Ethiopia, Saint George. It was the team with all the money and the best players. They were bankrolled by Ethiopia's only international businessman and multi- millionaire, Sheik Al Moudi, and he lavished money on his club, even paying for a foreign coach. This meant that every true aficionado of the beautiful game in Ethiopia hated Saint George with a passion, and that included me. The team was named after its sponsor, Saint George beer, which was an Al Moudi owned company. I refused to drink the stuff. The only thing I liked about them was their home strip of yellow shirts and red shorts. It was the same as Watford's.

You can't go to a football game and be a neutral. When I first started going to the Addis Stadium, I watched Buna play a few times, and I had warmed to their open, attacking style, even though it never seemed to earn them a victory. Then one particular game it all fell into place. Once again, Buna had carved out numerous chances to score but had somehow failed to find the net. With five minutes to go the opposing team, who had hardly had a kick all game, broke away and scored. With a groan I put my head in my hands and realised that for the last few weeks I had been watching the Addis Ababa version of West Ham. I had my team.

On many a Sunday afternoon I was the only *ferenji* in the stadium. I scanned the massed ranks of thousands of supporters for another white face and never found one. I became a regular and always sat in the same place, which was towards the back of the only shaded stand. The few hundred other football fans, who could also afford to watch from the shade of the stand, assumed that being a European I was something of an expert on the game. Whenever a goal was scored they leapt into the air, and then, as one, turned to see what the *ferenji* thought of it. As a wind up, sometimes I would shrug my shoulders as if to say "nothing special" and they would all sit down again. Not so much a Mexican wave, more of an Ethiopian slump.

I had met Danny at a conference on media and international development. Like most of the other delegates he had flown in specially for the conference and we had got talking over a coffee during a break in the sessions.

"Not much to do in Addis on a Sunday, I suppose," he said, Sunday being the delegates' day off.

"Depends," I replied, "I generally go and watch a football match."

"Really," he said, brightening.

"Yep, and it's a big one tomorrow, cup semi-final."

It turned out Danny was a sports journalist by background and an ardent Everton supporter. He was also the editor of the BBC World Africa website. The remit of the site was to cover all things African, but under Danny's command there seemed to have been a marked change in editorial policy with a far greater emphasis being placed on African sport, football in particular. His job was office based in Bush House in London. The only time he pulled rank, he told me, was to do the live commentary every year from the final of the African Cup of Nations. I imagined him standing on the half-way line Malawi or Lesotho, talking into an old-fashioned lip mic and wearing a sheepskin coat.

"If you're going, mind if I tag along?" he asked.

Buna were playing a team from Awassa. It was a game Buna were expected to win comfortably, but in typical Buna fashion we were making hard work of it. With ten minutes to the final whistle we were one nil down and facing a swift exit from the competition, when Yiordanos produced a sublime piece of skill and engineered a chance at the far post which our striker, for once, put away. At the final whistle the score stood at one all. There followed a nervy thirty minutes of extra time, with both sides failing to score, which led to the inevitable penalty shoot-out.

"I've got to tell you," Danny told me after the game as we drank a couple of beers on the terrace of the Hawi Hotel, "I've reported on football matches in every English league, and from quite a few African countries, but I've never seen anything like that."

I knew what he meant. I'd never witnessed anything quite like it either. Awassa took the first penalty and promptly scored. Then Buna equalized. Then Awassa tucked away their second penalty. Then one of Buna's strikers stepped up and scored. In this way, with none of the players failing to bury the ball in the back of the net, the score crept up to five all. Then it was six all, then seven all, then eight all and then incredibly, nine all. The tension was unbearable. As each player approached the ball, he was greeted with a barrage of what I can only guess was the more riper Amharic from the opposing set of supporters. As each goal was scored, the tension ratcheted up a couple more notches, not to mention the volume of abuse hurled at each player.

Not that any of the players were trying to calm the situation. In the rest of the world, after you score a goal you punch the air, or jump up and down, or go and hug your team-mates. Not in Ethiopia. After each player scored he ran straight over to the opposing fans, turned round, bent over, and wiggled his arse in their faces. Another universal aspect of the beautiful game is that football crowds can be pretty excitable groups of people. These supporters went ballistic. Shirts were ripped off and thrown in the air, followed by seats, and if I'm not mistaken on a couple of occasions, small people.

With the score at eleven each, it was left to the goalkeepers to take shots at each other. The Awassa keeper was up first. He took it pretty well for a goalkeeper too. His foot met the ball with a resounding thump that could be heard all over the stadium, and the ball arrowed low and fast towards the bottom right hand corner of the goal. Our keeper read the intention brilliantly and with the power and agility of a leaping leopard hurled himself full-length. As the ball threatened to rocket past him he managed to get a fingertip touch on it, deflecting it onto the foot of the post. Half the crowd went mad.

Now it was our turn. It was the first time in the entire match Buna had the chance to take the lead, and if they did, it was game over, we were through. The crowd went quiet as our keeper placed the ball on the spot. He took a few paces backwards, wiped his hands on his shorts, and then calmly stroked the ball into the back of the net. Cue ferocious arse wiggling from the entire Buna team.

Outside the stadium we fought our way through mobs of supporters who, it has to be said, were more content with hurling insults at each other rather than fists or anything more solid.

"Well," said Danny, "not the most sporting behaviour I've ever seen on a football pitch."

"Couldn't care less," I said, "we're in the final. My round."

Covering football in Ethiopia would be any sports sub-editor's dream. The teams aren't named after towns or places so you didn't get names like Addis Ababa United or Mekele City. They tended to be named after their sponsors, most of which were state run utilities or industries. Buna, for example, is Amharic for Ethiopia's largest export, coffee. Other teams were called Electricity, Insurance, and Banks. One team had the racy name of Investment. Try coming up with a chant to sing on the terraces for that one, I thought. There was a team called Cement and another called Wanji Sugar. Sadly, the English language newspapers in Addis Ababa never rose to the bait. So it was in vain that I would feverishly turn to the back pages in the hope of reading headlines like: CEMENT SOLID AT THE BACK; ELECTRICITY BUY MIDFIELD DYNAMO and BANKS PLAYERS ON LOAN. In another nail-biter during the earlier rounds of the knock-out competition, Buna narrowly managed to scrape a last minute winner against a team they should have beaten easily. Any decent sub on a Sunday tabloid would have coined: COFFEE STILL IN THE CUP. Buna actually went on to win it that year, but having struggled to score goals, rumours were rife that we were about to launch a bid to sign the twin strikers from the Wanji team. I had already written the headline: COFFEE WITH TWO SUGARS.

The other way of watching football was in a *footybet, bet* meaning house. I came across my first *footybet* walking home from a local bar one evening. It was pitch dark, the backstreets were deserted and suddenly from behind the wall of a compound came the unmistakable sound of an English football commentary. It stopped me dead in my tracks. I walked over to get a closer look and noticed a guard sitting on a low stool wrapped up against the night-time chill in an old army great coat. The sight of him took me by surprise and I immediately veered away to continue walking up the street, but he beckoned me over. I noticed that the wicket doorway in the compound gates was ajar which never happened in Addis Ababa, especially at night. He led me through and we entered the compound of a reasonably nice house. Lights burned inside the windows, the front door was open.

When I got to the front door I stopped. Being a *ferenji* in Addis Ababa meant you could walk in pretty much anywhere. But this was someone's private residence. But the guard gestured to me to go in, saying, "*Eshi, Eshi.*"

I made my way down a parquet floor hallway, past a side table with fresh flowers in a bowl, towards a door where the sounds of the football commentary were coming from. I suppose it was a living room of sorts, but instead of a couple of kids doing their homework, mum tidying up after the evening meal and dad reading the paper, the place was crammed with about fifty men, eyes fixed on an English premiership game on the television at the end of the room.

Normally, a *ferenji* suddenly appearing amongst a crowd of men in a house in the backstreets of Addis Ababa would get noticed, but I barely got a second glance. The room had been completely cleared and crammed with wooden benches and chairs. Those who couldn't get a seat perched on the window sill or sat cross legged on the floor. The one concession to me being a *ferenji* was that the man sitting nearest to me on one of the wooden benches got his mates to bunch up so I could sit down. A couple of minutes later a man appeared with a bunch of money in his hand and an expectant look on his face. I fished into my pocket and pulled out a small wad of birr and he took two single one birr notes. A few moments later a young boy appeared carrying a crate of beer. I gave him a five birr note and he did that thing of opening one bottle of beer with the cap of another. I looked up and there towering above me stood the owner.

"I'm terribly sorry," I began, "I was just walking past and I heard the commentator, and then your guard..."

"No problem, you are most welcome."

After the game was over he gave me a guided tour. Apart from the large living room there were two other smaller rooms on the ground floor that he had also cleared out and filled with seats and television sets. He explained that a satellite dish he had installed in the compound picked up the matches on a South African sports station. He had built up quite a mixed clientele: students, teachers, bus drivers and shoe shine boys all turned up regularly to hand over their couple of birr and watch the games. A hand scrawled note on a piece of paper stuck to the wall outside announced each fixture and kick-off time.

"What about your family?" I asked him.

"They live upstairs," he told me. Presumably when the English football season closed down for the summer months his wife got her downstairs back. I became a regular at the *footybet* where I was always made to feel completely at home. From then on the signs outside announcing the upcoming games were always written in both Amharic and English. As I never saw another *ferenji* in the place, I presumed it was purely for my benefit.

"Have you tried the Addis hash yet?" Dereggie asked me one evening as I was enjoying a beer with him in the bar of the Concorde Hotel. I almost spat it out across his lovingly polished bar.

Dereggie was the manager of the Concorde, which was close to the guest house and where I would sometimes stop by for a beer on my way home. He was always dressed smartly in a dark suit and tie and he had a thin moustache. I never saw Dereggie looking anything other than dapper. His uncle owned the hotel and worked him all hours. The Concorde was notorious throughout Addis Ababa for its nightclub downstairs, which every Friday and Saturday night was packed, wall-to-wall, with the most stunning hookers.

The club itself was in the basement of the hotel and looked like it had been designed by the same guy who did the sets for the movie Saturday Night Fever. It attracted two crowds, those who were there for the girls, and those who weren't. Both seemed to rub along on the dance floor comfortably enough though. Like oil and water they shared the same space but never quite mixed. The trick was to be able to pop in on your own for a couple of beers and hopefully meet a friendly western face or two without getting hit on by a succession of Miss World lookalikes who all wanted to spend the night with you. If one of them caught you glancing in her direction, she would lock onto you like a heat-seeking missile and drape herself all over you for the rest of the night. The best way to deal with them, I found, was to inject a sense of humour into the proceedings. So when one of them would sidle up to me and say, "*Ferenji*, you want sleep with me, two hundred birr." I'd look her up and down and say, "No, three hundred." This would tend to get a startled reaction and then I'd say, "But on second thoughts I don't think you can afford me."

It worked well. They got the message and I hadn't had to be rude about it, which they appreciated. The regular girls got to know me and would sometimes come over just to chat when business was slow, until the next prospect pinged on their radar.

So I knew the Concorde had something of a dubious reputation but I was shocked that Dereggie was in the business of pushing illegal substances.

"Quite a lot of the Brits here in Addis take part, you know. I've heard the British ambassador is a big fan." Blimey, perhaps these Foreign Office types weren't as stuffy as I'd previously thought.

Addis hash, or Hash Harriers, isn't a drug but a largely British institution that can be found in practically any expat community anywhere in the world – it's a running club. However, the emphasis isn't so much placed on fitness as socialising. I pitched up one Saturday afternoon at the Hilton Hotel car park, the hash's regular meeting place. A small crowd of expats were wearing t-shirts emblazoned with the words: A running club with a drinking problem.

Now these were "athletes" I could relate to. They were a mixed bunch and not exclusively British. Aid workers from Sweden chatted to diplomats from Korea and there were quite a few Ethiopians too. Those who had four-wheel-drives offered lifts to those who didn't and our little convoy snaked up and into the Entoto mountains. We arrived at a clearing on one of the heavily wooded slopes, the four-wheel-drives circling like a wagon train in a Hollywood western. Not that we had anything to fear from the locals. On the contrary, the sight of fifty, pink-faced, sweaty, overweight westerners in billowy t-shirts and gaudy bandanas, groaning as they tried to touch the tips of their Nikes, proved far too much for most of them and they fell about.

One man who took his running extremely seriously though was the afore mentioned British ambassador. The Red Letter Day in the Addis Ababa sporting calendar is the Great Ethiopia Run, which is the largest participation road race that takes place on the African continent. This was its third year and it had attracted a field of 18,000, both professional athletes and amateur charity runners. Ethiopia has a long tradition of producing world champion long distance runners, and the greatest of them all is Haile Gebrselassie. I doubt any country in the world has a sporting figure held in such high regard. For a country with such a negative image, to have an athlete taking on and regularly beating the world's best, inspires unprecedented levels of national pride and adulation. It's no exaggeration to say that when Haile runs, Ethiopia stops.

"So, how is it that Ethiopia produces such great runners?" I asked Dereggie over a beer one night in the Concorde.

"In Ethiopia we have a natural advantage," he said, "something that makes our long distance runners the best in the world."

"What's that?" I asked, rising to the bait.

"Lions," he said, slapping me on the back and spluttering in laughter. When he calmed down he explained that half of what he had said was true, Ethiopia did have a natural advantage, and it was altitude. This was plain to see the first time I saw Haile Gebrselassie in the flesh. He had thin arms, thin legs and a small head, and an absolutely huge chest housing an industrial size pair of lungs.

I had been to the last Great Ethiopia Run only a few weeks before, as a spectator. The course was a 10 kilometres route through the streets of Addis Ababa, which had been cleared specially for the day. Both the starting point and the finishing line was the same spot in the middle of Meskel Square, the only place in the whole of Ethiopia big enough to accommodate such a host and just as many spectators. Even so many of us spilled out into the streets that led into the square. The irony wasn't lost on anyone that bright, sunny morning that the only military hardware on display in the Derg's old parade ground was a starting pistol. Haile Gebrselassie, a riot of colour in his red green and gold national track suit, raised it above his head and the flat *Crack!* as he pulled the trigger was greeted by a huge roar from the massed ranks of spectators as the runners set off.

There were separate races within the race itself. In the elite athletes class it was a two horse race between the Ethiopians and their arch rivals, the Kenyans. Huge national pride was at stake. Unicef sponsored 2,000 youngsters in two separate age groups. Small NGOs were represented too. Even Gemini had runners in the race, teams of twins. But the race that held most people's interest was the ambassadors' race. Prestige plays an important role in the world of diplomacy, and I wondered if the successful outcome of talks on such issues as bilateral defence or the setting of a new carbon emissions target might hinge on whether we let the Chinese win.

Eight heads of mission lined up in a Grand International so to speak, including three lady ambassadors. The hot favourite for the event was the two times previous winner, the British Ambassador. However, this year there were rumours circulating that there could be a change in the leader board. A lot of the smart money was being dropped a highly fancied outsider, the Ambassador of the Netherlands, and some punters went so far as to predict a major upset in the form book.

This was in part based on the British Ambassador's rather poor showing a couple of weeks earlier at a charity football match at the Addis Ababa stadium. In a hotly contested battle between a European Union Representative Eleven and the Ethiopian Ministry of Foreign Affairs, our man in the right back position put in a distinctly lacklustre performance. Although, to be fair, he was up against a very nippy third Secretary for Trade and Cultural Development who played on the left wing and who seemed to delight in giving Her Majesty's representative to the Federal Republic of Ethiopia the total run around.

It took almost an hour to get the whole field away and I had visions of an almighty pile-up happening as the elite athletes, who set off first, re-entered the square only to run straight into the backs of the tail-end-Charlies who hadn't yet crossed the start line. But the Ethiopian organisers had done a brilliant job, and with the precision timing that would have made the Swiss ambassador proud, the last of the stragglers and fun-runners cleared the square just as the roar of the crowd told me the top athletes were approaching it from the other direction. The roar got louder as news was past down the line that the Ethiopian, Sileshi Selen, was in front, hotly pursued by a Kenyan. Sileshi crossed the line first and he even had the temerity to knock ten seconds off Haile's previous record, and in front of the great man himself. Addis Ababa went mad. In the women's event, Ethiopia notched up a remarkable first and second with the women's champion, Tirunesh Dibaba, beating her own sister into second place by the slimmest of margins.

And in the ambassador's race normal service, not to say honour, was restored when His Excellency, the British Ambassador, romped home in first place virtually unopposed, the clearly overrated Dutch threat having fizzled out at the halfway stage. Although a highly spirited debutant performance from the Indian Ambassador, who came in third, signalled what many thought would prove to be a very creditable Asian threat to European supremacy in the years to come. Most of all it had been a great day for the Ethiopians and that night the bars of Addis Ababa were packed as people celebrated long into the night. And I doubt if anyone partied harder than the light-fingered bastard in the crowd who had lifted my wallet.

Forays into expat life were actually infrequent and quite brief. Most expats in Addis Ababa worked with other expats, or were married to expats, and interacted with expats on a daily basis. Working at Gem TV my experience was somewhat different. For weeks I would be the only *ferenji* on the premises as it were. Occasionally, another film-maker would come out to work alongside me at Gem TV, but generally they would only be with me for a week or two. Or I might find myself sharing the guest house with a couple of choreographers working with Adugna, but for most of the time it was just me and Ethiopians, my Ethiopians, and that was precisely how I liked it. This was a rare privilege as it gave me a non-expat filtered view of life in Ethiopia and life in Addis Ababa didn't take place in an expat cocooned bubble. Experiences weren't diluted by being expat cushioned. I shopped in *habesha* shops, not the few westernised supermarkets that dotted the Bole Road and Churchill Avenue and which were always besieged by hordes of shiny four-wheel-drives parked outside, surrounded by street kids selling packets of tissues for a birr.

I rarely went to restaurants, when I got home in the evenings I ate *habesha* meals, prepared by Ghidey from whatever local produce was fresh at market that day. There was a great advantage to this which I only re-alised when I returned to the UK. One of the first questions people asked me when I returned was how did I cope with the food in Ethiopia. Actually, I quickly realised it was "coping" with the food in the UK that soon became the problem. For months Ghidey had cooked me the most wonderful meals all from natural foods and without an e number, a pre-servative or chemical in sight. My digestive system had been completely cleansed. But after a week back in the UK I was having distinct problems as my body reacted to all the crap, and lost tolerance of aforemen-tioned crap, that forms an almost unavoidable part of a normal, so called healthy diet.

All that said, expat living could be a bit of a lifeline from time to time, like coming up for air and taking a large gulp of oxygen before you submerged yourself again in all things Ethiopian for another few weeks. And, for me, that meant poker.

The Americans dominated the social scene in Addis Ababa and being very sociable Chris Purdy invited me to hang out with "the guys". And when American "guys" get together, they play poker. It's a big "guy" thing.

Money was never the object. Playing poker was a chance to drink beer and talk guy stuff – namely sport, cars and sex. We met once a week and people took it in turns to host the game. As well as providing the venue, the host also supplied a fridge full of cold beer, a couple of bottles of iced vodka and guy food, which was always pizza and freshly made guacamole. Guys, not being noted for their prowess in the kitchen, especially ones who had spent their entire working lives on overseas postings being cooked for, left it to their Ethiopian housekeepers to do the business with the avocados. They made a pretty good job of it too. Being guys, the gua-camole became almost as competitive as the poker itself. And it didn't take long for the gossip to circulate around Addis Ababa that Mac's Ethi-opian housekeeper's guacamole was now considered as good as Rudy's Ethiopian housekeeper's guacamole, maybe even better.

Although poker was never taken too seriously, on one occasion it did hit the headlines. It had been a rather unremarkable night up until the moment poker history was made. There were six of us round the table at Chris Purdy's place. Chris always did poker evenings particularly well. Leaving aside the guacamole making expertise of his Ethiopian house-keeper for a moment, what made poker nights at Chris's place special was that he had proper poker chips which made a satisfying *clack* sounds when you tossed them into the middle of the table. As well as Chris and myself there was Mark, who worked for a Catholic relief charity; Brendan, who was Australian and whose wife worked for an NGO; a South African, who was something in the tobacco industry; and a retired American who was in Addis Ababa doing voluntary work, and who gloried in the name of Wisconsin Dan. It was half way through the evening when it happened.

We were playing Five Card Stud when Wisconsin Dan won a meagre pot of less than a hundred birr. I had checked out earlier in the betting not being what you might call a "dyed in the baize" poker player. Suddenly the room went very quiet. I looked round their faces and saw that every mouth was hanging open. All except for Wisconsin Dan, who wore a look of what I can only describe as deep beatitude on his face. There on the table in front of him he had placed his winning hand, the ace, king, queen, jack and ten of clubs. He had arranged them in neat little fan, all the little club symbols appearing next to each other in the top right corners.

"Ooh look, you've got a matching set," I said. Wisconsin Dan had much more than that, he had a natural royal flush.

"You know what the chances of that are, guys," he drawled. We all shook our heads. "It's a six hundred and fifty thousand to one shot. I've been playing poker for over fifty years and that's the first time I've seen one."

That was the end of cards for the evening. There was no following that. We hit the vodka instead, and told ourselves we would tell our grandchildren that we had been there, that night in Addis Ababa, when Wisconsin Dan won a few birr with a natural royal flush.

Even then the excitement wasn't over. The South African lived in my general direction and offered me a lift home. As we drove through the dark, deserted streets of Addis Ababa he piled straight into a hyena as it slunk across the road. We sat in silence staring at the lump of dirty fur lying in a heap picked out by the four-wheel-drive's headlights.

"Do you think it's dead?" I asked him.

"Dunno, man," he replied. "But I'm not getting out to find out, ya. I tell you, one thing you don't want to be around is a seriously pissed off hyena."

Next week we convened at his place for the weekly game and he told us that the hyena had done some serious damage to the front of his four-wheel-drive.

"I had a raging hangover too," he told us, "and I tell you guys, I chucked up a couple of times picking bits of hyena out of my radiator grill."

It was almost enough to put you off his Ethiopian housekeeper's rather fine guacamole.

## SIX

# Faith That Carved Mountains

Gem TV had gone quiet for a week, and Selam had suggested I get out of Addis Ababa and go and see something of the country. The flight to Bahir Dar took less than an hour, just long enough for the Ethiopian Airlines flight crew to serve a breakfast of sponge cake and Coca-Cola. As we came into land one of the cabin crew came down the aisle closing the shutters over the plane's windows. Bahar Dar lies a short distance from the southern tip of Lake Tana in northern Ethiopia, half way between Addis Ababa and the Eritrean border, and the airport was playing a key role in the conflict as a staging post for military hardware and supplies being flown to the front. As I got off the plane, I was hurried quickly across the tarmac by soldiers with rifles, past military transports and attack helicopters that bristled with guns, the early morning sunlight glinting off slowly twirling rotors.

Inside I was met by the local representative of the National Tourist Office and we were joined by a couple who had been travelling on the same flight. We got chatting on the drive into town. Jan, a Norwegian, was a priest, and was travelling with his Swedish wife, Elsa. They had been invited to take over a mission in western Ethiopia.

"It is in a very remote place. We will have to learn the local language, there's no electricity and the post has been vacant for eight years," he told me. "My wife is not too keen on it."

Elsa nodded her agreement. "So why are you here?" I asked.

"I was born in Ethiopia, and I've never been back," said Jan. "And I've always wanted to show Elsa where I grew up. So when they asked me to take a look at the mission I thought, why not."

We piled into the NTO tourist bus, our driver cranked it into gear and half an hour later we drew up in front of the Lake Tana Hotel.

"My friend has a boat," said the waif like figure who stood before me. Dawit couldn't have been much older than his late teens. Earlier, I had seen him hanging around the hotel entrance when we arrived. His English was good enough to make preying on tourists a viable line of work for him. But he was polite and friendly and not too pushy.

"He can take you out onto the lake to see the monasteries," he told me and we did the deal. Dawit led me along a footpath lined with palm trees and thick swathes of bushes. Tropical Africa at last, I thought. Along the way we passed a compound ringed by a high wall topped with barbed wire. Beyond it I could plainly see a number of large corrugated iron huts that looked like barracks baking in the sun. Dawit caught me looking at it.

"It is the prison," he said, "it has more than one thousand men."

Further along we turned off the path onto a narrow track. We walked through a field where men toiled at breaking the sun hardened earth. In the doorways of huts, women squatted and prepared food and washed clothes, while young children played in the dirt at their feet. As we approached the lake shore, the track was swallowed by a wall of papyrus reeds that reached up to my shoulders and swayed in a gentle breeze off the lake. We emerged to find a wooden boat moored to a makeshift jetty. The boat was no more than ten feet long and covered in peeling paint that flaked off its sides like clumps of dandruff. How "lake-worthy" it was I had no way of knowing. A tattered awning promised a hint of shade and an outboard motor was mounted on the back. The curtain of papyrus reeds parted and the boatman stood before us. Dawit spoke a few words to him and then turned to me.

"You pay one hundred birr now, and fifty when we get back."

I couldn't work that one out. Was the idea that if we didn't make it back I wouldn't have to pay the extra, which under the circumstances would have hardly mattered. I handed over the money anyway. We slowly putt-putted along a snaking channel of water that cut through papyrus reeds. Dawit scoured the banks for a sight of basking crocodiles.

"It's too hot for them," he said. "At this time of day they like to stay under the water."

Herons stood on logs by the water's edge, drying their outstretched wings in the sun. When one spotted a fish it would dive under the water in a blur of movement, only to emerge seconds later with a wriggling flash of silver in its beak. Fishermen sat astride papyrus reed boats, which made them look like waterborne cowboys, as they paddled out onto the lake in search of *talapiya*, Nile perch.

"They are called *tankwas*," said Dawit catching my gaze as I looked at the curious craft, "the *Wyoto* people make them." It was easy to imagine that the basic design hadn't changed for a thousand years or more. Dawit explained that each *tankwu* had a life of little more than a couple of months. The reeds slowly absorbed the water until they became completely waterlogged and sank. As if to illustrate Dawit's point a few minutes later we passed a fisherman paddling out on his *tankwa* that was so low in the water he looked like he was actually sitting on the lake.

The water of the lake didn't move and stretched for miles. In the distance I made out the faint outlines of the first of the islands, small humps of green that broke the line of the horizon and shimmered in the heat haze. I dipped my hand in the water and it was surprisingly cool. The only sound was the gentle putt-putt of the outboard as we headed out across the vast watery plain. The horizon was a thin, barely discernible line where the lake met the sky in two similar shades of blue. The further we went out into the lake the more the horizon seemed to stretch before our eyes and wrap itself around us on all sides. If you were going to dedicate your life to the contemplation of God and his wonders, surely there could be no more peaceful place on earth to do it.

Everywhere I looked, the island was covered in a tangle of trees and choking vegetation. We stepped out onto a rickety jetty. A narrow path led up a steep slope. Fifteen minutes later, sweating and panting, we got to the top. The monastery was perched on the very top of the island in a patch of land that had been cleared of all vegetation. From a bird's eye view it must have looked like a monk's tonsure. The trees and vegetation had been cleared by hand, which must have been back-breaking work. Small fields of *teff* and vegetables grew in their place.

A monk approached us wearing a grubby robe and a saffron coloured scarf wrapped around his head like a turban. A large, rusty key hung from a piece of string around his neck. His face was cracked and creased like the dark brown leather cover of the Bible grasped in his hands, and wisps of silver beard sprouted from his chin. When he spoke his gapped teeth were the same colour as his headscarf. Visitors were rare but he didn't seem surprised to see us. He beckoned us to follow him, and turned and led us up the last few steps that disappeared into a wooden stockade that encircled the top of the hill. I had to bow my head to walk under the lintel. Emerging on the other side I saw two buildings.

The church was built in the round and next to it stood a square, squat ramshackle stone and wood building that looked like a barn. The monk led us over to the church. The outer ring was an open air cloister. As we approached it the monk motioned for us to remove our shoes. The walls of the cloister were covered with a brown, mud plaster. Then we stepped into the inner ring, which was a circular corridor surrounding the central Holy of Holies. It was gloomy inside and the monk went ahead of us and opened up one of the wooden shuttered windows in the wall. A bolt of sunlight streamed in illuminating on the opposite wall a floor to ceiling fresco of a king in royal blue robes wearing a gold crown. The colours were striking in their intensity. He opened another shutter. This time the light exploded across a painting of the Virgin Mary suckling the infant Jesus. Her face was serene and stared down at me with large, oval, unblinking eyes. The creaking of another wooden shutter heralded another burst of sunlight that lit up a crucifixion scene. Christ wore a crown of thorns, pain was etched into his face with black lines, and blood trickled down his body and legs. Window by window paintings were revealed: burning bodies twisting in hell fire, and ghoulish devils with horns and bat-like wings chopping off arms, legs and heads on the Day of Judgement. A small detail caught my eye. It depicted a peasant farmer ploughing a field with a wooden plough pulled by two oxen. From what I had already seen in the surrounding countryside, little had changed for Ethiopian farmers since these murals were painted over four hundred years ago.

Finally, the monk stopped in front of a pair of floor to ceiling, velvet curtains. They were shabby, thick with dirt, and what might have once been deep red had faded to grubby brown. The monk reached out, and as he balled a fistful of the fabric in his hand, he released a small puffball of dust into the air. Then he yanked the curtain back and the explosion of colour almost knocked me backwards. He repeated his action with the other curtain to reveal a tall pair of painted doors. They were covered in a riot of religious images, dominated by two larger than life-size angels who towered above me brandishing swords.

I have always thought of guardian angels as being benign figures, but these guardians were fierce, menacing, hostile. They were painted in luxuriant robes of red, blue and gold brocade. Large, unblinking eyes held mine in defiant challenge, and they held their swords high above their heads at the point where they were just about to strike me down. They may have been painted hundreds of years ago, but the No Entry message was stark and clear.

"This is the *maqda*," said Dawit, giving the Holy of Holies its Amharic name. the secret part of the church where the *tabot* was kept, hidden from the eyes of the world. *Tabots*, he explained are replicas of the tablets that bore the Ten Commandments which Moses brought down from the mountain and which were housed in the Ark of the Covenant. He explained that every Christian church in Ethiopia houses a *tabot*, which is what consecrates the church, and they are of enormous religious significance. They are paraded during religious ceremonies, the most important of which in Ethiopia is *Timkat*, the feast of the Epiphany which commemorates when Christ was baptized by Saint John the Baptist in the River Jordan.

"The people are not allowed to see them, only the priests," said Dawit in a hushed tone as if even talking about the *tabots* was akin to sacrilege. "The priests carry them on their heads wrapped in rich cloth, and the people sing and there is much celebration. In the night the priests say mass and bless the water of the lake and then we are all baptized again. It happens every year."

"Don't the *tabots* have something to do with the Ark of the Covenant" I said. Dawit needed no further prompting to share with me Ethiopia's version of the story of the Ark. It had nothing to do with Indiana Jones and Steven Spielberg. He told me that the Old Testament tells us that the Ark of the Covenant is the chest of gold built by Moses to house the Ten Commandments, and that he received from God on Mount Sinai. God then told Moses to build a Holy tent so that God could live among his people as they travelled across the desert to the Promised Land. The Ark was placed within the tent which became the most holy of places and where God would appear as a cloud. The Ark could not be touched by mere mortals and only chosen priests were permitted to go near it. When they travelled the Ark was carried on poles so that no one touched it.

"It was the Ark that had the power to cut the waters," said Dawit, recalling the parting of the Red Sea.

Later, King Solomon built a temple for the Ark of the Covenant in Jerusalem. The Queen of Sheba heard about King Solomon and journeyed to Jerusalem to learn from his wisdom. Makeda, as the Queen of

Sheba is known to the Ethiopians, was a powerful ruler of the Axumite Empire, which today would have had its heart in the northern province of Tigrey. Arriving in Jerusalem, she was greeted warmly by the great King and afforded many privileges.

According to legend Makeda was a woman of uncommon beauty and on laying eyes on her King Solomon instantly desired her. But Makeda made Solomon promise that he would not take her by force. He agreed but on one condition, saying that only if she did not take anything of his in return. Then he threw a banquet for the Queen where spicy food was served. Makeda woke in the night feeling thirsty and drank from a cup of water Solomon had placed by her bedside. This was all part of Solomon's plan and he immediately accused Makeda of taking that which was not hers, and then slept with her. When Makeda returned to Axum she gave birth to a son, Menelik, which means Son of the Wise. Years later, Menelik wished to meet his father, and he too journeyed to Jerusalem where he was greeted warmly by Solomon. But before Menelik left, God appeared to him in a dream and instructed him to take the Ark of the Covenant, which stood in the Holy of Holies in the Temple of Jerusalem, back with him to Ethiopia. Menelik and his small band of Ethiopians duly stole the Ark and fled Jerusalem in the dead of night. Solomon and his army chased them for many days but could not catch the young prince, and the most sacred of relics was lost to the children of Israel forever.

"So what happened to the Ark?" I asked Dawit.

"It is still in Ethiopia," he replied, "in the church of Saint Mary Zion in Axum."

This was not the first time this story about the Ark being in Axum had been told to me since I had been in Ethiopia. At first I had always reacted with outright scepticism, but I had learnt that this was very rude and disrespectful and had earned me many a reproving look. I was beginning to realise that in a country that had little in the way of historical documentation, belief played a more important role, and what I called legends took on a whole new meaning that couldn't be so easily dismissed. Dawit, like many Ethiopians, also believed that because God instructed Menelik to take the Ark, it's proof that Ethiopia is God's chosen country. This interpretation also explained one of the few things I had known about Ethiopia before I arrived, namely that Emperor Haile Selassie was the last of the Solomonic line of kings. He claimed he was the last ruler of Ethiopia who could trace his ancestry back to Menelik and the union of Solomon and Sheba.

"So why is Ethiopia a Christian country, and not Jewish?" I asked.

Again, Dawit had a story by way of an answer. "There was a Christian merchant from Tyre called Meropius," he told me. He told me how Meropius made a voyage to India, together with two boys he was educating, Frumentius and Aedesius. On their return they were attacked at sea by pirates and Meropius was killed. The two boys survived and were washed up on the Red Sea coast of the Axumite Empire. They were taken to the king who looked kindly upon the boys, and who later made Frumentius his Royal treasurer. When the king died he left his widow and an infant son as rulers. However, just before he died the king granted Frumentius and Aedesius their freedom, but the queen implored them to stay and help her and her young son rule the empire, which they agreed to do. Axum being a trading empire, Frumentius made contact with other Christian traders and encouraged churches to be built, planting the seeds of Christianity. When the king's son was old enough to ascend the throne, Aedesius returned home to Tyre, but Frumentius journeyed to Alexandria, which was a centre of Christian worship and learning. He sought out the patriarch and told him about how he had been spreading the faith in Ethiopia and pleaded with the patriarch to send a bishop to Ethiopia to offer spiritual leadership to this growing brethren of African Christians. The Egyptian Patriarch could think of no better qualified candidate than Frumentius himself, who returned to Ethiopia as its first Patriarch of the Christian Orthodox church, or *Abuna Selama*, Father of Peace, in 326AD.

"And that is why Ethiopia is one of the oldest Christian countries in the world," Dawit told me with obvious pride.

We left the church and followed the monk over to the other building. Two rough wood doors were held together by a band of iron held fast by a heavy padlock. The priest took the large, rusty key which he wore round his neck, thrust it into the lock and it yielded with a dry click. He pulled open the wooden doors on creaking hinges and beckoned for us to follow. It wasn't a barn at all but the church's treasure house, although a determined boy scout with a hairpin could have picked the lock in seconds. The room inside was lined with wood shelves. The light that spilled in from the opened doors revealed solid silver hand crosses, high domed gold crowns donated by past kings, and ceremonial robes sewn with gold thread. The monk reached forward and with both hands lifted a heavy wooden box off the top shelf and placed it on a small table. Then I saw that it wasn't a box at all, it was a Bible, as wide as it was high. The monk turned the goat skin pages one by one and Dawit told me that he said it was six hundred years old. The text was rendered in perfectly justified lines of exquisitely hand written *Geez*, the ancient, liturgical language of Ethiopia. The pictures were more than illustrations, each one was a painted work of art in its own right. In vibrant colours they told the stories of the birth of Christ, the epiphany, the temptation in the desert, the denunciation, the crucifixion and Christ's resurrection. They had a distinctive style in that the figures were rendered in profile and each face was dominated by a pair of large, oval, staring eyes, the defining feature of Ethiopian art. I couldn't begin to imagine the value of what I was looking at.

As we sailed back across the lake we passed the monastery of Tana Cherkos, which isn't an island but stands at the end of a promontory that juts out into the lake. Once again fact and fable merged together as Dawit explained that it was here that Menelik first brought the Ark of the Covenant when he took it from the Temple of Jerusalem, and that it resided there for six hundred years before it was taken to Axum.

"And Mary rested here when she escaped from Egypt to go to the promised land," Dawit added.

He and the boatman bowed their heads and crossed themselves as we went past, giving me no grounds to doubt their faith in the story.

After dinner Jan and Elsa had retired early to bed, and as far as I could tell we seemed to be the only guests at the hotel. But I was happy to sit on my own in the bar overlooking the lake. Despite, or maybe because of Dawit's extensive history lesson all afternoon, I had picked up a book in reception and started flicking through it.

If you had asked any schoolboy of my generation who discovered the Source of the Nile, we all knew that the answer was John Hanning Speke. In 1858, he discovered the source of the Nile, at Lake Victoria, in modern day Uganda. But that's the White Nile. The fact is the Nile has two sources and the other one – the Blue Nile – rises at Lake Tana in northern Ethiopia. The two merge at Khartoum in the Sudan and then flow north through Egypt to the Mediterranean. The Blue Nile is the more important because most of the water that flows beyond Khartoum is sourced from the Blue Nile. Also, it is the earth washed into the river from the Ethiopian highlands that contributes the silt that floods the alluvial plain every year and makes Egypt fertile.

This much I already knew, but as I read I learnt about a man I had never heard of before, James Bruce, a Scottish explorer, who discovered the source of the Blue Nile here at Lake Tana almost a hundred years before Speke even set foot on the African continent. Trouble was at the time no one believed him.

James Bruce, a Scot, was an extraordinary man. On November 10th, 1768, Bruce set out from Massawa on the Red Sea coast in present day Eritrea for Gondar, then the capital of Ethiopia, or Abyssinia, as it was then known to the Europeans. He attained the high plateau of the

Ethiopian highlands, and crossing it wrote about the herdsmen and cattle he encountered, describing them as "here in great plenty, cows and bulls of exquisite beauty, for the most part completely white". His diaries give fascinating glimpses into life at the time. He describes coming across three soldiers leading a cow. When they reached a river bank they tethered the cow and cut slices of meat from its side, which they ate raw. Then they "stitched" the gaping wound with small skewers, untied the beast and drove it onwards.

It took Bruce three months to reach Gondar, where smallpox had recently broken out. Bruce was something of an accomplished, though amateur, physician. He was summoned by the *Itege*, the wife of the king, in the hope of curing her two children, which he did. This established Bruce as a favourite at court and he quickly rose through the ranks. He made every effort to ingratiate himself, even learning Geez and the local language. Bruce had also arrived in Gondar at a time of civil war. The ruler, King Tekle Haymanot II, faced insurrection from various rebel groups. His chief general was a fearsome leader called Ras Michael. On one occasion, Bruce describes him returning to Gondar victorious at the head of an army of thirty thousand men. Each soldier who had slain a member of the enemy in battle was allowed to sport a red cloth tied to his spear. A more gruesome trophy was the stuffed skin of a rebel leader who had been flayed alive. Ras Michael's cruelty knew no bounds. He had captured forty-four rebel chiefs alive, and he had their eyes gouged out. Bruce then tells us that, "the unfortunate sufferers (were) turned out into the fields, to be devoured at night by the hyenas." However, Bruce managed to rescue three of them.

The Source of the Blue Nile is the Little Abey River, a small stream that flows into Lake Tana, and then emerges from the lake as the Blue Nile. Bruce's first glimpse of the river was the mighty *Tis Abey*, Blue Nile Falls, which lie about twenty miles south of the lake. He was fighting with the army at the time, and although desperate to follow the river back to its source, was forced to return to Gondar.

In 1770, he was finally allowed to leave the court and go in search of his prize. Together with a small expedition numbering only a few men, he climbed one of the high mountains, and on the other side looked down at the Little Abey, describing it with the words, "the Nile itself now only a brook that had scarcely water to turn a mill." Actually, Bruce wasn't the first European to discover the Source of the Blue Nile. History accords this honour to a Spanish Jesuit priest, Pedro Paez, who discovered it in 1618, but Bruce wasn't to know that at the time. So he can be forgiven for waxing lyrical when he finally stood at the water's edge, "standing in that spot which had baffled the genius, industry, and enquiry of both ancients and moderns for the course of near three thousand years."

Bruce was now even more desperate to return home and revel in the adulation he was convinced he so richly deserved. He was also getting heartily sick of the violence of life in Gondar. Every day saw him witness ever more barbaric tortures and executions. "Blood continued to be spilt as water, day after day," he wrote, "priests and laymen, young and old, noble and vile, daily found their end by the knife or the cord. Bodies were left to rot where they lay – and by night the capital was filled with scavenging hyenas."

Bruce caught malaria, but it proved to be his passport out of Gondar, the king giving him permission to leave on health grounds. It took him over a year to reach Cairo. When he finally returned to the UK the story of his epic discovery was treated with scorn. Humiliated, he returned to his native Scotland and wrote his memoirs.

Every evening, as I sat sipping a cold beer on the terrace overlooking the lake, I raised my glass to James Bruce in what became something of a ritual. I felt it was the very least I could do to honour the memory of the old chap.

The drive from Bahar Dar was along a rough, dirt road that cut across a dusty plain. An hour later we stopped at a small village. From there it was a half hour walk up steep banks and into rock-strewn gullies. We crossed a stone bridge over a river that had been built by the Portuguese in the seventeenth century. Portuguese Jesuits were amongst the first Europeans to make inroads into Ethiopia. Prior to the Italian invasion in the 1930s, it was one of the few permanent reminders of the rest of the world's fleeting contact with Ethiopia.

We passed through small hamlets of a dozen or so houses and each time we picked up small groups of children who walked with us, so that by the time we got there we had acquired over twenty of them, like the Pied Piper of Hamelin. Some of them knew a few words of English and tried to sell us trinkets, baskets, scarves, containers for butter made from gourds that had been dried. Patterns had been scratched into their surfaces and they hung from strips of cowhide. I bought a bamboo flute from a young girl who offered it in exchange for pens and an exercise book.

We heard the Blue Nile Falls as a far away whisper that steadily built the closer we got to them. By the time we climbed the last ridge, we had to raise our voices to hear each other and the spray was cool mist on our faces. The sweeping curve of the Blue Nile thundered over a sheer drop of a cliff into a vast bowl of thick green vegetation, where it broke and splintered into a dozen raging torrents that cascaded down channels of rocks and boulders. The force and volume of water churning over the rocky landscape turned the river into a raging white beast.

A permanent curtain of water droplets rose high into the air above the Falls where it diffracted the late afternoon sunlight into a perfect rainbow, as if the gossamer thin fabric of the atmosphere had been ripped open to reveal its underlying, true colours. But the real beauty of the Falls was that apart from the small crowd of children we had acquired, we had the place completely to ourselves.

Even the children, who saw the Falls every day of their lives, went quiet. Watching them I wondered if they realised that this Blue Nile, their *Tis Abey*, was the river that thousands of years before had breathed life into ancient Egypt and made it one of the greatest civilizations the world has ever known. That it had slaked the thirsts of the thousands that had toiled over long years to build the pyramids at Giza. That it had for three thousand years held the images of the temples of Abu Simbel and Karnak in the azure blue of its mirrored reflection. That it was the same river that Cleopatra's barge had sailed upon as she entertained first Caesar and then Marc Anthony. And that all these moments were mere pinpricks of time in the life of the river that thundered all around us.

In a leafy suburb of north London, not a stone's throw from Hampstead Heath, stands a red brick, Victorian pub. It's a popular haunt with trendy urbanites, especially at weekends when it serves gourmet pub grub. It's called the Magdala Arms, and I had frequented it over many years. In all that time I had never once given any thought to its curious name. But I was about to learn that it refers to one of the most bizarre footnotes in British Military history, and these events took place not far from Gondar in northern Ethiopia 1868, which was my next stop. As I relaxed into my seat on the prop job that was to fly the half hour hop from Bahir Dar to Gondar I opened up the history book that Jan had lent me.

For many years during the 19th century Ethiopia had been a leaderless land. Competing warlords fought for supremacy, and years of long and bloody feuding condemned the country to anarchy and chaos. From the ashes arose a mighty leader, Kassa Hailu, who subjugated much of what is today northern Ethiopia, and proclaimed himself, Emperor Tewodros. Tewodros was a complex figure. His early years were spent as a *shifta* outlaw, during which time he earned a reputation as being a brilliant commander.

Many armies were sent against him and he defeated them all. He also became something of a Robin Hood figure by nature of the benevolent way in which he treated the peasants in the regions that he kept conquered, and kept adding to his steadily growing kingdom. He was also a moderniser. His aim in conquering all of Ethiopia was to restore the country to its former greatness, and he made efforts to forge alliances with European powers. But there was also a darker side to Tewodros. He was unpredictable, his rages were fearsome and his cruelty could know no bounds. It was not unknown for him to order that people be whipped to death, or thrown from the top of his mountain fortress to their deaths on the rocks below.

Fearing that his newly forged Christian kingdom would be overrun by Muslim armies on his borders, he appealed to Queen Victoria for help. He wrote her a letter which he gave to the British Consul at his court, Charles Duncan Cameron, to deliver personally to "the Great Queen". However, while on the way Cameron received word from the Foreign Office to send the letter and in the meantime investigate developments in neighbouring Sudan. Consequently, when Cameron returned to Tewodros's court much later with no word from Queen Victoria, and admitting that he hadn't delivered the letter himself, the Emperor flew into a rage. The letter, it later transpired, made it into an in-tray at the Foreign Office in London, and stayed there.

Tewodros eventually lost patience, and in order to spur a response from the British Government, took Cameron hostage, together with the handful of other British and European citizens and missionaries at court. When news of what Tewodros had done eventually reached Britain, there was outrage. How dare an African tin pot dictator challenge the might of the British Empire. The hue and cry demanded that the government take action.

Under the command of Lieutenant General Sir Robert Napier, an army was sent from India, the likes of which had never been seen before. It consisted of thirteen thousand soldiers, twenty-six thousand camp followers and over forty thousand animals, including forty four elephants to carry the heavy artillery. More than two hundred and eighty steamships and sailing vessels transported the colossal enterprise from Mumbai to Zula on the Red Sea coast where an advance party had constructed a seaport to receive them. Railway tracks were laid across the lowlands and steam engines and rolling stock imported to ferry Napier's army into the interior. When the army reached the central massif, it took Napier another three months to trek up and across four hundred miles of mountainous terrain to reach Tewodros's fortress at Magdala.

The battle took place on Good Friday. It was a very one-sided affair. Men with spears and hide shields proved no match for the might of the British Empire's military machine. Tewodros's secret weapon was a large cannon he called Sevastpol, which shattered after firing its first round. A replica of it stands in the middle of a roundabout halfway up Churchill Avenue in Addis Ababa. I've driven past it numerous times in blue and white minibuses on the way up to Piazza, and every time it makes me think that Tewodros must have had absolutely no idea of what he was taking on when he challenged the British. The fighting lasted little more than a couple of hours. British casualties amounted to 20 wounded, two of whom subsequently died, while Ethiopian losses amounted to over 700 dead and twice as many wounded. In a last-ditch attempt to avoid total defeat Tewodros released the hostages, but the gesture was too little too late. With defeat and dishonour staring him in the face, his army destroyed and his once loyal troops slipping away, Tewodros bowed to the inevitable. He took a pistol, held it to his head, and pulled the trigger, an act which would make him a martyr to future generations of Ethiopians. Ironically, the pistol was a present sent to him by Queen Victoria. Then, with this vast kingdom at Napier's mercy, and at the beginning of the European powers' Scramble for Africa, the British commander did something truly extraordinary. He packed up and went home.

However, the British didn't leave completely empty handed. They looted churches and relieved them of illuminated manuscripts, Bibles and sacred *tabots*, many of which remain in the British Museum and private collections to this day. Successive Ethiopian governments have campaigned for their return. And on the rare occasion when a *tabot*, or other precious artefact is returned to the country, it is greeted like a returning hero by ecstatic crowds lining the streets. There was one other possession that Napier took back with him, Tewodros's son, Prince Alemayehu. Apparently, Queen Victoria was very much taken with the young prince, paying for his education and sending him to Rugby school. However, Alemayehu died in October 1879 at the age of nineteen. On hearing the news Queen Victoria said, "It is too sad. All alone in a strange country, without a single person or relative belonging to him. His was no happy life."

The drive from the airport into Gondar took us past a military barracks that had been built by the Italians in the 1930s on the outskirts of the town. It had been converted into a hospital for casualties of war from the Eritrean front. Wounded soldiers lounged around in the shaded grounds, and amputees propped themselves up on wooden crutches. Perhaps these were the lucky ones. In the centre of Gondar we passed a market. Country people sold fruit, vegetables, milk, butter, whatever they had to spare and would make them a few birr. They were mainly women and their daughters, the men and boys had stayed back to work their highland farms, the fathers looking after the crops and the boys tending the livestock.

In the seventeenth century the Emperor Fasilidas chose Gondar as his new power base. A highland city, it made for a natural fortress standing at the crossroads of the major caravan routes that stretched north to the Red Sea, Sudan and Egypt, and along which gold and slaves travelled. For centuries Ethiopia's kings had come from various bands of warlords fighting for power and who were always on the move. Fasilidas was the first to build a permanent settlement and for the next two hundred years and more, Gondar became the closest there had ever been to a capital. Its name derives from *Gon* and *Dar* meaning Great and City.

Fasilidas established his authority by building a great castle. He spawned a dynasty that ruled for many generations, and each king that followed him built his own castle next to that of his predecessor, so that today Gondar is known as Africa's Camelot.

Fasilidas's original castle is still the most impressive. It stands three storeys high and has four tall towers, one at each corner. The other castles are smaller but no less impressive in their architectural detailing, which betrayed Portuguese, Indian and Arab influences. The castles looked serene in the warm glow of the late afternoon sunshine. There was a fairytale quality about them, I thought, and they wouldn't have looked at all out of place as an illustration in a story by the Brothers Grimm. I wondered what James Bruce would have made of their benign appearance.

We stayed in Gondar for only one night, it was a stop-over on our way to Lalibela. Over dinner I asked Jan, who had been to Lalibela before, to give me a bit of background about the rock hewn churches I had heard so much about. "All you need to know" he said, "is that tomorrow you will see the eighth wonder of the world."

The darkness was so black inside the church it felt like a heavy thing. Suddenly the beam of a torch lanced out and there he stood before me, picked out in its wavering beam. The saint had been carved in bas-relief out of the rock wall of the church nearly eight hundred years ago. To the western eye the rendering was crude, but all the more imposing for it. A standing figure, it was life size, which was momentarily disconcerting because it meant that the saint looked me straight in the eye. Our Christian tradition places those we revere on high, they don't descend to our level and admonish us face to face. His features were strong and simple and bore the classic planes and lines of the African. His gaze was direct. He wore a headdress and flowing robes that reached to the floor. His left hand was concealed beneath the folds of his robe and his right hand held a prayer stick surmounted by a crucifix. All this had been revealed in a couple of seconds as the beam of the guide's torch played down the figure. I called to mind Howard Carter's words when his flickering match illuminated the interior of Tutankhamen's tomb for the first time. I, too, was gazing upon "wonderful things".

The rock hewn churches of Lalibela are a UNESCO World Heritage Site, and someone I had met in Addis Ababa described them as, "like Petra, but in a setting that's as wild and remote as Machu Pichu".

We flew in on a grey and cloudy day. It was a forty minute drive from the small airport to the town of Lalibela, perched at over seven thousand feet in the rugged Lasta mountains. The rains had turned the roads into squelching, clawing, clacking quagmires, and you could set your watch by the downpours.

We drove across a rocky and bleak landscape that reminded me of the backdrops I had conjured up in my mind's eye when I first read Wuthering Heights. The only sign of life we encountered on the entire drive was a lone shepherd boy herding goats, who stopped to watch us drive by. His legs were bare and the wind tugged at the leather cloak pulled tightly round his thin shoulders, but he seemed immune to the cold as he smiled and waved as we drove past him along the narrow, winding road that continued to thread its way around rocky outcrops and up over ever climbing switchbacks until we finally dropped down into the town. Apart from a handful of small hotels, there was nothing to suggest that Lalibela contained anything special at all. The roads were narrow and unkempt and the faces of the people were careworn with hard work.

In order to have faith, we sometimes have to suspend our belief in more familiar 20th century concepts such as science and technology. Here, in the 12th century, eleven churches were carved out of the surrounding, bare rock landscape. To this day archaeologists still don't know how they managed to achieve it. Being Ethiopia, perhaps there's more to be gained by looking to the realm of legend for an answer. It tells us that in the early 12th century a prince was born into the ruling Zagwe dynasty in the remote mountain town of Roha, in what is the present day region of Wollo. When he was born a swarm of bees descended on his crib and his mother recognised this as a sign that soldiers would one day serve her son. She christened him Lalibela, which meant that the bees recognised his sovereignty. But the king, Lalibela's elder stepbrother, became jealous and poisoned the young prince. As Lalibela lay fighting for life angels descended and lifted him up to heaven, whereupon God instructed him to return to Roha and build the greatest churches the world had ever seen.

The eleven churches are arranged in two groups separated by a rocky stream called the Jordan River. Lalibela abounds in references to the Holy Land. Most of the churches are *monolithic*, or free standing, which means they had been carved out of the rock on all four sides. Others are still attached by one wall to the surrounding landscape. They are linked by deeply carved trenches which give the site the atmosphere of a vast catacomb. Some of the churches stand over ten metres high and Bet Giorgis has been carved completely below ground level. Each carved church is unique in design, both inside and out, the interiors having been hollowed out and lined with sculpted reliefs and religious murals, and each church stands in its own cavernous courtyard. The churches not only constitute some of the most spectacular architecture ever imagined but can also be hailed amongst its most dramatic sculptures. The rock from which they have been carved is rusty red, and looks like sandstone, but is much harder and more unforgiving to carve.

Legend tells us that it took forty thousand people to carve the churches, and that's about all we know about how they came to be. Legend also has it that every night when the workers rested, angels descended from heaven to continue the work.

We began at the church of Bet Medhane Alem which means "Saviour of the World". It is the largest rock hewn church in the world. It stands in a courtyard six metres deep and we walked into it down a series of roughly hewn stone steps. As we descended the shadows deepened and the sounds of the town, above and beyond, muffled to silence. My eyes were fixed on the uneven steps all the way down so that when I got to the bottom and looked up at the church I was totally unprepared for the effect. From above I had got no idea of the true scale of the church or of its detailing. It was a very different story when you looked up at it though. The church towered above me majestically and its resemblance to the Parthenon in Athens was striking. Thirty-six pillars support the roof from the outside and another thirty-six line the walls of the interior. It was almost impossible to imagine that every square inch of the structure, both inside and out, and every lovingly rendered architectural detail and motif, had been carved by hand over eight hundred years ago.

The churches encompass the intimate as well as the impressive. From Bet Medhane Alem a short tunnel led us to another courtyard which housed three smaller churches, which were more like chapels. The one held in the highest affection is Bet Maryam, the house of Mary. Inside it was exquisite in its detail and had a richly decorated painted roof. Looking at Bet Maryam I began to recognise some of the architectural influences that must have been at work when the churches were carved. Windows were shaped in the form of *stelae*, the monumental funeral pillars of the emperors of the Axumite Empire. Everywhere I looked I saw crosses rendered in many forms: Latin, Greek, and even Maltese crosses, suggesting the influence of crusading holy orders. This raised an intriguing question. Did the crusaders hear tales of Lalibela in the Holy Land and journey to this remote, mountain kingdom to seek out its mysteries, I wondered. Or perhaps Christians from Lalibela took the cross and went on crusade to the Holy Land, returning with knowledge and ideas gleaned from European crusaders. Was it possible that once upon a time this forgotten corner of sub-Saharan Africa was a major cultural and religious crossroads?

In the middle of the church was a pillar covered by a richly embroidered cloth.

"Do not touch it," hissed our guide. "This is where Jesus Christ leaned when he appeared to King Lalibela."

He told us that the Ten Commandments are written in Geez under the cloth, and if anyone touches the pillar they will disappear. "Phut!" he added, as he splayed his fingers like a firework and rolled his eyes. Outside, in a small courtyard, stood a carved stone bath. "When the women have a problem making a baby this is where they come." he explained. The waters held miraculous powers and women who could not conceive would immerse themselves in its cold waters for an entire night.

The church of Bet Golgotha, named after the hill where Christ was crucified, had a powerful and resonating atmosphere. It is also the most sacred of the Lalibela churches. We approached it along a steeply carved ravine. The walls rose sheer on each side and the footpath was only wide enough for one person to walk along it at a time. The sky darkened dramatically and it began to rain. Inside the church the rock floor, walls and ceiling were anthracite black. This was where the carving of the saint had first startled me in the beam of our guide's torch. There were six other life-size figures of saints carved into the walls. Each time the guide's torch played across them they jumped out at us in stark relief, like holy jack-in-the-boxes.

"A place in heaven is now yours," our guide explained, before taking us over to a stone slab set in the floor. "Here lies King Lalibela," he said, lowering his voice.

A priest appeared wearing heavily brocaded ceremonial robes, holding a processional cross. "This is the cross of King Lalibela," our guide informed us in a hushed tone, "it is the church's most sacred relic. You may take photographs."

We lifted our cameras and the priest reached into the folds of his robes and produced a pair of wraparound sunglasses. A moment later I saw why. The flashes of our cameras fired, and bolts of light bounced off the walls like trapped lightning.

To get to the church of Bet Goirgis we had to walk across a rocky plateau. At first all I could see was a large, square, gaping hole the size of two tennis courts placed side by side. Standing on the edge the walls dropped sheer for fifteen metres. The church stood inside the carved chasm like a cross-shaped peg in a square hole. Legend says that when St George heard about the rock-hewn churches he was very angry that not one of them had been dedicated to him. He appeared to King Lalibela who promised to carve for him the finest of them all. So impatient was the saint to set eyes on his church that he rode his horse down into the cavern to see it, and the holes that pockmark the walls are said to be his horse's hoof prints. Less fanciful were the open graves that had been chiselled out of the rock walls and which housed the decaying remains of priests and monks.

As we left I passed a monk standing quietly by the entrance to the church. His weathered features were creased in prayer as he pored over a copy of a dog-eared Bible. The sight of him was a reminder that as well as being a place of huge historical and architectural significance, above all, to millions of Ethiopian Orthodox Christians, Lalibela remains a living religious centre, as important today as it was back in King Lalibela's time, and that for many Ethiopians life and religion have changed little here in over eight hundred years. In this wild and remote corner of Ethiopia faith had not moved mountains, it had carved them.

Back in Addis Ababa, having completed the DKT commercials, and seen them go to air, it was time to leave, my work was done. My business partners back in London had been very patient, but they were keen to get their new advertising agency up and running. On my last day at Gem TV everyone surprised me in Selam's office with a plaque depicting the Blue Nile Falls, the castles at Gondar and the rock-hewn churches of Lalibela. On the back they had written a message in felt pen: To Bob, from all the students at Gem TV. It hangs on the wall opposite my desk.

"They paid for it out of their own salaries," Selam told me later.

The next morning, which was a Saturday, Selam and Sintayehu arrived at the guesthouse with Getachew to take me to the airport. I said fond farewells to Ghidey who had looked after me so kindly. Then, just as we were about to leave, who should turn up but Misrak. I was touched. Or perhaps she was just making sure I left the country.

The first few weeks back in London flashed by in a blur of meetings. I moved into my new offices located off Carnaby Street in the heart of Soho, the capital of London's adland. Every morning I emerged from Oxford Street tube station and grabbed a cappuccino on my way to the office just like the thousands of others working in the "meedja". Lunchtimes were spent having catch up "Heh, I'm back" lunches with old friends, and the evenings saw me meeting up with young, hungry, freelance creative teams, assessing their portfolios of work and extolling the virtues of my new agency. Within the first couple of months we made our first TV commercial for a pizza delivery company. It was never destined to be an award winner, but it got my fledgling ad agency up and running. After slaving away in the business for twenty years, arguing with bolshie clients and clashing with creative egos, I had finally made it to the top. I was living every adman's dream. I was the creative director of my own agency. I was even interviewed by the marketing business press and had my photo taken, looking moody, standing on a fire escape. But I had managed to do my bit for Africa along the way. My conscience was clear, my prospects of making a lot of money were good and the future looked bright. So I quit.

It took me a while to realise but working with Gem TV hadn't got Ethiopia out of my system. It had planted the hook deeper. The experience had changed me and flogging pizza just wasn't going to do it for me anymore. This created a problem because it wasn't as if I could go back to Ethiopia. Gem TV didn't have another project for me to work on. I had been put on another path but unfortunately it wasn't leading anywhere. I think my new business partners realised my heart wasn't really in the new agency even before I did.

It took me six months to come to the same conclusion. They could not have been more understanding, and it has to be said that I had let them down badly. They had given me every support and backed my venture with the hard-earned reputation, and in return I had failed to deliver on the commitment I had made to them. I agreed to stay on for as long as it took to find someone to replace me and take over so that the business would seem to carry on as normal. I knew what I didn't want to do. More frustratingly, I knew what I did want to do, there was just no way of doing it. I was in limbo. I spent the next six months trying to chase up freelance work but there was very little going. My friends were understanding but I suspected quite a few of them thought I was mad to have thrown away my own agency – and for what? But it was impossible to explain to people how my Ethiopia experience had changed me. I hadn't fully worked it out myself. Especially, what working with Gem TV had meant to me. And then about a year later the phone rang.

"Hi Bob," said a familiar voice.

"Hello Carmela," I replied.

"We need help to make a fundraising film about Gemini. Are you doing anything?"

# SEVEN
# Gemini

I emerged from Bole International Airport and inhaled the smell of smoky butter which is the telltale hallmark of Ethiopia. I crossed over the road and walked the short distance to the car park where I knew Getachew would be waiting. His nut-brown face split into a huge grin as I approached and his gold tooth glistened in the blinding sunlight. We locked shoulders, like friendly rugby players, in the traditional gesture of welcome between men and patted each other's backs.

We loaded my bags into the four-wheel-drive and we took the now familiar drive to the guest house. It was a Sunday and the Bole Road was quiet as we left the airport and headed into town. In a few hours it would be back to a snaking, clogged, noisy ribbon of dented horn-blaring metal. Getachew turned into the Meskel Flower Road and the four-wheel-drive clattered over railway tracks of the old Addis Ababa to Djibouti railway that cut across the tarmac like livid scars, a symbol of the hopes of prosperity and modernisation from Emperor Haile Selassie's time, dreams that died in the dust.

A few minutes later, Gethachew turned into the first of the rough stone and pitted side roads, and we bounced along them like sailors tossed in a heavy sea, until with a final jolt as Getachew jumped on the brakes, we pulled up short in front of the all too familiar wrought iron gates that shielded the guest house compound from view. Getachew leaned on the horn and a few moments later a sleepy looking guard slipped the bolts and drew back the doors which opened with a teeth numbing clatter. It felt good to be back.

Being a Sunday there was no sign of Ghidey. The guest house was spick and span as usual and it appeared I had the place to myself. My room looked like it hadn't been touched since I left it. The next morning I woke to the clanking sound of the lock being turned in the front door, and a minute later I heard the rattle of pots and pans being put in the sink for washing as Ghidey got about her daily chores.

I lay in bed staring up at a couple of flies chasing each other round the paper light shade that hung from the centre of the ceiling, and my thoughts turned to the Gemini film we were about to make. Essentially, it would be a documentary, with a donor plea at the end. I was looking forward to making the film because it would introduce me to all the other parts of the organisation I didn't really know much about. I had always suspected that working at Gem TV I had only seen the tip of the Gemini iceberg.

As I listened to Ghidey laying the table for my breakfast I recalled the last time I had seen her, when she said goodbye to me as I left for the airport. I'm not the most organised person in the world, and every time I left the guest house to go to Gem TV I would either forget something, or have to send Getachew back for it later in the four-wheel-drive. I knew Ghidey found this totally bemusing, and it wasn't long before she took the matter into her own hands. Every morning as I left she did her level best to make sure I had everything I needed. She would stand before me and check me over like an over anxious mother sending her little boy off to his first day at school.

Not being able to speak any English didn't make Ghidey's task any easier and her inspections were accompanied by a series of sighs and little clucking noises she made with her tongue. When she was satisfied she'd usher me on my way with a wave of her hand. Even so, my haphazard approach to things would still sometimes defeat her best efforts. And many was the time Getachew and I hadn't driven more than a few yards when out of habit he would check his rear view mirror and then pull over. I would swivel round in my seat to see Ghidey, doing her best to run after us in her floor length skirt, waving a file of papers or a DVD of a film at us.

The day I left Ethiopia she had walked up to me, smiled sweetly, peered long into my eyes, stretched out her hand and touched me lightly on the cheek. It was the same gesture with which she greeted each of her four children every evening when she got home. Then, with a little sigh, she had looked across at Getachew with an expression that seemed to say, "And he's over here because he's from the *developed* world". This time I'm going to show Ghidey I can do better, I said to myself, and threw on some clothes and stepped into the kitchen.

"*Dehna*, Bob, *dehna*," came the traditional greeting, are you fine? But the only thing familiar about it were the words, because they hadn't been spoken by Ghidey, but by a large, smiling woman. "Shewaye," she said by way of introduction, pointing at her ample chest.

"*Dehna*," I said in response, I'm fine. "*Dehnanesh, Shewaye?*" I asked in reply, using the feminine form of address.

I didn't ask where Ghidey was as it didn't seem polite, but I knew that people were always being moved around Gemini from job to job. Perhaps she was now doing something else. I hoped it allowed her more time with her family. Later that evening Carmela took me out to dinner.

"So, where is Ghidey?" I asked her, as I prodded a succulent piece of African beef.

"Oh," said Carmela and then paused, "I'm afraid she died, probably AIDS related, but people don't talk about it."

The gentle woman who had been so kind to me was now just another faceless statistic on a UNAIDS spreadsheet. There were millions more just like her filed under "Ethiopia", and many more millions all over Africa. HIV/AIDS was just one of the problems Gemini was trying to tackle at grass roots level. All of a sudden the film we were about to make took on an even greater importance. Over the next hour I quizzed Carmela on Gemini to get the back story on what we would be filming.

"I came here in 1984 and worked as a paediatrician at the Black Lion Hospital," Carmela said, "and that's where it all started really."

This was also the year of the Great Famine, and while I was being shocked out of my lethargy back in London, as well as others like me all over the world, by Michael Buerk's news reports from the front line of the famine, Carmela's attention was focussed elsewhere. She was fighting a battle against poverty on a much smaller scale, one that never commanded the world's headlines. She explained that one of the first things she noticed was that twins born to mothers living in the slums of Addis Ababa faced a real struggle to survive. They were often born with frighteningly low body weight and their mothers, being malnourished themselves, couldn't breast-feed them.

"Many of them turned to bottle feeding with disastrous results," she said, "which led to severe diarrhoea and vomiting."

Back then in Ethiopia, one in every three twins died before its first birthday. And the birth of twins meant two mouths to feed rather than one, putting an extra strain on families already living in terrible poverty and struggling to survive.

"Very often, it pushed them over the tipping point," she said.

So Gemini started life as a feeding centre, which Carmela told me she started in an old shipping container in the grounds of the Black Lion Hospital where she worked. Over the years the operation expanded and by the time I became involved Gemini had become a well established NGO looking after the feeding, healthcare, housing, education and other welfare needs of over twelve thousand of Addis Ababa's poorest people. Until now, my only contact with the wider world of Gemini had been fleeting. I realised that making this film would reveal to me in stark close-up what being one of the poorest of the poor in the slums of Addis Ababa was like. Many of the families were households headed by women, the men having disappeared into the army years ago never to be seen again, or they had simply abandoned their families.

Carmela explained how they lived. Their houses were more like huts made of mud and straw and had corrugated iron roofs. Most of them didn't eat more than one poor meal a day. Three quarters of the Gemini households had no access to water in their compounds and a third of them didn't have a latrine. Another two thirds of the families had no income. Those that did work, and again they were mostly women, were forced into back-breaking labour as road builders or wood carriers.

Previously, on drives to Entoto, I had been shocked by the sight of these wood carrying women. Every day many hundreds of them would walk the ten kilometres from where Addis Ababa sprawled in the bottom of a vast volcanic bowl up into the Entoto mountains and return carrying heavy loads of firewood that they had scavenged in the forest. For many in Addis Ababa, firewood was the only source of fuel for cooking and this was the means by which it was harvested and delivered. Girls as young as fourteen and fifteen, and women as old as sixty or more, would struggle under loads that could approach their own body weight, and which were tied to their backs with string that cut into their flesh mercilessly, like cheese wire.

The road down from Entoto was punctuated with long, waist high, concrete plinths that the city authority had built for them, where the women could stop and rest their loads upon them. The women were no doubt grateful for the momentary relief they offered, but for me these concrete plinths came to symbolise an institutional acceptance of this appalling degradation of women. The sight of the old wood women was the most pitiful, bent almost double under the weight of their crippling loads, they shuffled from plinth to plinth, many of them in bare feet and under a blistering sun. Equally as crushing as the loads tied across their backs, and which were often as long as the women were tall, must have been the knowledge that this would be their existence every day for the rest of their miserable lives, or until their bent and broken bodies finally gave out and condemned them to starve.

Carmela explained that Gemini didn't just look after twins in a family, but entire families themselves.

"How do you feed or educate one child in a family and not the other?" she said.

The first thing Gemini did was make sure their families got enough to eat. So Gemini provided wheat, corn, soya blend, oil and milk, and they built a demonstration garden at the main Gemini compound to show families how to grow vegetables in a small urban space. Over the years Gemini's work expanded to include health, education and welfare, programmes which became life saving for hundreds of young children. Gemini built a rudimentary health centre, recruited and trained nurses, instigated health education and referred patients to hospitals.

Another problem was the large size of Gemini families. One of the pillars of Gemini's work was placing women at the heart of family life, empowering them with choices. So Gemini provided family planning services for its mothers, allowing them the opportunity to decide for themselves if they wanted to have any more children, and educated them about child spacing.

For the next few weeks I would be filming people who either worked for or were looked after by Gemini. Each one was a remarkable person in their own right, each one went to camera to tell their remarkable story, and each one spoke for many others just like them. Like a cutaway shot in a film, each story was like a piece in a jigsaw, which bit by bit slowly pieced together my growing understanding of Ethiopia; the country's recent history, its problems and challenges, but most of all the remarkable strength, belief and resilience of its people. The one story we would not be able to tell was Ghidey's.

EIGHT

# Cutaway to Yeshi

*In film, a cutaway is a shot that shows something different from the main thing that is being shown.*

Gemini's story didn't begin just with Carmela, but also with an Ethiopian woman called Yeshi Belay. Yeshi was the first Gemini mother. Hers is just one of thousands of lives Gemini has transformed. Like so many others we would interview over the coming weeks, we filmed her in the small house in the backstreets of Addis Ababa where she had managed to raise six children.

Her hair was braided and she wore a traditional white cotton dress. Yeshi was plump and smiling and it was hard to imagine that she had ever known hardship. As the crew started to set up their equipment I asked Adanech, who was directing, to get Yeshi to tell me her story. With Yeshi wiping away tears as she spoke, Adanech simultaneously translating, and me scribbling furiously in long hand, this is Yeshi's story – in her own words – as she told it to us.

My name is Yeshi Belay. I am the first Gemini mother. Dr. Carmela started helping my twins just as I gave birth to them in the Black Lion Hospital . I was in a big problem. Then she helped me. Thanks be to God. Now I am fine. All six of my children have finished school now. All of us work now. Long life to Dr. Carmela! She saved me from hanging myself.

When I was in labour I gave birth to the first one but I couldn't give birth to the second one. After I gave birth to the first one I told the doctor that the placenta should have come out with the boy, and so I asked him why the placenta has not come out yet. The doctor told me to just heave. But nothing happened, it wouldn't come out. Then I asked him again, "Why has the placenta not come out yet?" He then told me that I have one more child inside. I was shocked and I got up and sat down. I asked him how should I heave. He showed me and I heaved sitting there. But again nothing. I thought the baby would have to come out of my mouth. It was then that they rushed me to Dr. Fantahun who saw me and said that the child is misplaced and that they should hurry to save my life. They rushed me to the operating theatre and operated on me. They took out the child and I lost consciousness for three days.

Afterwards, when I woke up they brought me the children and the first question that came to my mind was 'what will I feed them?' and 'God why did this happen?' I told them to take the children away. But they told me to look at their faces. So I said 'Ok they look good, but take them away now'.

I had nothing to eat. I had no milk to give to the children. I couldn't breast- feed them. Since the children were twins I couldn't feed them both. Also, I had no income. I used to work as a daily labourer carrying things for a living. I had four other children. I was worried. My husband was sick and couldn't work. We thought the earth and sky had closed in over us.

There was this Swedish woman and she thought my children looked nice. So she brought me clothes. Dr Carmela used to come too and look at them. The help started then. Dr. Carmela got me milk and clothes for the children, even when I left the hospital. I have reached this far because of her. I went back to working as a daily labourer on building sites, carrying bricks and trays of cement. I decided to live one day at a time to try and rear my children. But when I have nothing to feed them I think it is better to lose my life than watch my children starve. I tried hanging myself three times. Then when I saw my children sleeping in their beds I felt sorry for them and told myself to just spend one more day with them. Dr. Carmela found me in this dilemma and rescued me. She told me that funds are being raised to help mothers with twins. So when I was in a tight situation, and when I was hungry, I went to Dr. Carmela and she gave me food. Then Dr. Carmela told me to stop the heavy daily labouring job. She told me that Gemini is going to be established soon and I will get work there. So when Gemini was established I started working as a cook for the day care children and spice workers. I used to make injera and cook the wot sauce.

Now my twins are twenty five years old. If Gemini didn't exist I wouldn't have existed. Gemini pays for school fees, buys uniforms, gives exercise books, and provides medical care. It even provides medical care and education for my children who are not twins. Gemini has done a lot of things for me. I don't have enough words to tell it all. Gemini has bought my life a hundred times. I love Dr. Carmela more than my own life. She wiped my tears away. She cried when I cried and laughed when I laughed. She is the one who suffered with me during those terrible times. So she helped me reach here, and taught my children and saved me from hanging myself.

# NINE

# Rastaland

Lisa and her friend didn't present business cards, I only wish they had, then perhaps I wouldn't have made such a complete fool of myself. They were dressed casually in baggy linen trousers and tops, and they wore sandals, all of which was standard attire for women NGO workers. They were both blond and blue-eyed. For the first fifteen minutes Lisa hadn't said a word, her friend had done all the talking.

"We are from the Swedish branch of Save The Children," she explained.

It turned out they did a lot of work with refugees in camps and used drama as a way of getting kids to open up about their experiences.

"Would you be interested in helping us make some drama films with these kids?" she asked.

Now if there's one thing film-makers like to do more than make films, it's talk about making films. So I promptly launched into a fifteen minutes long lecture about the power of drama and film-making to change people's lives. After all, I had been working in Ethiopia for a few months and had made some TV commercials, so I knew what I was talking about. I asked Lisa a question about Save The Children and she replied that she didn't actually work for them.

"I'm just here to help my friend if I can," she explained in a gentle American accent.

"What do you do back in the States?" I asked.

"I make films," she replied.

I had come across do-gooders like her before. They were always very nice and kept talking about "the community". But just because they had a camcorder and had filmed a couple of end of term high school plays it didn't exactly qualify them as film-makers. To be honest, most of the ones I had come across hadn't even been particularly talented amateurs. But this was Save The Children, one of the biggest international aid agencies in the world, who could become an important client for Gem TV, so I thought it best to play along as politely as possible.

"That's nice," I said, "and where do you do this?"

"In Hollywood."

Lisa Lindstrom was an A-list producer. The woman I had been patronising for the last quarter of an hour was a player, someone who, when she phoned Steven Spielberg, he interrupted his meeting to take her call. You couldn't take anyone for granted in Addis Ababa.

So when Teddy Dan walked into the office a couple of weeks later, and Wonde told me he was Ethiopia's greatest living reggae star, I was more than prepared to believe he was closely related to Bob Marley.

"Yoh, Barrrrrrrb," Teddy Dan greeted me. "Wonde here tells me you're the man to talk to about a video."

Next to him Wonde was almost beside himself with excitement. Reggae was his second passion after film-making, and he would give anything to direct this video.

Teddy Dan looked like central casting's idea of a reggae star. He was tall and his dreadlocks reached all the way down his back. His denims were faded and ripped, and he wore lots of ethnic jewellery and a woolly hat made up of three coloured bands, the red, gold and green of the Ethiopian flag. He drawled rather than spoke, and in all the time I knew him I never once saw him without a joint stuck in the corner of his mouth. And every time you saw him you never knew what kind of smile you were going to get. It depended on whether he had his false teeth in that day. Teddy wasn't alone.

"Meet the barrrnnnd," he said. He was flanked by two fellow Rastafarians who both hailed from Manchester. Alton was the drummer and
Spencer played keyboards. Spencer had also brought his girlfriend along,
who doubled as their road manager.

"I've written a song we want to turn into a video," Teddy Dan said.
"It's called United States of Africa, and I want the video to show Rastafarian life here in Shashamane."

Shashamane, I knew, was a major town about four hours drive south
of Addis Ababa on the way to Awassa. I'd heard it was a pretty rough
place. Everybody else in Ethiopia knew it to be the home of the Rastafarian community. Before I came to Ethiopia the only thing I knew about
the Rastafarians was that Bob Marley was one, but over the next few days
I learnt a lot more. The founder of the Rastafarian religion was Marcus
Garvey, who established it in Jamaica during the 1930s. About this time
a young, regional leader was coming to prominence in Ethiopia.

The Rastafarians believed that Ethiopia was the true land of Zion,
the resting place of the Ark of the Covenant, which is something they
shared with Ethiopian Orthodox Christian belief. So Ethiopia became
the spiritual home of the Rastafarians even though Marcus Garvey,
and practically every other Rastafarian for that matter, had never been
there. Later, after I had got to know Teddy Dan a lot better and we talked
about this, he said, "Yaaah, but the Bible says Moses and the Israelites
had never been to the promised land before they went there either."

He had a point. Ethiopia became the promised land for Rastafarians
from all over the world, who gave up their old lives and made the exodus
to Ethiopia. The regional ruler went on to become Emperor Haile Selassie, the last of the great Solomonic line of kings. The Rastafarians believed,
as they still do, that the Emperor was anointed by God as his representative on earth. So on assuming the throne, Haile Selassie found himself
to be not only the lord and master of millions of Ethiopians, but also the
subject of religious worship by a growing number of Jamaicans. As more
and more Rastafarians arrived in Ethiopia he realized he had to do

something with them, so he gave them a couple of hundred of acres of land around Shashamane, which has been their physical as well as their spiritual home ever since. When the Emperor was crowned he adopted the name Haile Selassie, which means follower of the Trinity. Before he was known by his title *Ras*, and his given name, *Tafari*, from which we get Rastafarian.

Nobody in the room, myself included, had ever made a pop video before, so in the finest traditions of Gem TV I said, "No problem, you've come to the right place." Then we all sat around and entered into a big group discussion about how we were going to do it. Fortunately, the high end production values normally associated with producing a music video didn't pose a problem. Teddy Dan didn't have much money. Not that we would have had a clue how to spend it if he did. This was one of the more challenging things about film-making in Ethiopia. It was never about budget or equipment, it was always about using your creativity and ingenuity instead. Everyone chipped in, including the band, and half an hour later we had a plan. The shoot would be dictated by the locations.

"Marrrn, we have a gig at Midora this Saturday," said Teddy Dan. Midora was a popular reggae bar in Addis Ababa. "So, I aaaaam thinking we could shoot the concert tharrr."

"Fine, but won't they want a location fee?" I asked.

"No praaablem," said Teddy Dan, "Midora is owned by Alton's sistaaar. The rest of the shooting we can do in Shashamane."

This was greeted by a round of nodding from the rest of the band. The one thing I did know about music videos was that you could shoot lots of different set-ups and get away with continuity flying out the window. There were a number of locations in and around Shashamane we could shoot in Teddy Dan told us, and most of them, it seemed, were owned by "Alton's sistaaar". Talk about looking after each other, I was beginning to think the Freemasons could learn a thing or two from the Rastafarians. The problem was how best to do it.

The band had a copy of the song on CD and Gem TV had a ghetto blaster. Put the two together, I figured, and we had a playback machine that the band could mime to when we were on location. They only potential hiccup was they would have to get the miming spot on, otherwise when we edited the footage to the good quality recording of the song on the CD, it wouldn't be in sync. Not very MTV, but there was no reason why it shouldn't work. Finally, I asked Teddy Dan to recite the lyric for us line by line, which I wrote down. Then I handed it over to Wonde saying, "Here you go mate, start thinking of some visuals to go with that lot."

I could have walked past Midora's without noticing it. It was hidden behind a high stone wall on a busy part of the Jomo Kenyatta Road. But if you were a Rastafarian you'd know where to find it. It was basically an empty room and we got there early to set up. There was a raised stage at one end and a bar at the other. In between there were no tables and chairs, just an open dance space. The walls were bare except for some Bob Marley posters.

A few hours later it was a sweaty, heaving mass of bodies. And a pretty mixed bunch they were too. Ethiopians, Rastafarians and young, western aid workers gelled together on the dance floor. Bottles of beer in hand, they moved together to the Trenchtown beat. Like a shoal of sardines, they swayed together to make one larger movement that was pulled this way and that by the current of reggae music that belted out of the speakers mounted on either side of the stage.

"Peopllllle," roared Teddy Dan into the microphone where he stood at the centre of the stage. He was greeted with a roar of acknowledgement.

"We give thanks to His Imperial Majesty, the Emperor Haile Selassie-eeeeee," he shouted, which was greeted with another roar from the crowd. "He is our one true Gaaarrrddd!"

Having built the crowd up to a pitch of excitement, he counted down the band and they launched straight into United States of Africa. Shewaddy hit the switches on the lamps, and Teddy and Sintayehu threw their cameras on to their shoulders and hit their record buttons.

Hand held they weaved in and out of the band on stage shooting crazy angles and big meaty close-ups.

From time to time they would dive into the gyrating throng to get crowd shots and p-o-vs, or point-of-view shots, looking back up at the band on stage. As soon as the number came to an end, Teddy Dan and the band launched straight into it again, as arranged, to give our boys on camera a second chance to get more coverage. The crowd quickly got into the idea of being in the video. So that when Teddy Dan and the band launched into it for the third successive time they were greeted by the biggest cheer of the night. It was like having the encore at the start of the performance rather than at the end. Sintayehu and Teddy finally emerged hot, sweaty and beaming from ear to ear, and Wonde gave Teddy Dan the thumbs up. The first set-up was in the can. The crew struck the lights, packed the cameras away into their silver boxes and locked all the equipment away in the four-wheel-drive and rushed back to get the rest of Teddy Dan's set. I did what all good producers do at the end of a successful location shoot. I got the beers in.

We arrived in Shashamane late in the afternoon. The Rastafarian enclave was on the outskirts of the town in an area known unsurprisingly as Jamaica. We drove along wide, tree-lined streets where not much seemed to be happening. The sun was high overhead and the place had the air of a sleepy Mexican town during the afternoon siesta. The only signs of life were a group of kids kicking a football, so we stopped and asked them directions to the Rift Valley Hotel, which is where we had arranged to meet the band. They insisted in showing us the way so they all climbed in and sat on laps and various boxes of equipment determined not to miss out on the chance of a ride around town in a four-wheel-drive.

The Rift Valley Hotel was something of a rarity for Shashamane, in that it was a decent place to stay. The rest of the town's accommodation consisted mainly of cheap hotels most of which doubled as brothels. Shashamane is a major crossroads and every night hundreds of truckers stopped there overnight before continuing on their journeys the next morning. In the cheap bars you could almost see the HIV virus swirling in the smoke-filled air, like the iridescent hues of petrol in a dirty puddle of water. We found the band in the bar sipping mango juice and watching the funeral of the Queen Mother on BBC World.

Even though the Rift Valley Hotel was owned by Alton's sister, the band's budget for the shoot didn't even stretch to her specially reduced rates. However, the band had a plan, they would put us up themselves at their own homes. I left the billeting to Wonde and Teddy Dan to sort out and it was decided that Wonde, Sintayehu and Joseph, our Gemini driver, would stay with Teddy Dan and his wife; and Teddy our camera operator, Shewaddy and I were invited to stay with Spencer and his girl-friend. It looked like I was going to live like a Rasta for a few days.

Not having had the chance to recce the town before we arrived, we made the shoot up as we went along. Spencer was having a barn built in his compound. His Oromo workers had only recently started the job and so far had levelled the floor, which stood as a platform of bare earth a couple of feet above the ground.

"That looks like a stage," I said to Wonde.

"You're right, and I like all the green in the trees behind," he added. "If we put the band in the same places they were in at Midora, we could cut between the two set-ups."

Wonde was getting the hang of directing music videos a lot faster than me. An hour later the band had changed into the outfits they had worn for the Midora gig, and we were ready to turn over. Wonde arranged them on the makeshift stage and the thumping strains of United States of Africa belted out from our ghetto blaster. Teddy Dan and the band launched into their set ignoring the fact they weren't performing in front of an audience of adoring Rastas, but three bemused Oromo labourers, two goats and half-a-dozen chickens.

For the next few days Wonde was in his element. Every morning we would pile the band and the gear into the four-wheel-drive and hit the road looking for locations. One morning we pitched up at the Rift Valley Hotel. Wonde wandered around the grounds looking for a set-up. A line in the lyric went, "Don't leave us with our backs against the wall".

"Look, we can put them in there," I suggested to Wonde pointing at an empty, derelict looking swimming pool, "it can look like a prison." Vegetation sprouted from the cracks in the floor and walls. Wonde liked the idea and ladders were found and a few minutes later, and with the now familiar strains of United States of Africa bouncing off the swimming pool's concrete walls, Teddy Dan and the band performed the number again. Wonde shouted directions at Sintayehu and Teddy who scurried around with their cameras perched once again on their shoulders, ducking and diving in amongst the band as they got their shots. I had warmed to Teddy Dan. He had total confidence in Wonde and never once did he refuse to do anything Wonde asked him to do, or question any of his ideas.

On another day Wonde took us out of town to Wondo Genet, about fifteen kilometres away. The road led through a landscape of trees and shrubs that created a world of green everywhere you looked.

"Genet means paradise," Wonde told me as we drove along, "the garden of Adam and Eve. The Emperor used to live here."

The Emperor's summer residence stood on a hilltop overlooking a natural spring that bubbled out of a hole in a sheer rock face and tumbled down into a natural pool below. People stood under the cascading water. Others swam in a pool or were content just to lie in the shade. For a few birr, you could tour the royal residence and see for yourself how the other 0.0001% lived. We drove past the Emperor's house and continued up a winding rock-strewn track. Wonde's head swivelled on his shoulders as he scanned both sides of the road for a possible location, the sweep of his gaze swishing back and forth. We bounced around inside the four-wheel-drive for a further five minutes before he called a halt. A fallen tree had caught his eye. It lay sprawled along the side of the road overlooking a plunging valley.

Teddy, Sintayehu and Shewaddy unloaded the camera gear while the band set up their drum kit, keyboards and speakers. By the time Wonde had arranged the band members, together with their instruments on various limbs and branches, a small crowd of children had gathered to see what was going on. Wonde hit the play button and United States of Africa, as recorded by a reggae band from Manchester, blared out over Emperor Haile Selassie's private Eden.

Spencer's house where I stayed was a typical Rastafarian house in Sasha-mane. It had mud walls and a corrugated iron roof. It consisted of a kitchen, living room and two bedrooms, which made it pretty palatial by the local Oromo standards. The house sat in the middle of half an acre of land where Spencer grew fruit and vegetables. It was bounded by tall trees, a sturdy fence and large double gates. The bathroom was a tap and bucket in the compound and there was an outhouse with a drop toilet. It may have been basic but was surprisingly comfortable, and was made more so by the genuine warmth of Spencer and his girlfriend's welcome.

"I come from Moss Side," Spencer told me, one of Manchester's more notorious and violent inner city estates. He was showing me around his plot where neat rows of beans and tomatoes grew next to lines of fruit and vegetables I didn't recognise. "To me this is heaven on earth," he said as he proudly surveyed his garden which looked like a tropical version of a council allotment. Like most Rastafarians in Sashamane, Spencer had arrived with nowhere to live. All he had was a little bit of money and a dream. They purchased the land and built their home from scratch.

"We wouldn't have survived here without the help of the other Rasta-farians," he told me.

The Rastafarian community had put down firm roots in Shashamane, and Spencer was just one of the thousands of Rastafarians from all over the world who had chosen to build new lives for themselves. As well as English Rastafarians, there were Jamaican Rastafarians, American Rastafarians, German Rastafarians and so on. And within the national groups there were smaller sub-groups.

For instance, the English Rastafarians included the Brixton Rastafarians as well as the Manchester ones. For all I knew there could have been a branch of the Chipping Norton Rastafarians knocking about somewhere as well. There was one thing they all shared in common though they all believed they had returned to their spiritual home, Ethiopia.

There wasn't much for a *ferenji* to do in the evenings. Wonde and the rest would take themselves off and I spent the time talking late into the night with Spencer and Teddy Dan about their lives here. Rastafarianism, I learnt, isn't a strictly unified religion. Rastafarians belong to different "houses" but they all hold to the Bible, and their interpretation of it is central to their way of life.

However, the people who had actually lived there for the last couple of thousand years or so didn't always see it the same way. The Rastafarians might have been black, but to the local Oromo they looked as foreign as I did, which meant that the Rastafarians were rich *ferenjis* and therefore deserving of being ripped-off at every opportunity. This must have been confusing for the early Rastafarian settlers, who returning to Africa expected to be welcomed with open arms by their brothers, only to find they were more interested in picking their pockets instead. Most Rastafarians had learnt to treat the local Oromo people with a healthy degree of suspicion, an attitude which it turned out was entirely mutual. However, the two communities seemed to rub along together reasonably peacefully, each keeping a wary eye on the other.

On the one hand the Rastafarians have been very good for the Oromo. They provided employment and many of the Rastafarians were more than happy to pass on skills like carpentry and computing and help the Oromo children improve their English. But some Oromo complained that their children had taken up smoking marijuana, although it had to be said that a lot of Oromo farmers made money from growing the stuff and selling it to the Rastafarians in the first place. However, their biggest fear was that many more Rastafarians would come and take over. Meanwhile, the Rastafarians were busy lobbying the Ethiopian government to be afforded full Ethiopian citizenship.

I enjoyed my time being part of the Rastafarian community. I had been accepted warmly by everyone I met. People had been very open too, happy to talk and share with me anything I wanted to know about their way of life. Even when I asked a question that was very direct or personal, no one failed to answer me politely. They wanted to help me find out more about the Rastafarian way of life. Would they have been met with the same patience and understanding in my world, I wondered. Somehow I doubted it. Knowing that we would be leaving first thing next morning, Teddy Dan and Alton came over to Spencers's house to say goodbye to me. We sat in the garden cloaked by the dark, royal blue of the Ethiopian night. No street lights polluted the night sky, and with our necks craned we stared up at the starscape over our heads that stretched interminably to the waxy glow of the Milky Way, just about discernible in the furthest reaches of the infinite night sky.

The silence was total, and was punctuated only by the barking of dogs inside compounds, as hyenas skulked through the deserted streets outside. A sweet, heady fog of ganja hung heavy in the air. I was always invited to take part but politely declined, simply because I was already pleasantly zonked just by breathing in the trailing plumes of smoke as spliffs were passed from hand to hand under my nose. And there I sat long into the night discussing life, religion, music, Ethiopia, and the new-look Manchester United back four, with a group of guys wearing brightly coloured tea cosies on their heads.

# TEN

# Cutaway to Adugna

When Andrew Coggins came to Ethiopia to make a documentary for the BBC, he was so moved by the plight of street children he decided to make a film that documented their lives. As well as being the inspiration behind Gem TV, this encounter also gave birth to another idea. Andrew persuaded two well-known community choreographers, Royston Maldoom and Mags Byrne, to come to Addis Ababa and put on a dance performance featuring street kids. For four weeks Royston and Mags rehearsed over one hundred street children to dance a specially choreographed performance of Carmina Burana, which was created from scratch in seventeen days. In the audience hundreds of street kids in dirty football shirts rubbed shoulders with ambassadors and senior NGO officials in smart suits and ties, and as one they all gave the performers a standing ovation. Addis Ababa had never seen anything like it. The Adugna Community Dance Theatre Company was born.

Adugna was set up with Royston Maldoom as its Artistic Director, assisted by Mags Byrne, and eventually came under the wing of Gemini in much the same way as Gem TV. Carmela quickly grew to become passionate about both projects and watched over their development with a stern but motherly eye. Many times I have heard her address a group of visiting aid workers or potential funders saying: "I have always believed that a sustainable way out of poverty depends on the education and development of Ethiopia's disadvantaged youth." Gemini has pioneered this approach in Ethiopia, also establishing a music and an art group for Gemini youngsters.

"Adugna" is an awkward word to pin down in English, it means something between fortune and fate. It certainly went on to enrich the lives of the eighteen young people who were initially recruited into the dance training program. Choreographers from Ethiopia, Africa and overseas worked with the dancers on short-term assignments. I often shared the guest house with Royston, and on many occasions I stayed up late into the night as he shared with me his many experiences of working with women in prisons in the UK, the disabled, and the poor and illiterate all over the developing world.

Having directed numerous voice over artistes in my previous life making TV commercials, I'd have given a year's salary to have discovered Royston years ago. His voice was deep and sonorous and can only be described as "dark brown". If you heard him reading out the telephone directory you'd still want to stop whatever you were doing and listen to him. Royston had this elusive quality in abundance, or perhaps it was the underlying passion he conveyed about dance's potential for personal development that people found mesmerising.

"You have to be incredibly self-disciplined to be a dancer," he told me, "the training demands it. You also have to have complete faith and trust in your fellow dancers, and sometimes these things are completely new experiences for these kids, but when it happens it's magical. You can change your life in a dance class."

Royston invited me to come and see the work Adugna were doing at their compound in Kanzanchis, an area of Addis Ababa dominated by the European Union and United Nations headquarters. Adugna's compound was not much more than a small field with a few shanty buildings and the dance studio itself was a barn. Normally a dance studio would have a sprung floor. This one had a concrete one covered with thin matting. The Adugna dancers leapt and pirouetted on it for hours every day, five days a week.

Remarkably, from this humble studio and with the help and support of many dancers and choreographers from across Europe, Adugna produced performances that not only entranced audiences in Addis Ababa's theatres and back street *kebeles*, but with the help of organizations like the British Council and Alliance Francaise, they performed at dance festivals in Paris and London, and to standing ovations and critical acclaim.

Under the most difficult of circumstances, Royston and his dedicated team of choreographers coaxed, and at times cajoled, the most extraordinary performances out of the Adugna dancers. Royston was extremely demanding, not just because he had to be but, I suspected, because deep down he knew that the only way to do something worthwhile was to give it everything you had. I don't think I ever saw Royston when he wasn't wearing combat pants and Doc Marten boots, and he had a haircut that wouldn't have looked out of place on a US Marines drill sergeant. As he rehearsed a particular move with them time and time again, it was plain to see he was held in the greatest respect.

So when we came to make the film about Gemini it was obvious that we included the Adugna dancers, especially as one of them had just made international headlines. One of the leading lights of Adugna was Junaid Jemal Sendi, and at the age of 20 he had just won the Rolex Award, the most prestigious prize in the international arts world. He was also the first ever African recipient of the award.

This got me thinking about the role business sponsorship can play in the developing world, which to be honest wasn't a million miles away from my advertising background. This had taught me that sponsorship is only truly successful when it works for *both* parties. They should both get something out of it. To be really successful there should also be a synergy between the company doing the sponsoring and the individual or organisation receiving the sponsorship. This was clearly the case with Rolex and Junaid. Despite Royston's best efforts to educate me about contemporary dance during our late-into-the-night chats in the guest house, what I had learnt you couldn't squeeze into a tight-fitting tutu.

But even I knew enough to appreciate that you can't dance if you can't keep time.

Rolex are brand leaders in the world of time keeping. Their products are all about "precision movement", and the same could certainly be said about Junaid's dancing and choreography. Just as importantly, the arrangement was mutually beneficial. With the financial support of Rolex, Junaid got to travel abroad and work with his mentor, the top Japanese choreographer, Saburo Teshigawara. This helped to further develop his artistic talent. In return, Rolex got their name associated with a headline-grabbing artist whose range of work and expression perfectly echoed their own brand values. It was a classic win-win situation. In Junaid, it has to be said, Rolex also got an outstanding spokesman who handled the media attention that followed him wherever he appeared in the world with remarkable aplomb for one so young.

But more than this, Junaid is also an ambassador for Ethiopian youth, a responsibility I thought he clearly took very seriously. Previously, when I walked down a street in Addis Ababa I would pass hordes of scruffy looking *listro* boys shining shoes, or gangs of feral looking slips of girls selling packs of chewing gum, and I wouldn't give them a second thought. But after meeting Junaid, each time I hurried past one I said to myself, wait a minute, here is a young person of extraordinary potential. The question that always formed in my mind was would they ever get the chance to develop it? Of course, it's good that companies like Rolex sponsor young people like Junaid, and it's quite right that they get a commercial benefit from doing so, otherwise why would they bother?

But shouldn't it be Ethiopian companies that are getting the commercial benefits of such sponsorship, I wondered. It doesn't have to be on a grand international scale like Rolex, and few could afford it anyway, but couldn't commercial sponsorship work just as effectively in a domestic market as it does on the international stage, I wondered. Surely, most Ethiopian companies would be proud to be associated with someone like Junaid, and there have to be thousands of other Junaids out there waiting to be discovered and who just need a chance to show what their talents can do. Gemini, of course, was doing its bit in a small way and with very limited resources, and although everyone was fiercely proud of Junaid's success, it wasn't the only measure. Each dancer's artistic development, no matter how small or incremental, was seen as being just as important.

This was especially true of the Adugna Potentials, Ethiopia's first group of mixed ability dancers. Sadly, physical disability is viewed with fear and suspicion in Ethiopia and people with physical problems are often hidden away. The Adugna Potentials play an influential role in combating this prejudice and harmful stigma by appearing on stage in Addis Ababa, either on their own or together with the parent company. I sometimes shared the guest house with another choreographer, Adam Benjamin, who specialised in working with mixed ability dancers and who regularly worked with the Adugna Potentials choreographing special pieces for them to perform. Much later Junaid, together with another Adugna dancer, Addisu Dimessie, would form their own dance company called Destino. They would go on to perform their own choreographed pieces on dance stages all over the world, but they always held true to their Ethiopian roots, and saw dance not just as a means of artistic expression but also as a way of inspiring others like themselves to develop their talents no matter what their backgrounds or circumstances.

# ELEVEN

# Mercato

From a camel to a Kalashnikov, I had heard it said, everything is for sale in Mercato. They say you can even barter for a new soul.

Adanech and Fikirte were both from Mercato and were fiercely proud of the fact. To hear them talk about Mercato was like listening to cockneys talk about the East End of London. But for *ferenjis*, Mercato had a fearsome reputation that effectively put it off limits. The more people told me about Mercato, the more I convinced myself it belonged more in the pages of Joseph Conrad rather than the Lonely Planet. But I was determined to see Mercato, and that meant taking a guide.

"I want to go shopping Adanech, can you take me?" I asked her one morning.

Adanech immediately started talking about the *ferenji* shops on Churchill Road, so I stopped her. "No, not that kind of shopping," I said, "I want you to take me to Mercato."

"Thank you, Bob, it would make me very proud to show you," she said.

We arranged to meet at the Europe hotel, opposite the football stadium. I was sitting at a small table inside the door sipping a coffee.

"*Denaneh*, Bob?" she asked as she sat down. Are you fine?

"*Dehna*, Adanech, I'm fine," I replied. She ordered a coffee for herself, and outlined what she had planned.

"Saturday is market day everywhere in Ethiopia," she said, "Mercato will be very busy today."

"Busy is good, that's what I want to see," I replied.

"First I will take you to Mulugeta's shop. He is my boyfriend and he will come with us." She made it sound like we needed a minder. "But there is so much I want to show you," she said, brightening. "*Ineet*, shall we go."

From the centre of Addis Ababa we had to take two minibuses to get to Mercato. The journey took an hour, so we talked, and Adanech told me a little about her life. Perhaps it was being out of the office that made her feel comfortable to talk to me. I was about to get a small glimpse into the lives of my new colleagues at last.

Adanech, which means saviour in Amharic, joined Gem TV when she was twenty years old. She isn't a twin herself, but the eldest daughter in a Gemini family. She has two younger brothers who are twins. She also has a younger sister and another younger brother.

"My father left home when I was very young," Adanech told me as we were jostled together on the small bench seat of the minibus, which I could barely squeeze myself into, as it bounced over ruts in the road and through pot holes. "My mother had to raise us on her own."

Their home was a two room dwelling in a compound in a crowded back street of Mercato. They had electricity but no running water. Instead they shared a standpipe with the other families in the compound who lived just like they did. Desperate to feed and clothe her family, Adanech's mother decided to rent out one of the two rooms moving the entire family into the one remaining room. When the *kebele*, the local city authority, heard about this they confiscated the room saying that if they could rent it out it must be surplus to their requirements. Adanech told me that her mother also suffers from diabetes and mental health problems, but at least she had a job working as a cleaner at the main Gemini office compound. Unlike most people in Addis Ababa, which is in the heart of the Amhara region, Adanech and her family are Gurage, a small ethnic group who come from the south-west.

"The Gurage people have a reputation for being good business people," she said.

However, it was obvious from an early age that commerce was never going to be Adanech's destiny.

"I was a big problem for my mother," she said, "she was always saying what will happen to you? Who will look after you?"

Adanech left school when she was sixteen. At first, she had a full-time job coping with her sick mother and being a substitute mum to all her brothers and sisters. When she wasn't caring for the needs of her family Adanech would sell *kolo*, fried barley, on the streets of Mercato. Another thing that marked her out was that although they were Christian, Adanech and her family weren't Orthodox like the majority of Christian Ethiopians, but Protestant. What scraps of spare time she found for herself she spent at her local church where her singing quickly established her as a key member of the choir.

Through Gemini she was offered a place at Gem TV. She was the last one to join. Although she had the basics of an education, she was desperately shy and couldn't speak a word of English. She had joined Gem TV five years ago, and it was hard for me to conjure up the image of a nervous youngster. It was obvious to me that even in the short time I had worked with her that she was an accomplished director. However, learning all the technicalities of the job had been a mountain for Adanech to climb.

"It was a big thing for me just to touch a camera," she said, laughing at the memory of her first days at Gem TV.

An even bigger challenge had been building up the confidence to have a point of view and express it in her films. For a young woman this was almost unheard of in Ethiopia, where for generations women had been denied any kind of a voice at all.

The years of hard work had paid off handsomely in Adanech's case. A first major film was called *Stolen Childhood*, and to this day it perfectly encapsulates what Gem TV was all about. The film is a drama documentary and tells the true story of a young girl from the countryside called Kebebush. She was married off to a farmer when she was twelve years old. Early marriage is an established cultural practice in Ethiopia where it's not uncommon for girls to be married off as young as ten or even younger. Kebebush's story was typical. Her parents arranged for her to be married to a man twenty years older than her. The bride price paid for Kebebush was a donkey, and maybe her parents were acting in what they thought were in their daughter's best interests. As it turned out it was a straight swap, one beast of burden with four legs for another with two.

Many of these girls become little more than domestic slaves either of their husbands or mothers-in-law, living lives of fetching firewood, carrying water, cooking, cleaning and caring for other family members from dawn till dusk. Often these girls are pubescent girls and sexually unready for married life. They die giving birth because their frail young bodies are unable to withstand the trauma. And sexual intercourse often results in fistula, a tear in the bladder that leads to incontinence and permanent urine leakage. Fistulas blight the lives of thousands of Ethiopia's women who become social outcasts in their own villages. They live alone on huts and exist on paltry handouts.

Like many girls before her, Kebebush ran away to her parents. They beat her and sent her back. This happened many times before Kebebush realised that the only way to escape was to run far away and seek a new life in the city. It took her many weeks but eventually she made it on foot all the way to Addis Ababa. When she arrived she had no education, no possessions apart from what she stood up in and carried in a small bundle, and no hope. Like hundreds of other girls from the countryside, she ended up living on the street. She was spotted by a wealthy woman who offered her a job as a maid in her house. At first things were all right. She was fed, safe, had a roof over her head and went to sleep every night in her own cot in a corner of the woman's kitchen.

The work wasn't hard but the hours of cooking and cleaning and fetching and carrying were long. In the countryside she had been used to that. Even so, every night before she went to sleep Kebebush would offer up a prayer of thanks to her maker for her good fortune. Some time later the wealthy woman's cousin came to stay. He was kind to Kebebush. He would send her on little errands and reward her with a few coins. One day he appeared next to her where she was washing clothes in the compound. He had a present for her, he said. He beckoned for her to follow him. She stepped into his room and he closed the door behind her. He reached under the bed and took out a pair of shoes. They were bright blue, old and well worn and made of cheap plastic. Cinderella couldn't have been happier with her glass slippers than Kebebush was at that moment. The hardships of her life had not prepared her for such an act of kindness. As Kebebush reached out and took the shoes in her hands a smile lit up her pretty, young face. It lingered there for the merest fraction of a second before he clamped his hand over her mouth, wrestled her onto the bed, lifted the skirt of her ragged dress and raped her.

Kebebush became pregnant and when she could no longer work the woman threw her out. She ended up back on the street where she gave birth to a baby girl. She managed to get a job in a bar washing glasses. Then she was promoted to selling the men beer. It wasn't long before she was selling them her body as well. She got pregnant again. Once more she lost her job and was thrown back on the street. Only this time she had a young child to support and another on the way. Kebebush ended up working the streets as a prostitute in one of the red light districts of Addis Ababa. And it was here that Adanech found her and approached her to be the subject of her film.

Making *Stolen Childhood* was a daunting experience for Adanech. Nothing in her life had prepared for her for the world she was about to enter. She had never set foot inside a bar before she started researching the film. A burning sense of anger and injustice overrode her fears. The most memorable scenes are when Kebebush talks directly to camera, recounting her life story. Adanech inter-cuts them with dramatised reconstructions that show Kebebush in a short skirt, bare legs tucked into a pair of cheap, shiny high heels, standing at the side of the street at night, trying to flag down the men who drive past slowly in their cars. The last shot is a close up of Kebebush. It is the face of an old woman on a young girl's body. All she wants to do, she says in a barely discernible whisper, is sleep.

What makes *Stolen Childhood* such a seminal Gem TV film is that shortly after it was made it was shown to an audience of Ethiopian members of parliament. The great and the good, the most influential in the land, sat down and watched a film about a child prostitute made by a young woman that used to sell *kolo* on the streets of Mercato. After *Stolen Childhood* was made, Adanech kept in touch with Kebebush. Then, after a while, Kebebush moved on. No one knows what became of her and her children.

The minibus fought its way along one of the many broad streets that led into Mercato, which was clogged with hundreds of other buses. It was early morning and already Mercato was operating at full throttle. The temperature was nudging the high thirties and the sweat of dense crowds of people mingled with the smells of petrol fumes, spices, animals and open sewers. It created a fug that stung the eyes and which was almost visible in the hot, heavy air that was steadily being cooked by the midday sun. This was air you could get your teeth into.

We had to dodge around hordes of trolleys piled high with sacks of grain, bolsters of richly coloured cloth and all manner of household goods: pots and pans, plates and cups and bars of soap. The trolleys were all the same, shaped like the capital letter A with a small wheel at the point. Rough wood planks were nailed across the pointed half of the A to form a platform, and the pushers stood between the two long wooden staves that thrust back, pushing the loads for all they were worth. They reminded me of the luggage *wallahs* who worked the platforms of Indian railway stations. This was how thousands of people made their living every day in Mercato, and many of them were women.

Watching them shift heavy loads reminded me of a conversation I had had with Habtamu, one of the Gem TV camera operators, the day before. Habtamu was quiet and shy and he struggled with English more than the others. He was always smiling and he was one of the most willing members of the crew. Nothing ever seemed too much trouble for Habtamu. His father was a weaver and Habtamu had four brothers and two sisters, two of which were twins. One of his brothers was a weaver like his father, another one was a bus driver and a third worked in a government office having studied law thanks to a Gemini education programme. One of his sisters was living and working in Beirut and the other one worked in the Gemini library and played in the Gemini music group. A younger brother was showing all the signs of developing into a talented artist and was a member of Gemini's art group, and the two youngest were still in school.

Habtamu was lucky in that he had been to school, leaving at grade five at about the age of fifteen or sixteen. But since the age of seven he had always worked. To help the family he had got a job in a market close to where they lived, where he carried heavy goods. Every day he would rise at 6.30, do an hour's work, then go to school until lunchtime, and then go back to the market and carry heavy loads on his back for another five or six hours before going home.

"The people would give me small money, fifty cents or a birr every time I carry something," he told me. "When I was fourteen I carried a sack of grain and when they weighed the sack it was 113 kilos. I always remember that one," he added with a shy smile.

On first appearances Mercato looked like an endless shanty town sprawl, but I discovered that beneath the surface chaos there was a grand plan at work, which was like lifting the lid on the human equivalent of a beehive. Every inch of its twelve square kilometres was subdivided into areas, or *teras*, which were defined by what was made or sold there. So the *sifaet tera* sold baskets, the *kibe tera* sold spices, the *atakilt tera* sold fruit and vegetables, the *shekla tera* sold pottery and so on for mile after mile after mile of narrow streets and alleyways.

In the *kibe tera*, where butter was sold, scores of market stalls stood in the open air under a canopy of pieces of different coloured tarpaulins, which cast rainbow shafts of amber, blue and emerald green diffused light. Slabs of pale, yellowy butter sweated gently in the heat; their sides scored with oozing rivulets, and the air was filled with the faintly nauseous smell of milk that had gone off. In the *kibe tera*, spice area, large sacks of ground spices stood side by side, or in conical piles of vibrant colour, and gave off the aroma of ginger, cinnamon and many other spices I couldn't identify.

In the *coricha tera*, saddle making area, I watched dozens of artisans sitting cross-legged on mats while they carved saddles, whips and belts out of strips of leather. Everything was done by hand and eye with tools that looked like they had been handed down from father to son for generations. Whereas in the *chid tera*, straw area, it was the women who were doing all the work; their nimble fingers plaited and interwove thin strips of dried grass into baskets and mats of different shapes, sizes and design.

"The *chid* is what is left over from the *teff* after we take the grain to make *injera*," explained Adanech, bending down to grab a handful of the pale yellow grass stalks. "The most highly skilled *chid* weavers come from Harer," she said, referring to the thousand years old Muslim city that stands overlooking the Ogaden desert that stretches all the way to the ill-defined border with Somalia. The baskets were breathtaking in their artistry. However, it seemed to me that everyone knew how to weave the *chid*. I had often seen children weaving dolls for fun. But everyone could weave *chid* it seemed to me, and this skill really came into its own on Palm Sunday, when they would weave the most intricate crosses. Two strands would be left long and these would be used to tie the crosses around their heads, with the cross centred in the middle of the forehead looking like a religious version of a miner's lamp.

"What are those?" I asked, pointing to what looked like a round table with a domed, pointed hood that was decorated with intricate and colourful zig zags.

"*Mesobs*, they are our tables for eating," she replied. The *mesobs* were about three feet high and round. Each one was an individual piece of work and the workmanship was extraordinary.

"We use them every day, but they aren't all as beautiful as these ones," Adanech said, as she got the stallholder to lift a couple down from a shelf for me to take a closer look at.

"If I buy one will it make you like *injera*?" she asked, with a chuckle.

My biggest regret about my time in Ethiopia was that I didn't like the traditional food. Lunch at Gem TV was a ritual. Everyone would get together to eat *injera* and *wat*. On my first day, naturally I was invited to join in. It was an eye-opener because I was fresh off the plane and had no idea that in a country that I mistakenly associated with famine, food played a central role in the culture.

I shuffled myself into a tight space between Fikirte and Mehbratie as fourteen of us crowded around the table. Kebe did the honours of coming round to each of us in turn with a pitcher of water and a bowl. She approached Wonde first and poured a steady stream of water over his right hand, in which he held a small sliver of soap. Then he dried his hand on the towel that was slung over Kebe's shoulder. It's a ritual which is as gracious and refined as anything you can imagine being performed by a *geisha* in the imperial Japan of the *Shoguns*.

The meal consisted of what looked like small, grey, rolled-up towels, which were unfurled and laid out in the centre of the table. It was *injera*, the flat bread that is like a pancake and is the mainstay of all Ethiopian cooking, and which gives it its highly distinctive flavour. Onto the *injera* were ladled half a dozen other dishes which stood in little piles, slowly soaking into the *injera* below.

"We call these *wats*," Selam explained. "This one is *doro wat*, which is chicken," she said pointing out the pile of chicken pieces in a buttery gravy. The others included *tibs*, fried strips of beef, and different vegetable *wats*. My favourite became *shiro*, a brown, soupy *wat* made from lentils.

They bowed their heads and mumbled grace, making little crucifix gestures over the food with their right hands. Then fourteen hands started ripping the *injera* apart and demolishing the *wats*, and in no time what had moments before looked like an elegantly arranged meal, good enough to be photographed for the cover of an eco-tourism brochure, resembled the culinary equivalent of a war zone.

Selam tore off a strip of *injera* and held it in the tips of her fingers, hovering over the *wats*. Then her nimble fingers pounced on the choicest morsels, and gobbled them up until she had made a small *injera* food parcel. Then she turned to me and said, "Open up." With everyone watching I gingerly opened my mouth, and quick as a flash she popped it inside.

"We call this *gursha*," she said, "when you feed someone like an honoured guest or loved one."

Spicy flavours exploded like a firework inside my mouth, which burned with the zing of *berberie* pepper. I coughed, I spluttered, my eyes streamed. Teddy thumped my back and Fikirte dashed to get my bottle of water. Everyone else rocked with laughter. Then the underlying taste of the *injera* kicked in. It's made from *teff*, which is like wheat and grows in the highlands of Ethiopia. It's pounded into flour, mixed with water and yeast, then left to ferment for a few days. This is what gives *injera* its distinctive, bitter aftertaste. It's cooked on a *mogogo*, a round, flat, frying pan, in much the same way as a crepe. Over the following weeks I developed quite a taste for the *wats*, but never could get to like *injera*. From then on I always ate my *wats* with a bread roll.

"They're beautiful Adanech," I said as I admired the *mesobs*, "but sadly not beautiful enough to make this *ferenji* like *injera*."

The other daily ritual was *buna*, but in Ethiopia it isn't a drink, it's a ceremony, and an everyday part of the culture. The coffee ceremony takes place everywhere and is performed in exactly the same way in the

President's Palace as it is in the hut of any peasant farmer. Ethiopia is the home of coffee where it was first cultivated in the *Kaffa* region, hence the similarity of name, as far back as the ninth century. Legend has it that a goatherd noticed how his goats became frisky after nibbling the coffee bush's bright red berries. His name was Kaldi, and Addis Ababa's most popular chain of coffee shops is named after him. Coffee is Ethiopia's gift to the world.

The first time I had *buna*, Selam made sure I watch the whole ceremony from beginning to end. "There's no such thing as grabbing a quick cup of coffee in Ethiopia," she said.

Faneh, Gem TV's maid, sat on a low stool. In front of her the floor of the office had been covered with *getema*, strips of grass, a traditional sign of welcome. Also in front of her stood a *rekebot*, a low tray on which she had placed *sini*, ten small, handle-less coffee cups arranged in neat rows. Next to her stood a *yekasal mandeja*, a small stove filled with glowing charcoal. First, Faneh roasted the coffee beans in a pan over the heat, shaking it and making the beans rattle.

From time to time she would lift the pan and pass it under our noses. She offered it to Selam first and she fanned the aroma towards herself with her hand and uttered the traditional words of appreciation, "*Egzabiher yistelegen*", God bless you. Then Faneh offered the pan to me so I could appreciate the aroma, and one-by-one to the others as well. When she was satisfied that the beans were ready, Faneh removed the pan from the stove and replaced them with a *jebena*, a traditional clay coffee pot, filled with water to boil.

Next she returned her attention to the coffee beans and ground them in a mortar with a pestle, which made a rhythmic crunching sound. When a steady plume of steam began to rise from the thin stem of the *jebena* she added the ground coffee. Then, holding the *jebena* high above the tray, she poured the rich, dark brown liquid into the cups. Being the honoured guest, the tray was passed to me first. I picked up a coffee cup that was filled to the brim with the tips of my fingers. Next Faneh passed the tray to Selam and so on round the group.

"You drink three cups," said Selam. "The first one is called *abol*. It is the strongest in flavour, and we say it is for health. The second one we call *huletenya thani*, and it is for love, and the third one, *baraka*, is for good fortune."

The many hours we spent drinking coffee were the times I felt most at home with Gem TV. Normally, they would always speak English whenever I was around, but never during *buna*. Only if they wanted to ask me something specifically would they address me in English. This wasn't rudeness, far from it, it was a compliment. I always felt I was taking part in something distinctly Ethiopian, and that they wanted to share the moment with me. I was always more than happy to switch off and be lulled into thinking my own thoughts by the lilting music of their Amharic.

"I want to buy a *jebena* as a souvenir," I told Adanech, adding, "so I can always remember having *buna* with Gem TV."

"Then we must go to the *shekla tera*," she said.

In row upon row of small stalls men sitting behind potters' wheels were conjuring pots out of wet clay with skilled hands. Raw clay came in at one end which was fashioned into all kinds of pots, before handles and spouts were fitted, and then the completed pots were fired in kilns. Finally, they were put on display, thousands of them, piled on top of one another and each one having been individually made by hand. The *shekla tera* wasn't a row of shops, it was a highly productive production line.

"Is there anything else you want?" Adanech asked as I returned having successfully negotiated the buying of a *jebena* from a formidable looking Mercato woman.

"Yes, there is actually, I'd really like a Queen of Sheba painting."

I had seen this iconic image everywhere. Known as the Cycle of the Queen of Sheba, the painting told the story of Makeda's journey to Jerusalem where she had lain with Solomon and begat Menelik who would later steal the Ark of the Covenant and bring it to Ethiopia.

Every rendition was the same in that it was divided into 44 individual frames, each with a caption underneath, so every painting looked like a storyboard for a movie. No wonder Adanech and her Gem TV colleagues were such natural film-makers, I thought, having been brought up surrounded by such cultural icons.

Adanech led me to the modern part of Mercato, *Adarash*, which means the hall. "This is where we'll find the artists," she said. It was a covered, modern built section selling imported goods. At the back of *Adarash* we found a number of small market stalls selling artworks, relics and curiosities. It was an Aladdin's Cave of goatskin Bibles, beautifully illustrated and written in *Geez*, the ancient liturgical language of Ethiopia; hand carved Bible stands that were painted with scenes from the lives of the saints; small devotional diptychs and ornately hand-wrought silver crosses. There was also a stall selling imperial coins, military medals and hippo hide shields. "Adwa," said the stall holder, proudly beating one of the shields, referring to Ethiopia's most famous victory, when in 1896 they defeated the Italians. He left me in no doubt that the shield he was trying to sell me had seen action at the famous battle.

One particular Queen of Sheba painting caught my eye. I made an offer and the stall holder rolled his eyes and we started to haggle. I thought I was holding my end up pretty well and was about to close the deal when Adanech took hold of my arm.

"Come, Bob," she said, gently pulling me away, "this is not a good price."

Reluctantly, I shot a despairing glance over my shoulder at the painting as Adanech led me away. She was a Mercato girl so I wasn't going to argue with her.

We heard the *biret tera* long before we saw it. The tip-tapping grew in volume the closer we approached it, until finally, it echoed all around us.

"This is where things are recycled," said Adanech, adding, "nothing is wasted here." She almost had to shout to be heard above the growing din. "In Mercato we take everything old and make it new again."

Walking into the *biret tera* was like stepping into a scene by Heath Robinson painted by Hieronymus Bosch. Hundreds of artisans toiled away beating and hammering assorted bits of discarded metal to fashion all sorts of new tools and household items. Tin cans, bedsprings, railings, wheel hubs, and lots of other bits of old metal were being transformed into *injera* frying pans, trays, cutlery, saucepans, blades for shovels. I watched as a welder worked. All he had for protection was a cardboard box he wore over his head and shoulders. He'd cut a letterbox shaped hole in the front of it, from which he stared out from behind a pair of sunglasses. Sparks of white-hot solder spat at him and enveloped him in a ghostly shroud, to which he seemed completely impervious.

There was no pretence in hiding the origins of the items made here. Tin cans which had once contained powdered milk and were emblazoned with the distinctive red and blue US AID logo were cut open down one side, rolled out, beaten flat and remodelled with bits of gauze to become sieves for sifting flour. No attempt was made to conceal the logo. On the contrary, it became a design motif in its own right, a proud symbol of resourcefulness and ingenuity. It said someone threw this away, but look we made something useful out of it. The *biret tera's* raw materials created a landscape of mound after mound of discarded bottles, glass, tyres, rusting pipes, oil drums, sacks, plastic sheeting and discarded furniture. They stood like slag heaps in an Ethiopian version of a Welsh valley in the days of coal. Men crawled over them wrestling out the things they needed to create something new, a piece of pipe here or a rusting railing there. Even bottle tops were horded in vast piles, maybe a million of them, who could tell. Walking into the *biret tera* was like ripping the top off a human version of a termite mound and peering inside.

Mercato, I discovered, is many things, often contradictory. It's Christian and Muslim, a church and a mosque stand side-by-side in the heart of Mercato, which for many symbolise Ethiopia's religious harmony. It's town and country, rich and poor, hi-tech and handicraft, artisan and artist, but it's always buyer and seller, and it all works.

After an exhausting day Adanech finally led me back to where hordes of minibuses stood waiting to take the army of shoppers back to all parts of Addis Ababa and beyond. A *wayalla* cried out "*Stadium*" and I managed to fight my way into the minibus and squeeze into a seat at the back next to people laden down with bulging bags and boxes tied with string. One day in Mercato had taught me more about Ethiopia than all the time I had spent in the country. I felt I'd seen more of Ethiopia's different ethnic peoples than if I'd spent months travelling around the country. I'd gained more of an appreciation of Ethiopia's culture than I would have learned in any museum. And having arrived in Ethiopia with the image of a begging bowl country in my head, one day in Mercato had shattered that illusion completely.

But before we left Adanech took me to look at the two great churches that dominate Mercato, symbolising the religious harmony that largely exists in Ethiopia. Although Ethiopia is primarily a Christian country, over a third of Ethiopians follow Islam and the two communities live in peaceful coexistence. In amongst the heart of Mercato's people-packed streets, the Christian Cathedral stood in the shadow of the Great Mosque.

Although Christian herself, Adanech was proud to tell me how in 615 AD the Prophet Muhammad and his followers faced persecution in Arabia. He gathered a group together under his cousin, Jafar bin Abi Talib, and pointed them towards Axum in northern Ethiopia, saying: "Yonder lieth a country wherein no one is wronged, a land of righteousness. Depart thither, and remain until it pleaseth the Lord to open your way before you." They journeyed to Axum where they were well received by King Armah. However, they were pursued by their persecutors who demanded that the king hand them over. But King Armah refused saying: "If you were to offer me a mountain of gold I would not give up these people who have taken refuge with me." One of them was a young woman, Umm Habibah. When she returned home years later she became the Prophet's wife, and told him all that had occurred in Axum. On hearing how his people had been so warmly received, the Prophet declared that the "Abyssinians should be left in peace" and excluded from *jihad*.

A couple of days later I was in the office when Adanech came up to me with a rolled up canvas. I knew immediately what it was and as I unfurled it I recognised the vibrant colours and the faces, with large eyes painted in profile, of the Cycle of the Queen of Sheba. It was the painting I had haggled over with the Mercato stallholder.

"He was wanting *ferenji* price," she told me, "so I went back to buy it for you." Perhaps there was more native Gurage in Adanech than her mother gave her daughter credit for.

# TWELVE

# Cutaway to Tigist
# and Haimanot & Tigist

The more I saw and understood about Gemini, the more I came to realise that used properly aid and donations can galvanize whole communities and empower people to work themselves out of poverty. That said, the spirit of Mercato was to be found everywhere throughout the organization. Nobody I came across in the whole of Gemini wanted a hand out, they just needed a hand up.

All they really wanted was a decent chance to improve their lives and those of their children, and they were prepared to work every second of every minute of every God sent hour to make that happen. And no one worked harder than Carmela to hold the whole thing together. The weight of responsibility on her shoulders was enormous. If a CEO of a large corporation gets things wrong then the stockholders lose a few cents off the value of their shares. But if things went wrong on Carmela's watch, people lost their homes, or got sick, or went hungry and died. There were times when, despite her best efforts to hide it, I suspected Carmela was buckling under the workload and the responsibility of holding so many people's lives in her hands. In its own way it was a burden as heavy as that borne by any of the women carrying firewood on the long, torturous, twisting road down from Entoto.

The shanty towns of Addis Ababa are a world away from the rural villages of Bangladesh, but they have a common link, micro finance.

The first micro finance institution was the Grameen Bank launched in Bangladesh by Professor Muhammed Yunus, who believed that collateral free loans, aimed at rural communities, could become powerful income generators by allowing poor people to start their own small businesses. Grameen means village in Bengali and since the Grameen Bank was launched, micro finance has transformed the face of development, especially for women. Loans are extended to small groups of people one at a time. When the first person pays off their loan, the next loan is extended to the next person, and so on.

This makes the system self-policing, as all subsequent loans depend on the previous one being repaid. When Professor Yunus first suggested this micro finance business model he was roundly laughed at and the financial establishment said that poor villagers would never repay the loans. The Grameen bank has a repayment failure rate of less than 3%, far lower than any established bank. The vast majority of people taking out loans are village women. They don't have big plans to take on the corporate world. The small businesses they set up with micro finance loans enable them to feed and educate their children. Professor Yunus's pioneering approach to fighting world poverty earned him the Nobel Peace prize in 2006. His idea has spread all over the developing world, including Addis Ababa, where Gemini has initiated micro finance initiatives of its own and had helped to launch one hundred and fifty small businesses.

We filmed Tigist Bekele in her small shop in Mercato. She was a small, slightly built woman with a lined face that belied years of hard work and worry, and she spoke in a high-pitched voice. Even as she talked to us she was never still, she seemed constantly on the lookout for things to do as if taking a moment's rest would bring her business crumbling down around her ears. She told us her story in between serving customers at her busy tea shop, washing cups and stoking the fire to put more water on to boil.

## Tigist's story

I am a mother of twins. I was a very young girl when I had my children. I lived in a poor place and I had no way to feed my children. I had nothing. Then I heard about this organization that helps families with twins. I joined Gemini when I was sixteen years old. Gemini helped me with feeding for my children and education for them. But I wanted to support myself as much as I could, and my family.

I had this idea to sell tea. I went to Gemini and explained this idea to them and they gave me a loan of 200 birr and with that I started selling tea. I worked all day and every day and still had to look after my family, but I was very grateful for this opportunity. It took me a long time to pay back the loan, but slowly my business started to do well.

Next I took out a loan of 500 birr and with this I rented a small shop. With Gemini's help I have been able to raise my children. One of my sons has graduated from university and has a good job. And one of my daughters is at Dire Dawa University. The other children are still at school. This shop is all I have, but it has given me everything. I couldn't have done this without Gemini.

Later the same day we filmed an even more remarkable Gemini business success story. Haimanot and Tigist Demtaw are the twin daughters of one of the Gemini guards who watched over my guest house. They were in their early twenties at the time. Slim and striking with long black hair, wide expressive eyes and sculpted lips that parted to reveal radiant smiles, their faces would have graced the cover of any fashion magazine. But as I soon discovered there were serious brains behind the beauty, and no little artistic talent, not to mention a deeply felt sense of caring and community. Scarcely out of their teens themselves, already they employed sixty Gemini women in the jewellery making business they had set up from scratch, and with a little help from Gemini.

We caught up with the twins and filmed them at the NGO Bazaar, a gathering that takes place on the last Saturday of every month in Addis

Ababa, where local artisans take tables and sell art and craft works to the international NGO community. It wasn't difficult to find them at the crowded bazaar, Adanech told me we just had to look out for the largest crowd of *ferenji* women. Their business success story, they told us, started in one of the rusting shipping containers in the Gemini compound, which served as a classroom, and ended up on the World Wide Web.

## Haimanot & Tigist's story

When we were young we used to spend half the day in school and half in Gemini learning English. A volunteer called Rebecca Fisher came and asked us if we had any interest in making jewellery and we said OK. We started because of her. She then started teaching us how jewellery is made. Later, other volunteers came along also taught us different other things like making bags. Some of the first jewellery we made was from recycled newspapers. We worked with what we had. Now we have been making jewellery from our own designs for four years now and have our own company called Habesha Designs.

We make a lot of jewellery and have unique works. We mix different beads and materials that we get from here and abroad to make our own beautiful designs. After we make the jewellery we come and sell it here at the *ferenji* bazaar. Some of our trainers take our jewellery and sell it for us in the countries where they come from. So now we have sold our jewellery in the USA, Australia and England, and we recently went to a trade fair in Burkina Faso and sold our jewellery there. Gemini have helped us in different ways. For example, at first we didn't have plenty of places to sell our work and our work was limited. Gemini helped get us a table at the NGO bazaar. So now we take along any design we want and present it here. And people see our jewellery and come to our little shop that Gemini has given us and the people buy other things they see there. Gemini also helped us by giving us marketing courses and this helped our business grow. We are now members of the Ethiopian Export Association, and we have trained and employ sixty women in jewellery making who have been affected by Fistula problem. They would find it difficult to find work if we did not employ them, but now they can support their families. One day we want our jewellery to be internationally recognised and we are trying to get a market on the internet.

# THIRTEEN

# Piazza

**H**er whole upper body quivered. Every muscle jerked and twitched at a speed faster than the eye could count, and her shoulders shuddered up and down in a blur of movement. It was as if she had been hit by a bolt of twenty thousand volts. Strangely, her mouth wasn't contorted into a teeth clenched rictus grin. Her face was serene. Her head, perched above her manically shaking shoulders, twitched with a jerky, chin-jutting movement. Only her eyes gave away the intensity she was feeling – they blazed. Her arms slowly began to rise, lifting the two halves of the sash she wore tied around her waist. Arms fully extended, she looked like an angel with embroidered wings. At her throat she wore a heavy collar of chunky chain jewellery, which bounced and flew to the tremors that continued to wrack her body. Her head began to jerk more violently, and her long, beaded, jet black hair whipped across her face. Slowly she sank down onto her knees as if exhausted. But then her movements intensified, as if an unseen hand had cranked up the electricity coursing through her slender frame. With her head tilted to one side, her shoulders increased their juddering tempo causing her breasts to jump up and down. She was clothed top to toe in a traditional, white, cotton dress. Even so, it was pure sex – it was *ishkista*. The "electricity" was the high-tempo driving beat of a four-piece band. The musicians also wore traditional, white pyjama suits with embroidered collars and cuffs. A couple of them also wore sashes across their chests, the red, gold and green of the Ethiopian flag shone vibrantly. They played traditional

stringed instruments and the drummer held the set together with a re-
lentless, driving rhythm that hammered away unrelenting at the insides
of my head.

"What's that?" I asked Wonde sitting beside me, pointing to a long
necked stringed instrument that ended in a bowl made of wood and cloth
which emitted a sound like a lyre.

"A *karar*, it's Ethiopia's oldest musical instrument."

*Ishkista* is the dance of Ethiopia, and everyone can perform its high-
speed shoulder shaking. Watching her reminded me of classical flamenco
dancers I had seen – only upside down. In Flamenco everything happens
below the waist, *ishkista* is the complete opposite, everything happens
above it. Her feet hardly moved apart from when she took small steps to
turn her body around so that she faced different members of the audience
as she danced.

Wonde and I were in an *azmaribet*. It stood in a compound ringed by
a high, corrugated iron fence. From the outside it looked no different to
any of the other compounds in the dimly lit side street in the Kazahchis
area of the city, which is where, Wonde assured me, all the best *azmaribets*
were to be found. Inside, the walls were covered in woven fabrics and
tapestries, and spears hung next to shields, dating back to days of glory.
People sat around *mesobs* on carved, wooden stools covered with strips of
cow hide, watching the girl dance. Wonde had promised me a night out
on the town in Addis Ababa.

After the dancer had finished a man took centre stage. A hushed expectation descended and Wonde leaned close to me and whispered,
"He is the *azmari*."

*Azmaris* almost defy definition. An *azmari*, is a singer-songwriter, musician, story-teller, social commentator, stand-up comedian, philosopher,
satirist and keeper of the flame of Ethiopian culture, wit and wisdom –
all rolled into one. Both men and women can be *azmaris*, and *azmari*
traditions are handed down from father to son and mother to daughter.
Their songs contain a mixture of *semina* and *worq*, wax and gold,

double or hidden meanings, which *azmaris* weave into their cleverly improvised songs with consummate skill.

He had emerged from the shadows wearing the same white cotton trousers and shirt as the other performers. He must have been six and a half feet tall and there wasn't an ounce of fat on him. His sharp features poked out at angles making him look like a walking, talking portrait by Picasso. He announced his arrival by playing a long, high-pitched note that put my teeth on edge.

"What's that?" I asked Wonde, referring to the strange looking single string instrument he carried.

"It's a *masinko*," he said, "all *azmaris* play this."

The *azmari* warmed up by singing a couple of songs. Then he started to work the audience. He walked over to a group of people, broke off from his song and started to chat with them. Having mined some interesting material and a few personal details, he resumed his song, only now it was about one of them. When he sang the punch line the place burst out laughing. Insult by insult and put-down by put-down the *azmari* worked the room, chatting to customers and then skewering them with a witty putdown in song.

No one took offence. On the contrary, it seemed people liked being ridiculed. Cries of "*Tetchawet*", enjoy, accompanied his performance. Embarrassing physical attributes, dodgy reputations, peculiarities of any kind, nothing was off-limits. I watched as vanities were exposed and egos lacerated in a tradition that dates back to the days when *azmaris* were court jesters to Ethiopia's kings, and to a time when they could get away with murder, so long as they were being funny. Nowadays, the targets may have been softer but the humour seemed to be as sharp as ever.

"Is being insulted by an *azmari* an honour thing?" I asked Wonde.

Before he had a chance to answer the *azmari* appeared towering above us where we were sitting near the bar. He started talking to Wonde but it was obvious I was the subject of the conversation. It appeared to be open season on me too. He launched back into his song, everyone in the room clapping along in time with the rhythm. After a stream of Amharic I heard him say "*ferenji*" and then after another burst of Amharic the words, "Bill Clinton". Whereupon everyone in the place roared their heads off. A few of the men came over and clapped me on the back, and one of them even bought me a beer.

"What was all that about?" I asked Wonde who like everyone else was convulsed at what the *azmari* had said. He looked at me and just shook his head. "Go on, tell me," I urged, but Wonde was too embarrassed.

"Now you must give him ten *birr*," said Wonde.

"So you actually pay good money to get insulted here," I replied.

I fished in my pocket and handed the *azmari* a ten birr note which he accepted with a gracious bow. I didn't mind. It was worth it just to have seen the *ishkista* dancer.

"Do you like beer?" Wonde asked me. The commercials were about to go to air so perhaps this was Wonde's version of a wrap party. That's how he and I ended up in the *azmaribet*, but it wasn't the end of the evening, it was only the beginning. Half an hour, and a hair-raising taxi journey through narrow ill-lit streets later, we found ourselves in Piazza, an area which stands at the end of Churchill Road, overlooking the city from a lofty eyrie. Piazza was developed by the Italians when Mussolini's troops occupied Addis Ababa, and Italianate architecture could still be seen wherever you looked. It was also the glitzy part of Addis Ababa, and a popular haunt for the young and late night revellers. Apart from that it was a place very close to Wonde's heart, and he was keen to show me around.

"This is where I lived when I first came to Addis," he told me, "after I escaped from Wollo."

It was curious, I noticed that Wonde often used the word escape when he meant left. But then as he began to tell me his story I began to think that perhaps he had used the word deliberately. Wollo is in the north of

Ethiopia, and it was here on a small plot of land that Wonde grew up. His family were poor farmers, peasants really, eking out an existence that more resembled the lives led by serfs in medieval Europe than anything that belonged to the modern world. Even from an early age, Wonde was driven to better himself.

"All I wanted to do was go to school," he told me, "but every day I had to be with the cows." From dawn to dusk he would tend the few, thin cows his father owned which were the economic lifeblood of the family. Still, he managed to grab some schooling and in the evenings he would take himself off to the shade of a tree with whichever book he had managed to get his hands on.

"My father didn't like to see me reading," he explained. "A cowherd doesn't need to know how to read."

Wollo was on the route the army took on their way to the front in the war with Eritrea. Wonde was working in the family's field alongside his father one morning when the army passed through. They were desperate for men and they conscripted his father there and then. Wonde was just too young to be taken.

"When they took my father, they did not even let him say goodbye to my mother," he said.

Wonde's father was never heard of again, and Wonde believes he probably died at the front in the bitter trench warfare that was the hallmark of the fighting that cost hundreds of thousands of lives on both sides of the border.

"I knew if I wanted to get an education I had to go to Addis Ababa, and I had an aunt who lived there."

Wounded soldiers from the front were constantly being ferried through Wollo in big, open army trucks on their way back south. Wonde seized his chance and hitched a ride on a truck of wounded soldiers heading to Addis Ababa. For three days he bounced around in the back of the truck as it made its slow, grinding way through the mountains with its cargo of shattered bodies. Many of the wounded soldiers were conscripts like his father had been. Some had bullet wounds, others were the victims of landmines or shrapnel. Some were amputees, victims of field hospital surgery as much as weapons. They had been patched up as best as possible before being loaded onto the truck. Wonde was soon given a job to do, change their blood-soaked bandages. He was fourteen years old.

"I will never forget the screaming," he said.

When the truck finally discharged its bloody cargo in Addis Ababa, Wonde set off in search of his aunt. All he knew was that she lived somewhere in Piazza. He went there and asked around until he found her. It took him three days. She lived with her daughter, Elsa, in a single room in a compound, but of course she took him in. At first he supported himself, and helped his aunt, by selling cigarettes on the street. Still hellbent on getting an education, he somehow managed to come to the attention of an NGO which was running education programmes for a few hours a day. Through the grapevine he heard that another NGO, Gemini, was starting up a film school. It was through Wonde that I learnt about the early days of Gem TV.

Having had the idea to set up the film school, Andrew worked to raise funds, and left the recruiting of the students to a local film-maker, Alemayehu, and another freelance producer, Bill Locke, who happened to be living in Addis Ababa at the time. Much later, back in the UK, I had lunch with Bill Locke. By then Bill was a highly successful TV producer working for a large independent production company making documentary TV series for the BBC and other international broadcasters. I met him at his company's offices near Hammersmith in West London. It was a world away from Gem TV.

"I had been at the BBC making children's programmes," Bill told me, "and my wife got a job in Ethiopia to do leprosy and TB research, so I went along as a dependent spouse. I'd been there about a year when I heard there was this bloke Andrew Coggins in town who was doing this very ambitious film project. They'd somehow managed to get some good equipment together but now they needed someone hands-on to train these people, so they asked me would I be interested. I explained that I had about another nine months to go in Ethiopia, before my wife and I would be returning to the UK, but that yes I would.

Alameyu and I held auditions with about ten in each session. They were largely uneducated, some of them had been living on the street, they spoke little or hardly any English and only one of them had actually taken a photograph before so I didn't have much to go on. With Alameyu translating, the crunch question I asked every one of them was, "What was the day you'll never forget?" If they said something like, "Oh my birthday was very nice last year," I excluded them. What I was looking for was a sense of story-telling."

The story Wonde told Bill was how he had got himself to Addis Ababa from Wollo in a truck full of wounded soldiers.

The first bar Wonde took me to was on the main square where scores of blue and white minibuses were lined up two and three abreast. The bar was small, very small. It was about the size of the square you're supposed to serve the ball into in tennis. Not surprisingly, it was standing room only and there must have been twenty men in there, and one overworked woman who dispensed draught Meta beer in a constant stream from a barrel in the corner. Although the bar counter, such as it was, was only about six feet away from the door it still took us a good minute to get there because the throng of drinkers was that thick. Wonde started elbowing his way bar-wards enthusiastically and I followed in his wake muttering "*yikertas*", or "excuse-mes", at the disgruntled drinkers Wonde left in his wake as he barged through the throng. We sank four beers in under half-an-hour. Being the veteran of many a rugby weekend in Dublin, I can handle the pace when called upon, but this was pushing it. Here we met Wonde's friend, Said.

"Said is from Wollo also," said Wonde, by way of introduction. "I was the best man at his wedding."

Said was neat and dapper, dressed in a grey suit and a white shirt and black tie. He had a small moustache tucked under his nose. It didn't extend wider than his nostrils but was trimmed so that the edges tapered down towards the corners of his mouth. It looked like a Hitler moustache, wearing flares.

"Said is an accountant," said Wonde proudly.

The three of us staggered out of there and headed up past St George's Cathedral and the large equestrian statue of Emperor Menelik which formed the centrepiece of a busy roundabout. By way of contrast the next bar was practically empty. It was ten times the size of the previous one and completely deserted save for three other drinkers leaning against the wall by the end of the bar. Wonde and Said knew them so we joined them there, all of us huddled together shoulder to shoulder in the corner of a large empty space. We must have looked like the drinking equivalent of battery hens that had just been let out of the coop for the first time, and hadn't worked out yet how to run around the farmyard.

After three more beers Said dropped out. Either the pleasure of the company of his new wife waiting at home was proving too strong, or more likely, he had been out on the lash with Wonde before and had a good idea of the direction in which the night was heading, and didn't welcome the prospect of being divorced before he had celebrated his first anniversary.

"Now, we go and meet Abush," said Wonde. "He is my best friend and he is a DJ."

We headed off into the night and down a dark, narrow lane that looked like the sort of back street that all good guidebooks say on no account should you ever go down. There were no street lights and we skulked past dark, silent compounds of shanty shacks and little hole in the wall shops lit by naked light bulbs. Wonde stopped at one to buy three loose cigarettes.

A few minutes later we stopped under an orange neon sign that stood above a battered wooden door in a peeling concrete wall. We ducked our heads and went in. We stepped into an open courtyard that was lined with tables and chairs leaving a small dance area at one end. The walls were brightly painted in cheerful colours and were decorated with posters of rock legends including The Clash, Eric Clapton and Bob Marley. About half the tables were occupied by young couples. The bar was in a separate room behind the courtyard.

The bar was bedecked with Christmas lights, from floor to ceiling it twinkled. We bought a couple of beers and Wonde led me back into the courtyard. A raised terrace ran down the length of one wall and at the end of it stood a wooden hut, the type where my dad used to keep his garden tools. Wonde knocked on the door, which opened with a creak and a big head emerged. Abush was big all over. He had big eyes, a big smile, a big voice and a big laugh. He was about the same age as Wonde and where Wonde was passionate about filmmaking, Abush was just as mad about music, all kinds of music. We sat down at one of the tables and three more bottles of Meta appeared from nowhere.

Abush wanted to know everything about life in the UK. We talked about politics, fashion, football, work, but most of all music. But most of all Abush wanted to know what I thought of Ethiopian music.

"The only artist I've really heard of is Gigi," I told him.

Gigi was Ethiopia's biggest star, a woman singer-songwriter who lived and recorded in Washington DC. I heard her music everywhere in Addis Ababa, a fusion of traditional Ethiopian songs and laid back jazz.

"And do you like her?" Abush asked, a serious critical look crossing his features for the first time.

"Yes, very much," I replied.

"Oh thank-you, Bob, thank-you," Abush said, slapping his hand over his heart. If there was one thing that was as important to Abush as music it was his pride in all things Ethiopian, and he was never happier than when the two went hand in hand. Much though I liked Gigi, I told him that I first got into music in the seventies. Abush dashed into his "rock shack" and within a few moments *Hotel California* was blaring out. What his regular clientele of young Ethiopians thought of it I had no idea but they didn't seem to mind. For the next couple of hours the beers flowed and the classics kept coming: T-Rex, David Bowie, Led Zeppelin, Roxy Music, Free, Phil Collins, Rod Stewart, early Elton John and the late Jimi Hendrix. Plus plenty of Santana. The three of us hammering out the heavy rock rhythms on the table top with our bare hands, making the steadily building band of empty beer bottles dance.

It was well past midnight and the bar was about to close, but the rest of Piazza was still going strong.

"First we find my girlfriend," volunteered Abush, "and then I know another bar with good music." The road that led from the main square to the Itegue Hotel was lined both sides with bars that were still doing roaring trades.

We popped out heads into three or four before we found Abush's girlfriend. She was surrounded by half a dozen men at the bar, and didn't look particularly pleased to see Abush. She was tall and shapely and wore a tight, figure-hugging top, and even tighter jeans which showed off her long legs perfectly. She was also completely off her face.

We huddled round a small table and she tottered over to us a couple of minutes later, after she had managed to prize herself away from the male fan club who had probably been buying her drinks all night. Abush was something of a celebrity in Piazza and the way he looked at her it was obvious that he had strong feelings for the girl and that she was much more than just a trophy girlfriend. But he deserved better. How could I tell? Because while Abush told her how much he loved her, she rested her beautiful head on his shoulder, while underneath the table her hand fondled my groin.

The next bar was small and packed with young, trendy Addis Ababans, the guys in designer sunglasses and the girls aping the latest fashions from the well-thumbed, imported glossy magazines that were sold in Piazza.

They sipped cocktails and tried to talk above the pounding beat. They tried desperately to look uber-cool, all of them that is except the two young women in skimpy tops and skin-tight jeans who were having a fight. I actually saw it kick-off. One of them was minding her own business sitting at the bar chatting to a couple of guys when the other one strode over, grabbed a fistful of her hair, and yanked her out of her seat. Wonde told me later that one of the guys was the attacker's boyfriend, and she obviously took exception to the other girl talking to him.

The sight of her stiff, stick-up ponytail obviously proved too tempting to resist. The girl with the ponytail immediately reacted with a stinging right hand slap to the face that was loud enough to be heard above the booming track of Timmy Thomas singing, ironically, *"Everybody's Got To Live Together, why can't we live together?"* Everyone, including the combatants, froze for a split second before the two girls leapt at each other in a fury of hissing, scratching and punching. Friends, sisters and passing waiters piled in vainly attempting to pull them apart, but the girls were having none of it. People managed to force them out the door on to the street where the two girls gamely continued to try and knock seven bells out of each other. They sent tables flying, knocked over chairs and demolished a wooden fence before ending up in a writhing, spitting heap on the pavement. I couldn't be sure, but I think the girl who did the hair pulling in the first place just about shaded it on points.

It was certainly more entertaining than watching *Buna* the way they had been playing lately. The small crowd that had followed them out of the bar eventually managed to prize them apart. However, it didn't include the boyfriend who had remained at the bar the whole time, sipping something green from a tall glass that had a paper umbrella in it. Girls, I thought to myself, he's not worth it.

Things felt a bit flat after that so we decided to move on. It was now nudging three o'clock in the morning and Piazza was still buzzing.

"It's not unusual for a Saturday night out in Addis to go on until dawn," he told me.

Down by the Itegue Hotel the bars were quieter. The taxi drivers were beginning to look desperate and the prostitutes just plain bored. The Itegue is the oldest hotel in Ethiopia and was built around the turn of the last century. It was where Evelyn Waugh stayed when he covered the war in Abyssinia, which gave him the material for his comic novel *Scoop*. What Waugh would have made of the bar next door was anybody's guess. Inside the floor was of peeling lino and a line of beer sodden men sat on stools at the bar. Remarkably, they all swayed drunkenly in unison like a row of trees being buffeted by the same wind. Half a dozen bar girls were trying to drum up some trade but clearly their hearts weren't in it. The vast majority of the clientele were clearly well past it.

By now I was beginning to feel as flat as the beer in the bottles on the bar so I left Wonde and Abush and his girlfriend to it, and stumbled out of the bar, and thankfully, straight into a taxi.

Addis Ababa is a great town, but it was also a good place to escape from at weekends. The trouble was that every Friday afternoon half the expat population of Addis had the same idea, and there was only one place to escape to, Lake Langano, one of the largest of the Rift Valley Lakes. The roads in and around Addis Ababa were always choked with battered cars, minibuses, flocks of sheep and herds of cattle at the best of times, but on late Friday afternoons they were joined by just about every other four-wheel-drive in the city as hordes of NGO and aid workers headed out of town for the weekend, with all of them hell-bent on getting to Langano first and bagging the best spot at the lake.

There were only four main roads in and out of Addis Ababa and they ran north, south, east and west. Langano lay on the Kenya Road, so named because that's where it went. Of course, these weren't the only roads in the country, they were just the only ones with tarmac on them.

It was a four hour drive to the lake, which had to be done in daylight because driving at night was too dangerous. With no street lights, the roads were a minefield of deep ruts and pot holes, and the last thing you wanted to do was hit a cow or hyena in the pitch dark at eighty kilometres an hour. The drive was spectacular. The Kenya Road snaked down out of the Addis Ababa highlands and descended into the Great African Rift Valley. The dry, dusty plain stretched to the horizon and was dotted with acacia trees. The further we went, the more the signs of civilization receded.

At first, the road hugged the Addis to Djibouti railway line that had been built by the French. It was opened during the reign of Emperor Menelik II, the founder of modern Ethiopia, in the early years of the last century. It became a vital link with the trading port of Djibouti on the Red Sea coast. Previously, it had taken mule trains six weeks to make the same journey, but now the railway had fallen into disrepair. Only certain sections of the track were operable, and the line brought it within reach of Ogaden rebels and *shifta* bandits in the east of the country. Grass grew between the sleepers and some of the rails were cracked and broken.

We drove through Debre Zeit and Ziway, nondescript towns where all life seemed to be clustered along both sides of the road that cut through them. The towns gave way to small villages and eventually hamlets of a few round huts of wood poles lashed together with thatched roofs, corralled behind fences of thorn bush to keep their animals in and the hyenas out. We past *garis*, traps pulled by emaciated looking horses, their drivers flicking at their bony haunches with rawhide whips.

It was usual to drive for miles and not see another car. You could drive for fifty kilometres and not see another living soul. Then up ahead a man would appear as a ghostly apparition, slowly swimming into focus as the mirage that cloaked him seeped away. I often saw them walking along the side of the road carrying a *dula*, the short, stout stick all travellers in Ethiopia carried to protect them from bandits and inquisitive hyenas.

They carried the *dulas* across the back of their shoulders with their arms stretched out and looped over them.

From a distance they looked like slowly moving crucifixions. I saw one emerge from the shimmering heat haze and realised that we had not passed a single sign of habitation in the last twenty miles. After we passed him it was another twenty miles before we encountered a few ramshackle huts. Where these people came from, and where they were heading to, was always a mystery to me.

Heading south of Addis Ababa took us into Oromo country. The Oromo are the largest ethnic group in Ethiopia. They also pride themselves on being good horsemen and we passed lone riders on the road, resplendent in their traditional lion's mane headdresses and richly embroidered saddle covers, looking like they had just ridden out of the pages of a novel by H. Rider-Haggard.

If people had something to sell they simply set up shop at the side of the road. They sold pineapples, mangoes, papayas and other fruits; bags of charcoal and flasks of honey. We passed men holding up recently cured leopard skins. Often we would have to slow to let herds of cattle cross in front of us. They were herded by boys whose job it was to guard them from dawn till dusk, as if their young lives depended on them.

At our approach they would beat the slowly plodding cattle with sticks to clear them from the road. Each *thwack* would lift a cloud of dried mud into the air from their earth-caked rumps. The cows never took a blind bit of notice. Whenever we slowed down, it gave the boys a chance to stare in through the windows at us and wave. They wore western hand-me-down clothes that had been reduced to rags, and the younger ones would be running around naked. Their thin legs were coated in a dirty grey film of dust, they seldom wore shoes and their heads were shaved to the scalp to ward off lice. When I waved back their faces split into big grins.

Two hours into the drive, the first and smaller of the crater lakes appeared in the distance out of the left hand window, patches of dark brown. The lakes have a high mineral content which gives them the colour of stewed tea. Further south we passed small, gaily painted tombs that were decorated with colourful, geometric designs.

Even their roofs had been painted and the walls were decorated with scenes from the deceased's life. Mosques, built from sheets of corrugated iron painted green, and no bigger than village huts, stood by the side of the road, their flimsy minarets topped with crescent moons. They may have been made with the most basic materials that came to hand but there was evident pride in the workmanship.

The resort itself at Lake Langano was a bit of a disappointment. A number of small bungalows were centred round a restaurant and bar on the shore of the lake. Some of the older Addis families owned large villas, which had been occupied by the Derg and used by them in the same way as the Soviet Politburo chiefs escaped to their luxury dachas by the Black Sea. Nowadays, they were rented out to high level UN people. Most people opted to camp in the shade of the acacia forest that hugged the shoreline. Langano was a chill out place. There wasn't much to do except go for walks and sit and chat with friends in the shade of the spreading acacia trees. Swimming was the other big attraction because Langano was the only Rift Valley Lake that was bilharzia free, a condition caused by a nasty little worm that can cause severe bladder and liver damage.

At weekends Lake Langano became *Addis-sur-mer*, and it wasn't unusual to bump into people there that you had been vainly trying to track down in Addis Ababa for weeks. At night the long strip of lakeshore became a party town. Bonfires lit up the shoreline and the golden fingers of their reflections in the moonlight reached out across the dark waters of the lake. You didn't need an invitation to wander into any of the villa compounds and join whatever party that was going on, everywhere was open house. Laid back reggae throbbed gently from ghetto blasters and the air was spiked with the sweet, heady aroma of spliffs. Blue-eyed, blonde girls on their first postings overseas melted under the gaze of handsome, dark-skinned, Ethiopian men, and the adventure of many a passionate affair took its first, faltering steps.

But this wasn't the only way to visit Langano, for the lucky few there was a far more luxurious alternative, Bishangari, a private eco-lodge set in hundreds of acres of private land. And fortunately for me it just happened to be owned by Omar Bagersh.

"Bob, you will be my guest, I absolutely insist." Omar was being as charming and persuasive as ever. We were sitting in his office after a meeting about the DKT campaign. We'd made Cactus look good and Omar was keen to show his appreciation. I reasoned it would have been churlish to refuse, and the chance to spend an all expenses weekend at Ethiopia's most exclusive retreat was not to be sniffed at.

"It's not just a place for *ferenjis*," said Omar, "the idea is to preserve the natural environment and help the local people."

A few days later I found myself driving out of Addis Ababa on the familiar road to Lake Langano. My Gemini driver was Negussie, a slightly built man in his early forties. He was quietly spoken and had an easy smile. He had been a captain in the army during the time of the Derg. Negussie hadn't seen any fighting because he worked in administration. Even so he had been sent on training secondments to Moscow and Havana during his army career. He was married he told me but his wife and four children all lived in Toronto. Why he didn't live with them I never understood. When the Derg were deposed he lost his job and had been working as a driver at Gemini ever since.

Bishangari lies a few miles off the main road and by the time we found the track to take us to its gates, night had started to fall. It took us the best part of an hour driving across rough country in the pitch dark before we found the entrance to the Bishangari estate. We lurched and bumped, our headlamps throwing up stark images as we crawled past huts and fences that suddenly loomed out at us from the African night. No other source of light was to be seen, everyone had retired to their beds soon after nightfall. These were country people who lived their lives by the natural cycle of sunrise and sunset. When the headlamps picked out the shape of a solid looking structure immediately ahead of us, Negussie jumped on the brakes and we came to a skidding halt. It was a box bridge over a shallow river. It had been made by knocking through two cargo containers and welding them together. We had found Bishangari but there was no one to greet us. Two sheet metal doors marked the entrance to the bridge and were padlocked shut.

"If anyone is nearby they will have heard us," said Negussie as he killed the motor.

We waited, but nobody showed up. I slipped out of the four-wheel-drive to stretch my legs but was driven back within in a minute by swarms of insects. Negussie lent on the horn and mournful blasts drifted out into the night. The air was warm and the sky was clear flooding the landscape in pale moonlight. Half an hour later there was still no sign of life and we resigned ourselves to bunking down as best we could in the four-wheel-drive. Then across the river twin headlights glowed in the distance and slowly grew larger. The lights stopped on the other side of the bridge and a minute later the doors of the bridge swung open with a rusty grating. A tall figure approached. As he stepped into the twin beams of our headlights I saw that he was wearing a military overcoat and had a Kalashnikov slung over his shoulder. He shone a torch into my face and then gave me a wide, gap-toothed smile. He looked across and spoke a few words with Negussie before he stepped back and waved us onto the bridge. Negussie gingerly edged the 4WD forward and carefully aligned it with the narrow entrance of the bridge before gunning the engine and driving it up a short ramp that led into the rusty containers.

As I explored Bishangari over the next couple of days, Omar's vision was slowly pulled into focus. I stayed in one of the nine *godjos*. From the outside they looked like traditional huts but were beautifully furnished inside. Each *godjo* stood in its own secluded patch of acacia forest looking out over the lake. A small terrace slung with a hammock was all that separated you from the surrounding wilderness.

From the outside they may have looked like traditional dwellings, but inside they were a very different story. They were fitted out comfortably and simply. Even the toiletries in the bathrooms were made from local ingredients. The *godjos* had been built by local Oromo craftsmen. They had used only natural materials such as dried grass for the thatch on the roof and mud finishing for the walls. Omar had an eye for detail. He had recruited an anthropologist with an understanding of native Ethiopian craft and artwork to design the interiors and furnishings, which, naturally, were made from local fibres and hand made fabrics. It had taken him months of travelling throughout the region to find the right furniture and artefacts.

Bishangari's green credentials were just as impressive. A waste management plant digested all waste products and converted them into methane gas for cooking. The digested waste was then composted and used as fertilizer, and the whole lodge was powered by solar electricity.

Unsurprisingly for an adman, the first thing Omar did was commission some market research amongst the local community to find out what they thought about his Bishangari idea. He also wanted to understand the cultural, social, economic and demographic make-up of the area. So he went out and talked with village elders and other members of the community, and involved them in the planning of Bishangari. He learnt that one of the problems for them was that the only work many of them could get was as farm labourers. This was seasonal work and involved a great deal of travelling. Bishangari, he told them, would offer people permanent employment closer to home. As well as creating jobs for the locals as builders, cleaners, cooks, waiters and housemaids, he trained local people to become guides, furnishing them with an extensive knowledge of the local wildlife and flora. He arranged for them to have English lessons and sent some of them to college. His aim was to convince the local people that there was more to be gained from protecting the beauty of the environment rather than simply living off it. Practically unheard of in Ethiopia, he introduced a workers benefits package which included fixed working hours, social security and free medical insurance for all Bishangari's staff and their families. Finally, when he asked them what did they need most, they said a medical centre. So he built them one.

But for the visitor, Omar had created an African Garden of Eden. I woke long before breakfast and walked the fifty yards from the door of my *godjo* to the lake. Picking my way through acacia trees, I emerged onto a sea of frozen lava that had bubbled up from the bowels of the earth and cooled here thousands of years ago. It stretched in both directions along the lake shoreline in twisted shapes and looked like a lump of the moon had fallen to earth. Herons and pelicans took to the sky, and a flock of white birds exploded out of a tree as I approached, squawking their anger at being disturbed so early in the morning. The flapping of their wings became a fluttering echo as they headed out over the vast expanse of the lake.

The dining room, where I had breakfast, wasn't a room in the conventional sense at all. It had been built in a clearing in a patch of forest overlooking the lake. It had no walls and was completely open to the surrounding wilderness. Only local woods had been used in its construction and the beams that supported the vast thatched roof were lashed together with hemp ropes. The tall, locally cut timbers rose thirty feet or more into the air. Half the space was laid to dining tables and chairs and the rest was given over to a lounge and veranda, which was stocked with locally made wooden furniture decked out with thick bolsters and cushions and billowy, native fabrics. It was a masterpiece of local design and had been built without a single nail. It formed the heart of Bishangari and was where guests gathered for all their meals and to chat and swap stories at the end of the day.

At night it was even more spectacular when it was lit by paraffin lamps, and we had to raise our voices to be heard above the cacophony of insect crackle and chatter that surrounded us on all sides.

After breakfast two of Omar's guides took me on a horse ride into the equatorial forest that sprawled over many acres. There were so many indigenous types of tree even the guides didn't know how many there were. Many of them were hundreds of years old. Baboons, the size of rottweilers, slunk through the undergrowth and chattering colobus monkeys spied on us from lofty branches overhead as our horses walked along narrow, dapple-shaded pathways. Our approach put up exotic birds, their plumage a riot of petrol blues, mustard yellows and emerald greens, with dashes of lipstick red, their urgent *kaw-kawing* fading as they rose into the cavernous, green canopy overhead.

I returned to the forest many times to walk its pathways alone, and it was on one of these walks that I encountered one of the waiters who worked at Bishangari making his way home. He spoke a little English, but we communicated more by smiles and gestures, and he invited me to come with him and see his home. He led me into the heart of the forest and we came to a small, fenced-off patch of land. He pushed open a wooden gate and we stepped through.

There were half a dozen wood huts standing on individual smallholdings of tilled land. He led me over to one and a woman came out to greet us, wiping her hands on a scrap of cloth which served as an apron. She had a young girl with her who played and skipped around her ankles. She extended her right arm to me with the palm turned down towards the ground. I recognised the gesture and gently held her arm at the wrist, which is the traditional way of greeting someone when their hands aren't perfectly clean. The waiter explained to me that the woman was his sister and the girl was his daughter. His wife had taken their six head of cattle off for grazing. He gave me a tour, not that it took long, and showed me the wooden pen next to his hut where he kept his goats and a few chickens, and the plot of land where he grew maize.

This was how his father had lived before him, and many grandfathers before that. But working at Bishangari meant that he could earn considerably more money and that his family would have medical care and his children would be educated. He had no ambition to change his traditional way of life, he just wanted to improve it. Bishangari was giving him that opportunity.

In the late afternoon, Negussie and I walked along the lake shore to a pool, surrounded by high reeds, where we had been told we had a good chance of seeing hippo. It was the time of day when they emerged from their watery slumber and began to graze. We crossed the lunar landscape and emerged on to a flat plain of watery meadowland, the grass squelching beneath our feet.

Earlier, a brief thunderstorm had lashed Bishangari, and was now moving out across the lake. The receding curtain of rain looked like a grey wash, hastily sketched in by a watercolour artist's brush. The water of the lake was the colour of pewter and seemed to suck the daylight out of the air, save for glints of reflected light that were begrudgingly tossed back by ripples of wind-whipped water.

We approached a tall bank of reeds, which parted and two young men, perhaps aged about sixteen, emerged carrying long, vicious looking spears. Negussie spoke to them and then told me they were goatherds, explaining, "The spears are to protect the goats from baboons, who kill them and carry them off." They beckoned us to follow and crouching we climbed up a gentle rise. As we neared the top they quietened us with a gesture and slowly we peered over the lip. Twenty yards below us a group of five hippo floated on the surface of the lake, only their nostrils and ears broke the surface of the water, their ears twitching constantly to ward off the clouds of dragonflies that hovered around them.

We lay on our bellies and watched them for half an hour as one-by-one they dragged themselves out of the shallows and lumbered off to graze.

Their deep, snoring grunts made the air tremble and water cascaded off their mahogany brown hides. Their heads were massive and disproportionately large compared to the rest of their bodies. When one of them yawned it revealed two front teeth that were longer than my forearm. In a hushed whisper Negussie told me that hippo kill more people in Africa than any other animal. "Never get yourself between a hippo and the water," he told me. So many people die because in rural areas everyone congregates at water holes and riverbanks. "It's the same with crocodiles," he said, "water is life in Africa, but for the unwary it can also mean death." And violent death at that.

There was something decidedly strange about standing in the vastness of the Great African Rift Valley, a few clicks north of the equator under the midday sun, taking a hot shower. But then that's what you did at Sodore.

Sodore was another escape popular with *ferenjis* from Addis Ababa and Ethiopians who went there for the thermal springs. If one of the Gemini drivers wasn't doing anything at the weekend, quite often they could be persuaded to take us there. Getachew arrived at the guest house very early one Sunday morning to collect me, together with Dawit and Teddy who also fancied a day out.

It was a four hour drive, and once again it meant driving down into the Rift Valley. But this time the scenery was much more dramatic. The distant horizon was a sheer wall of solid rock hundreds of metres high. On the way we passed small villages, shepherds, cattle and donkeys laden with firewood and sacks of grain. The only stop we made was at a small village where the others bought their lunch, a freshly butchered hunk of beef chopped from the leg of a cow, and a large sheaf of *khat*, a mildly narcotic chewing leaf. The haunch of beef dripped blood and was wrapped in a few pages of newspaper. Dawit placed it on the back seat beside me. As the four-wheel-drive bounced along the rough road, blood oozed from it soaking into the bold Amharic headlines, merging them into indistinct black blobs.

We arrived at Sodore and drove straight to the thermal springs, located half way up on a rock-strewn hillside covered in scrub, bushes and stunted trees. Two concrete, open air shower blocks had been built into the hillside, one for men and the other for women. There were a few cabins dotted about but we stripped down to our shorts by the side of the car. Teddy was too shy to join Getachew, Dawit and me in the showers, so I gave him my camera to look after. We picked our way gingerly along the rocky footpath to the springs.

I was the only *ferenji* and the sight of my pale body caused something of a stir. There must have been fifty or more men in the shower pit, and we stood in tightly packed groups up to our knees in hot, soapy water, waiting for our turn to stand underneath the hot, thermal waters that cascaded down from a row of pipes overhead. When it came to our turn, the three of us huddled under a streaming jet and the water stung my face as the sun scorched my back. Typical, I thought, I'm going to get sunburnt taking a shower. Just then a man approached me pointing to Teddy who stood to the side holding my camera. The next thing I knew he had put his arm round my shoulders and swung me round to face Teddy and barked an order at him. Teddy gave me a pleading look and I returned it with a nod of approval. Teddy lifted the camera to his eye and fired off a shot.

Next thing everyone wanted their picture taken with the *ferenji*. The fact that they knew they would never see any of the photographs made no difference whatsoever. It was all very good natured, and in an attempt to get my own back as each man came up to me I rubbed my thumb and fingers together and said, "Ten birr". This was always greeted with lots of laughter and bouts of hearty back-slapping, but never any cash.

The resort was five minutes away from the springs. It was built around a large swimming pool that looked like it had been designed by the same people who built the outdoor lidos of north London that I used to go to as a kid. The pool was large and square and had a two-tier diving board at one end. It was surrounded by a well-kept lawn where people stretched out and relaxed. There was a cafe selling cold drinks and snacks but most people had brought their own picnics.

A chest high concrete wall defined the perimeter. The need for it became immediately clear to me when I wandered over there and had a look at what lay beyond. On the other side ran a slow flowing tributary of the Awash river, and on the opposite bank a large crocodile stared straight back at me. But curiously it wasn't the crocs you had to watch out for, it was the monkeys. If you turned your back on a cheese roll for a second, one of them would be down a tree and have it away in a flash.

It was lunchtime, so Dawit unwrapped the meat from the blood-stained newspaper, held it up, inspected it, brushed away a few, gleaming white chips of bone, and handed it to Getachew. He took it in both hands, lifted it to his mouth and sank his teeth into it. His bite must have been incredibly strong because he had to gnaw at the carcass to rip off a lump of raw meat, and then he began to chew slowly, wiping the blood off his chin with his hand. Then he passed it to Teddy who grabbed it and sank his teeth into it, tearing at the flesh until he too managed to rip off some of the carcass. Next it was Dawit's turn, and in this way they passed it from one to the other until they had picked it clean like vultures. I nibbled on a banana.

Then they produced the sheaf of *khat*. Dawit and Teddy picked off the small green shoots and popped them into the sides of their mouths and chewed. Getachew declined to indulge, more I think because he was driving than for any other reason.

"Try!" said Teddy offering me a bunch of the green leaves.

*Khat* is a naturally narcotic leaf that is cultivated and consumed in many parts of Ethiopia. It is sold quite openly and I often saw people selling *khat* on the streets of Addis Ababa. It comes in small bushels that look like large clumps that have just been cut out of someone's hedge. You pick out the smaller, greener shoots to chew, popping them into your mouth one after the other and chewing without swallowing so that you build up a plug of *khat* in the corner of your mouth, like chewing tobacco. It creates feelings of mild euphoria, increased energy and enhanced self-esteem.

Research suggests that chewing *khat* is far from harmless and it has been linked to increased risk of heart attacks, strokes and liver failure. Like smoking cannabis, *khat* has also been linked to inducing psychosis. For many Ethiopians it is a part of the culture and people go to *khat* rooms, to chew and socialise. These sessions can last anything from a few hours to a few days.

The effects, I was told, are often mildly hallucinatory but like all recreational drugs, there is a downside and *khat* chewers can become torpid and hungover, and the effects can last for a day or more, making the chewer not much use for anything. As a result there are many in Ethiopia who want *khat* banned. This poses something of a dilemma, because as well as being part of the culture, growing *khat* supports many subsistence farmers and *khat* is also a huge export earner, running into many millions of dollars. At the same time *khat* also plays a very different role. Like tobacco, it is an appetite depressant and is chewed in many rural areas where people don't always have lots to eat. To get the full effect you have to chew the leaves for hours while taking small sips of water. I accepted Teddy's offer but gave up after about half an hour simply because my jaw muscles weren't up to the constant chewing, and were beginning to ache painfully. To get off on *khat*, I concluded, you needed the chewing constitution of a cow. I left them to it, wandered over to the cafe and got the instant hit of a double espresso instead.

Not by any stretch of the imagination can I be said to possess any psychic sensibilities, but I always felt the fluttering of something strange and distant deep within me whenever we ventured into the Rift. Perhaps it was the landscape, because it's impossible not to be affected by the sheer grandeur of this colossal crack in the earth that stretches all the way from Lebanon in the north to central Mozambique, a distance of some 6,000 kilometres. The part of the Rift Valley that stretches across Ethiopia is spectacularly dry and rugged, a yellow scrub dotted with flat-topped acacia trees looking like God's nails pinning the savannah landscape to the surface of the earth. Here, about six and a half million years ago, a split occurred in our evolutionary cycle that saw our path diverge from that of chimpanzees and gorillas.

However, for the next half a million years or so, we continued to swing through the trees. Then we began to walk on two legs. It took another two million years before we developed a brain which at the time was no larger than a chimp's. By then we had climbed out of the trees and were living in grasslands and had developed teeth to chew food with. We carried on in this way for another one and a half million years, by which time we had evolved into more recognisable prototypes of what we are today. Homo habilis, as we were then, had brains about half the size of the ones we have today, but were developed enough so that we knew how to use primitive tools. By two million years ago we had developed larger brains, were probably making and using hand axes, and had learnt how to make fire. Then we started pedalling like mad on the evolutionary cycle. Shortly afterwards saw the emergence of homo erectus, the first hunter-gatherer. By half a million years ago, our brains had developed to be much as they are now. A quarter of a million years ago, Neanderthals arrived in Europe.

A couple of hundred thousand years ago, homo sapiens appeared for the first time, but it would take another fifty thousand years before we developed language. And a hundred thousand years ago, homo floresiensis, the diminutive "Hobbit" people, appeared in Indonesia, the precursors of what we have evolved into today. Right in the middle of all this appears Lucy, the bones of the world's oldest hominid, that were discovered near the Awash river in Ethiopia in 1974. She was quite simply the most significant anthropological discovery of all time, and she bestows on Ethiopia the epithet of being the cradle of mankind. The Hadar region of Ethiopia, which lies in the Rift Valley, had been identified as being a good place to search for fossils and primitive artefacts that could help explain the origins of mankind. On the morning of November 24th, 1974, Donald Johanson, an American anthropologist, was bored at the prospect of making field notes. Instead he grabbed graduate student Tom Gray, and drove his Land Rover over to a little explored area to search for bone fragments. They spent a couple of hours under the merciless sun picking over the arid plain but came up empty-handed.

Then, acting purely on a hunch, Johanson decided to explore a small gully. It had been checked over a couple of times before but nothing significant had been found, yet some instinct drew him to the site. They scoured the ground but again nothing interesting came to light. Seasoned anthropologists looking for bone fragments are like the San bushmen of the Kalahari in that they are expert trackers and can spot the most minute details in a landscape. As they turned to leave, something caught Johanson's eye. A small fragment of arm bone lay on the slope. He bent to inspect it and saw close to it another fragment that belonged to the back of a skull. He and Gray searched more of the slope and found fragments of a thigh bone, vertebrae, pieces of jawbone and part of a pelvis which indicated to Johanson that the bones belonged to a female. Could it be possible, Johanson hoped, that they all came from one individual. Such a discovery had never been made before. It took the entire team a further three weeks to collect all the fragments. Together they comprised 40% of an entire skeleton, by far the most complete hominid that had ever been unearthed.

When all the bone fragments were pieced together in the anthropological equivalent of a jigsaw puzzle, Lucy emerged as a mature, female hominid, who when she lived would have stood just under four feet tall and weighed about sixty-five pounds. Her bones are 3.2 million years old, and she would have looked more like a chimpanzee than a human.

From the waist down her bones were almost identical to ours, proving that three million years ago hominids walked erect. They knew there and then they had unearthed something extraordinary. Her name comes from the Beatles song Lucy In The Sky With Diamonds, a popular song at the time, which was sung around the campfire as they celebrated long into the night. Lucy's Amharic name is *Dinkanesh*, which means you are wonderful. Whatever you choose to call her, she is everyone's greatest ever grandmother.

Then in 2000, Ethiopia rocked the anthropological world again. The bones of a three year old girl, 100,000 years older than Lucy were discovered in Dikika, not far from where Lucy was found. Selam, as she is known, is a more complete skeleton. She was found embedded and largely preserved in sandstone, and her bones had to be gently enticed out of the rock's grip grain by grain. Already, Selam has revealed tantalizing new details and scraps of knowledge about how we evolved. Scientists and anthropologists continue to pore over her, and slowly Selam is revealing further clues of how we used to be. Perhaps there is a little bit of Ethiopian in all of us.

FOURTEEN

# Cutaway to Fantu

The compound was made up of five one-room shacks. The shacks were made of stripped wood poles, plastered with mud and dung, over which a cheap screed of rough cement had been scraped. In some places the cement had peeled off revealing their method of construction. The roofs consisted of overlapping sheets of corrugated iron that were either nailed down or held in place by large stones.

'Each house will have maybe six people living in it,' said Adanech, catching my gaze.

Fantu held open the door to her house and we filed into a single room. One third of the interior was taken up with twin bunk beds that extended from wall to wall. She slept in one with her youngest, the other was for her three children. There were two chairs in one corner made from wooden frames and lumps of foam, a table and a wardrobe on which Fantu had piled three suitcases, the top one wedged up tightly against the ceiling. She had done her best to turn it into a home. The walls were painted plain blue, like you might find in an NHS waiting room and a small, wicker *mesob* table stood by one of the chairs, its vibrant, woven design was the only splash of colour in the otherwise drab interior.

There was electricity though because Fantu flicked a switch and two bare, low wattage, overhead bulbs leaked pale light into the gloom. Cooking and washing was done outside in the compound. I saw no sign of a standpipe so guessed there was no running water for any of the families. Water must have come from a more communal source outside somewhere, shared by other compounds just like this one. I was beginning to realise that this was how most of the people in Gemini lived. There was so little space in the now crowded room so Habtamu ditched the tripod and decided to shoot hand held. But before we turned over we went through Fantu's story, Adanech translating as with the others, and me writing down her words.

'When I was young my father died and my mother married another man,' Fantu began hesitantly. 'But my stepfather was a bad man. He raped me. Later he arranged for me to get a job. He said it was a good job with a friend of his, and this is what he told me and my mother. I went there but it was not good. His friend had a bar and he forced me to work there as a prostitute. Then I became pregnant with twins and I ran away. After that my stepfather deserted us. He deserted me and the two other children he had with my mother as well. But I came home to help my mother and now there were six of us living in this house. It was soon after I started to get sick a lot. But because I had twins I had joined Gemini. I had been to the health education classes they have there. Because of this awareness I went to have an HIV test. I tested positive. Gemini gave me counselling and helped me get antiretroviral drug therapy, and with this help I gradually began to accept my status.

Now I am working at Gemini, trying to build up myself, and be a model for other people living with HIV. I distribute food and cooking oil to other HIV positive families in Gemini. I take the sick to hospital, and I have been taught to teach about HIV and prevention. I share their situation and show them that living with HIV is possible. If it had not been for Gemini I would have hidden myself away and gone back to working as a prostitute to raise my children. If I had done this I would be dead by now. Gemini has given me hope and life by showing me that an HIV positive person can work and make an important contribution.'

# FIFTEEN

# Face To Face With Famine

In an advertising career spanning twenty years I'd seen my fair share of business cards, but never one like this. The name, Dale Bills, was ordinary enough, it was his title that was intriguing: Director of Public Relations for the Church of Jesus Christ of Latter Day Saints. Dale Bills was the Brand Manager of the Mormons.

"I need a film," said Dale in a soft mid-western accent, "and somebody said I should talk to you."

Dale was in his early forties, his hair was greying and he was dressed casually in khaki combat pants and a check shirt. He also wore a broad brimmed hat to protect him from the sun. He may have looked like a comic strip cowboy but he was very serious.

"How can I help?" I asked. Selam was away for a few days and had left me holding the fort.

Dale explained what had brought the Mormons here. Two weeks ago they had seen a CNN news item back in Salt Lake City. It had reported a famine in southern Ethiopia. It wasn't a big one like the Live Aid famine of 1984, so it hadn't grabbed the attention of the world's media. It was just one of those small, largely unreported, little famines that parts of Ethiopia experience from time to time. The Mormons were quick off the mark. Within days of the broadcast they had organised large quantities of food to be delivered to Addis Ababa. A group of the Church's elders also arrived with the shipment to oversee its distribution, together with

Dale who also had the task of finding someone to film the Mormons' mission to Ethiopia for broadcast as a documentary back in the US.

A couple of days later I found myself, together with Adanech, Kebebush and Habtamu, and our driver Negussie, bouncing over rough, pitted roads a couple of hundred miles due south of Addis Ababa.

*The way to dusty death* is a line from Macbeth. We travelled along it to a place called Yetabon. The road was a strip of bare rock and rubble and was only passable by heavy trucks and four-wheel-drives. On either side fields stretched to the horizon. Well, that's what Negussie called them. The landscape was one vast dustbowl.

As we sped along I saw a farmer whipping a pair of emaciated oxen in a vain attempt to plough a furrow. The rough wood plough threw up a plume of grey dust that hung in the air behind him, like a dirty vapour trail. In Addis Ababa, surrounded by restaurants and food markets, it was hard to comprehend that the spectre of famine stalked the land only half a day's drive away. This knife-edge existence was normal for millions of Ethiopians.

The feeding station was a makeshift affair and had been set-up under the shade of a large acacia tree on the edge of the village.

When I walked across the fields my shoes stirred up clouds of dust that clogged my mouth and lined my throat. It was impossible to believe that anything had ever grown here, or ever would again. The rains had failed for the third year running. In the shade of the acacia tree hundreds of women and children huddled on the ground. The men were nowhere to be seen. They all waited patiently for the food supplies that they had been told were on their way. Mothers tried to breastfeed scrawny babies but their milk had dried up long ago, and older children tried to amuse younger brothers and sisters who were bored, bad tempered and suffering from cramps and hunger pains.

As soon as we arrived the crew set to work, Kebebush setting up the camera and Habtamu checking his microphones. Adanech stood by silently contemplating the scene that spread out before her. A telltale plume of dust a couple of miles away told us that Dale and the others were on their way. By the time the others arrived we were ready to turn over.

"The malnourished can't digest whole grains," Dale told me, "so we give them this stuff. It's called Atmit."

The Atmit was a bland but nutritious mixture of oat flour, powdered milk, sugar, salt and supplementary vitamins and minerals. When mixed with water it made a porridge.

"It can also be made into bread," Dale told me as his experienced eye took in the scene before him, "it goes further that way."

Dale was a veteran of many famines and disasters relief programmes but he told me had never grown immune to the shock of encountering starving people.

What I didn't realise was that you can't just fly in, pitch up and start feeding starving people in Ethiopia. First you have to go through a government department. The Disaster Prevention and Preparedness Commission (DPPC), has the job of overseeing all famine relief and food distribution, so they had sent their man along as well. He stood by and watched as a well rehearsed operation swung into action. Wooden stakes were hammered into the ground and ropes were strung between them to form "corridors" to channel the flow of people.

A crossbeam was lashed across two poles and a weigh scales suspended from it. While this was going on I noticed one of the women from the Church as she walked amongst the Ethiopian mothers sitting on the ground. She was a mother herself and had her young child with her, a blond, chubby boy who looked in the rudest of health. She bent down next to an Ethiopian woman with a boy of about the same age who was severely malnourished. For a couple of minutes they "talked" to each other despite the fact they shared not one word of a common language. The universal language of motherhood took over, as each seemed to recognise in the other the hopes and fears all mothers share for their children, whether they come from the third world or the first.

The Ethiopian child was the more extrovert and he reached out to touch the blond kid who shied away. Little by little the blond boy gained in confidence and soon they were playing pat-a-cake with their hands, both mothers looking on with smiles. Two children, alike in so many ways, but whose prospects could not have been more different.

The DPPC has strict guidelines which determines how much food supplement each mother can receive, determined by the number of children in each family, and each child's size and weight. A child came forward and he was lifted and slipped into what looked like a nappy, an old canvas sack that had been cut in half with two holes cut in the bottom corners for the child's legs to poke through. Two straps were looped over the hook of the weigh scales and the child was dangled from it.

Under any other circumstances it would have looked like a fun ride for a toddler at an amusement park. Next his height was recorded. Planks of wood had been nailed together and a wooden step had been nailed across the bottom. Lines had been scored across the planks so that the children's heights could be read off. I watched as the child was placed lying down on its back in the wooden half box. The child was terribly thin, and as gentle hands lifted it and placed it lying down on the wooden slats to be measured, it let out a wail of pure anguish, and its brittle-thin legs kicked weakly. Fear was etched into its face. It was probably just plain scared. I'm sure I wasn't the only one who thought it looked like the child was laid out in an open top coffin, perhaps a gruesome premonition of the child's immediate future.

Once the children had been weighed and measured, the man from the DPPC gave the mother a ticket and ushered her to where she would be given her allocated amount of Atmit. Adanech, Kebebush and Habtamu set about the task of filming them. Adanech's normally smiling face was etched with concern. Time and again she knelt down to talk to the mothers sitting in the dirt with their listless children lying in their laps.

And one by one she gently coaxed them into telling their stories so that the camera could record them.

"These people used to be rich," said Negussie, the Gemini driver, as he and I watched from the sidelines. By that he didn't mean that they were ever wealthy, just that when the rains didn't fail the land was good enough for the people to live off it and feed themselves.

I had no idea what Adanech was being told, the one thing I could see for myself was that not being able to feed their children had stripped these women of all human dignity. The Ethiopians are a deeply devout people, and God weighs heavy on the Ethiopian mind. Children are his greatest blessing and every mother's deepest joy, and for an Ethiopian mother to watch her child die slowly, in front of her eyes, and be powerless to prevent it, is a terrible thing to witness. The crushing effect this was having on the mothers was almost as hard to see as the ravages of the famine. But food brings life, and where there's life there's hope. This was plain to see on the faces of the women as they led their families away clutching their precious bags of Atmit.

The day ended sadly though. The food relief operation had been well organised, but it was a long and protracted process. The people had been waiting for many hours, and some may not have eaten anything for days. As the day wore on the crowd grew ever more restless. The sight of so much food so close, yet still out of reach, was putting nerves on edge. Many times the man from the DPPC had told them to be patient, to calm down, or else the food distribution would be stopped.

"It is for their own safety," he explained to me. "Sometimes these things get out of control, turn into riots, and people get injured, even killed."

As the afternoon wore on, the mood grew uglier and he felt he was left with no alternative but to close it down. It was bizarre watching aid workers remove food from in front of starving families in a famine zone. However, the man from the DPPC was quick to assure the crowd they would return the next day. Driving away from Yetabon we passed groups of mothers and their children making their way back to their huts.

Some carried food back with them, others didn't. Once again, a case of the haves and the have nots, only this time not between the first world and the third, but between neighbours who had met earlier in the day under the shade of an acacia tree in a small, unheard of, famine-struck village in Ethiopia.

How could famine happen again in Ethiopia of all places, I asked myself. Hadn't we learnt anything since Live Aid? Back in Addis Ababa this question nagged at me for weeks. So I went back to the Live Aid famine of 1984/85 in search of some answers. I spent countless hours in internet cafes scouring the internet for any scrap of information. From aid agencies, Human Rights groups and various media outlets, I was able to stitch together the whole sorry story piece by piece. And the deeper I delved the more I began to realise there was a lot more to the causes of the famine than drought, and that when I had watched Live Aid all those years ago, like the other one and a half billion people watching all around the world, I thought I knew what was going on and what to do about it. None of us had a clue really.

My researches revealed a more complex, and terrifying picture. Drought was only a contributing factor. It was the last playing card to be removed in a fragile house of cards that for years had been poised to come tumbling down. A maniacal despot, armed rebel insurrections, Cold War international politics, beleaguered aid agencies and the machinations of the western media all played a part in the tragedy. So too did a handful of remarkable individuals.

It seems that no matter how hard Ethiopia tries, it can never escape from an unrelenting cycle of drought and famine. More people live directly off the land in Ethiopia than in any other country in the world, a staggering eighty five per cent of a population of eighty million people. Most of them eke out a precarious existence farming small plots with nothing more than hand tools. They grow sorghum and teff and raise goats and chickens. The more "well off" may have a cow or two. They live in huts held together with a mortar made from mud and cow dung, and the roofs are sheets of corrugated iron. Even the furniture is made from the same mud and dung that plasters their walls. Whole families of up to eight or more will live in these one room dwellings. They have no electricity and no running water. Even at the best of times, when the rainfall is reliable and harvests are good, their existence is precarious.

Twice a year, the pattern of the prevailing wind system that affects East Africa shifts. Far out in the Indian Ocean, towering air masses begin to build, spiralling and swirling thousands of metres high. Winds pick them up, rotating them with a corkscrew action, and herd them like a pack of wild hunting dogs towards the East African coastline. As these giant air masses travel over the surface of the sea they soak up water vapour turning the air into blotting paper.

Somali camel herders are usually the first to know when the rains are coming. A faint breeze will pick at their goat skin cloaks, their camels will grunt and the temperature will drop. But rain won't come. The swirling air masses are on a journey and their final destination lies far beyond Somalia's border with Ethiopia to the west, and across the vast Ogaden desert. The nomadic camel herder shifts the weight of the Kalashnikov on his shoulder and presses on in his search of thorn bushes to feed his animals. It may take him days to find them.

In Ethiopia, in the ancient walled city of Harer, which stands on a promontory overlooking the western edge of the Ogaden, a woman in the market is bent over the basket she is weaving. Next to her a taxi driver is slumped on his haunches leaning against the wall chewing *khat*. They may look up as wisps of cloud begin to form high above them. But still no rain will fall. The woman resumes her weaving. The taxi driver shrugs and returns to his chewing. But journey's end is near. Warm air, heavy with water vapour, stays close to the surface of the earth. When it rises it cools, and cooler air cannot hold as much moisture, which is released as rainfall.

When the air masses collide with the vast, volcanic citadel of the Ethiopian central highlands, they are pushed up high into the sky, which turns deeper and deeper shades of grey. When the first raindrops fall, they are heavy and make distinct slapping sounds as they hit the hard, baked earth. Within moments the skies open and for the next three hours rainfall will hammer down, turning the streets of Addis Ababa into torrents of red, clacking mud. The corrugated iron sheets of the roofs of the houses rattle and ping in a cacophony that echoes throughout the city.

There are two rainy seasons in Ethiopia. The *belg* are the short rains that fall on the Ethiopian highlands between February and March and are followed by the *keremt*, or big rains, that fall between June and September. Both are vital to the agricultural sector. However, records show that the rains fail on average once every ten years. During the resulting periods of drought, farmers and nomadic herders are forced to sell off their meagre assets, or animals, to buy food. This leaves them with little or nothing with which to buy food or replace livestock. It can take up to five years to recover after a drought. Climate change is making the local microclimate even more erratic. Ethiopia, which constantly teeters on the brink of food security, never knowing when the next drought will strike, is one of the countries least responsible for climate change, but stands directly in the firing line of its consequences.

This is how the vast majority of people in Ethiopia have lived for hundreds of years. It was how they lived in 1984, and also how they had lived ten years earlier when another famine played a role in bringing down Emperor Haile Selassie, heralding the rule of the Derg, the brutal, Marxist military junta that ruled Ethiopia from 1974 to 1991.

By the early seventies, Emperor Haile Selassie, Elect of God, King of Kings, direct descendant of King Solomon and the Queen of Sheba, had been ruling Ethiopia for nearly sixty years. His word was law, his power absolute. When he was driven through the streets of Addis Ababa, people bowed down in the dirt as he passed by. He resided over an autocratic and antiquated regime propped up by the Orthodox Church, the aristocracy, and a vast web of patronage and intrigue.

At the age of eighty-one he was showing increasing signs of senility. The Emperor cultivated the image of being something of a moderniser, but in reality Ethiopia remained a backward country. When waves of protest broke out all over the country there were mutinies in the army over conditions, and students took to the streets of Addis Ababa protesting over proposed education reforms. Teachers, taxi drivers and trade unions went on strike. The Emperor was largely conciliatory in his response, but his concessions were too little too late. A system of government that owed more to medieval Europe than the twentieth century slowly unravelled.

A year before, the journalist, Jonathan Dimbleby, had been travelling in Ethiopia and filmed a famine in Wollo. Elements opposed to the Emperor managed to get the resulting documentary, *The Hidden Famine*, screened on Ethiopian television. It showed the Emperor, dressed in all his regal finery, feeding his pet dogs in the royal palace with cuts of fresh meat, served to His Majesty by a servant on a silver salver to give to them. These shots were intercut with footage of the starving and the dying. This wasn't the last time the media would focus attention on the problem of famine in Ethiopia.

Into this growing power vacuum stepped a group of dissident military officers. They met in secret calling themselves the committee, or *Derg*. At first they pledged to uphold the existing regime. However, they soon realised that opposition to them was weak and power was theirs for the taking. Very soon the *Derg* became dominated by one man. Colonel Mengistu Haile Mariam is not as well known to history as Idi Amin, Pol Pot or Sadam Hussein, but his crimes against humanity were no less brutal or widespread.

Mengistu possessed all the attributes of a dictator, his ambition was boundless, he pursued his goals with ruthless efficiency, and he had no respect for human life whatsoever, being prepared to let millions of his countrymen die in his headlong pursuit of power. His origins were humble. His father worked as a guard at a rich man's house, and his mother was the illegitimate daughter of a member of the nobility. The young Mengistu grew up with a deep-seated hatred of the aristocracy and the establishment. He wasn't well educated but possessed a natural intelligence, which might be more accurately described as animal cunning. At the age of fifteen he was enrolled in the army, where he quickly developed a reputation for being wilful and difficult to control. Mengistu fitted the classic psychological profile of the outsider.

In the course of little over a year, the *Derg* seized complete control of the country, nationalising the banks, all rural land, industry and abolishing the monarchy. In 1976, Mengistu held a mass rally that filled Meskel Square in Addis Ababa. In front of thousands of people he hurled bottles to the ground containing red liquid that represented the blood of "imperialists" and "counter-revolutionaries". The bottles exploded and splattered people all around. The Red Terror had begun. As groups, opposed to the Marxist doctrine of the Derg emerged, they were eradicated with Stalinist efficiency. Loyalist army officers, government ministers and high ranking civil servants were the first to be summarily rounded up and executed as enemies of the state. Next came the academics, teachers, doctors and professional classes, until it seemed that no rank of society was left untouched.

One of the more efficient Mengistu inspired killing machines was the *kebeles*, the local government committees that met regularly to draw up death lists. People sat in judgement on their neighbours, and many old scores and feuds were settled in blood simply by scrawling a name on a list. In scenes that echoed anything perpetrated by Idi Amin, Chairman Mao or Pol Pot, over one hundred thousand people were murdered in Addis Ababa during the purges of the Red Terror.

The city lived under a curfew of fear. Night after night death squads roamed the streets and the silence was split with the crackle of rifle shots.

It wasn't unusual for people to wake and find the bullet-ridden bodies of their neighbours lying in the streets. Wives and brothers who went to retrieve the bodies of their loved ones were forced by *Derg* soldiers to hand over a few birr for the body – the price of the bullet that had been "wasted" in killing them. Many relatives were simply taken away and executed themselves, their only crime being a counter-revolutionary by association.

Soon bodies lay in the street where they fell or were thrown, and the streets of Addis Ababa reeked of the stench of decomposing flesh left out in the sun. No one was safe and anyone could be next. Children became a particular target of the *Derg* soldiers. At the time the Secretary General of Swedish Save The Children said that "one thousand children have been massacred in Addis Ababa," and estimated that up to 150 young people – some as young as twelve – were being murdered every night. Students were rounded up wholesale and slaughtered in far larger numbers. In Addis Ababa people said you learnt "not to trust your own shadow".

Those who were able to leave the country fled, robbing Ethiopia of its most educated, skilled and professional people, a legacy that continues to hamper Ethiopia's development to this day. The death squads went to work for two years, and the horrific scenes witnessed in Addis Ababa were repeated in villages, towns and cities all over the country. Amnesty International estimates that half a million people died as a result of Mengistu's Red Terror.

While the *Derg* was systematically taking over the country, Mengistu was tightening his stranglehold on the *Derg*. When rival factions broke out within the *Derg*, Mengistu lost no time in displaying the ruthlessness that was to become the bloody hallmark of his rule. At one meeting he and his supporters got up and walked out leaving seven members of the *Derg*, who Mengistu considered to be opposed to him, sitting round the table. Soldiers walked in, marched them at gunpoint down to the basement, and in a scene reminiscent of the Saint Valentine's Day Massacre, lined them up against a wall and machine gunned them to death.

Mengistu personally took part in the slaughter. Next it was the turn of the Emperor himself. Haile Selassie was placed under house arrest in the Grand Palace, while Mengistu pondered what to do with him.

Meanwhile, there were other people lower down Mengistu's hit list who more urgently demanded his attention. They numbered sixty high ranking figures including two ex-prime ministers and Haile Selassie's grandson. They were all executed. Stripped of all support and contact with members of his family, the Emperor became an increasingly isolated figure. However, he remained a potent symbol of opposition to Mengistu's Marxist revolution, a rallying flag for Ethiopian nationalism and the thousands of years of tradition the deeply conservative Ethiopian people still adhered to, especially in the countryside. His days were numbered, and being an old man he was easy to dispose of. The *Derg's* official statement said he died of circulatory failure. Supporters claim he was suffocated with a pillow, some say at Mengistu's own hands. His body was "buried" under a toilet in the Grand Palace, where it remained until the *Derg* was eventually overthrown, sixteen years later.

The intervening years, which led up to the 1984 famine, saw Mengistu institute economic and agricultural policies that were taken straight out of the Marxist economics textbook. The *Derg* nationalised all rural land. In doing so it may have freed Ethiopia's farmers from the yoke of the private landlord, the old style aristocrat, but the policy only served to impose another form of tyranny upon Ethiopia's millions of farmers. Now the government was the landlord. Mengistu's overriding priority was to make sure that the army, together with the towns and cities, were fed first. He knew from his own experience that concentrated populations were more fertile breeding grounds for opposition and dissent.

To keep these populations quiet he instituted a policy where they received food at subsidised prices, the farmers picking up the bill by having to deliver fixed quotas of grain. If they failed to hit their quotas their assets were seized or they were imprisoned. The farmers were left with no alternative but to dig into their own food supplies, or sell precious livestock, to buy grain on the open market, and at a higher, non-subsidised rate, which they then sold to the government at a loss.

Mengistu had also introduced a system of state farms, a programme which swallowed up most of the agricultural budget every year. But they were inefficiently run and delivered less than five per cent of the country's annual agricultural output. Mengistu's policies conspired to wreck an already fragile agricultural sector. For the farmers all over the country, already struggling to survive on what they produced, this was crippling. If this wasn't enough, two separate regions struggled with an even greater problem.

Opposition to the *Derg* didn't die with the Emperor. Since Mengistu came to power, he had been fighting armed insurrections on two fronts: in the Oromo speaking area to the south of Addis Ababa, and more importantly, in the provinces of Tigray and Wollo in the north, the heartland of the Tigrayans Peoples Liberation Front (TPLF), who represented the greatest threat to Mengistu. In the years leading up to the famine, Mengistu had launched six separate military incursions against the TPLF. Each of these major assaults by the army lasted for many months. The land was subjected to widespread bombing and shelling. The army torched grain stores wherever they found them and slaughtered livestock in droves, so that they couldn't sustain the rebels.

In 1991, Africa Watch published a report entitled: *Evil Days: 30 years of war and famine in Ethiopia*. It included first-hand accounts of what happened during the rebel insurgency. A woman survivor described what happened at the village of Edaga Habret.

*We heard that the army was coming at 2 a.m. in the morning from people who had run to our village from neighbouring settlements where the army had already been. Then around 6 a.m. we heard firing between the kabrits [TPLF scouts]. As soon as we heard the news, we tried to prepare foodstuffs for the future. You can't take injera for a long period of time as it breaks and dries. We roasted chick peas and cereals to make qolo, took the food and fled. Two of us went up the mountain two hours away and we could look down and see the Derg [soldiers]. First the troops lit one house using a match, then they took burning grass from house to house. All the houses were burned, houses belonging to a hundred and thirty five heads of families. Nobody stayed behind. We had tried to take important materials to the bushes surrounding the village, but these were discovered by the Derg -- house materials, plates, jerry cans, soap, salt, sugar, pepper, cloth, sewing machines. Three sewing machines were destroyed and all seven oil presses were burned. My two beds were burned and the small garden destroyed. A lot of grass had been collected for feeding the animals for the summer. It was all burned. Seven people were killed and twenty wounded in the area. We stayed for three days in the bushes and on the third day the troops left. There were so many of them that there was a two and a half hour line of them marching out of the village. When we went back into our homes we found that all the grain in the village had been burned. I lost three sacks of sorghum and 12 sacks of sesame.*

A *Derg* Lieutenant captured by the TPLF and held as a prisoner recalled.

*I can think of four incidents in Tigrey I have witnessed. One was in Sinkatta where four men were questioned about the TPLF. They said they did not know anything, and they were then shot. Another time a thirteen or fourteen year old girl was raped. A third occasion was when soldiers went to a group of houses near the church in Hausien. Three old people came out, and the soldiers chose one and shot him. There was also a time when we were stationed at a village near Samre, and the villagers came and brought us roasted maize and beer. They treated us very well, probably hoping we would do the same to them. The order to leave came in the middle of the night, and the soldiers burned the whole village asleep in their beds as they left. It is taken as read that these sorts of atrocities are all part of the job. Anyone who questions them, or talks about what is done, is picked up by the welfare people. The soldiers are trained to act like machines or animals and not have any thoughts of their own. There is no training in torture techniques or anything like that: soldiers are just given boxes of matches and told to get on with it.*

Market towns were targeted specifically by the *Derg*. The market at Chilla, near Axum, was where some of the worst attacks occurred. Later, a TPLF fighter described what he lived through when Chilla was bombed.

*You cannot believe what you saw. It was not something for anyone to see. The blood was flowing like rivers and sitting in pools, and there were crushed bodies thrown everywhere, the blood of the people was mixed with the blood of the animals that had been hit. You could see a head there but you couldn't find the body, it was thrown some meters away. The children were hysterical and screaming even after some hours. The helicopters chased them and they couldn't get away. They cry now even if they hear a plane. If they have seen a massacre when they are only four or five years old, they will remember forever when they shut their eyes that they saw their mothers being killed*

Another survivor of Chilla recalled: *Four helicopters blocked the exits from the market and machine gunned the market place. MiGs then finished this work. Even two weeks later we could still observe bomb splinters on the rocky ground and the smell was unbearable. The ground was strewn with various broken fragments, spilt cereals and corpses of donkeys. Everywhere there were traces of blood on the ground and on rocks where people had tried to escape. Here and there were the unknown graves of more than a hundred local people who had been massacred.*

In a series of hundreds of little Guernicas like Chilla, the *Derg* military systematically destroyed food supplies and the means of food production in the region that harboured concentrations of rebels, with no thought of the millions of civilians who were in the way, leaving devastation in their wake. Drain the sea and you kill the fish was the maxim. A region that in good harvest years had been Ethiopia's bread basket, was reduced to a scorched-earth wasteland.

Many farmers, who had once been able to support their families, became refugees fleeing to other parts of the country. Many more had no option but to remain. By the beginning of 1984, years of disastrous agricultural policies, and almost constant warfare, had left eight million

Ethiopians teetering on the edge. When the *belg* rains failed in the spring it was the final straw. It pushed them over the brink.

Mengistu had a strange relationship with the famine, as did his government, no doubt taking their cue from their megalomaniac leader. As Mengistu pursued his military offensive against the rebels in the north, he must have been aware of the effects this was having on the rural population. Then again, Mengistu was not a man given to be overly concerned with awkward consequences. When Mengistu told his military leaders to get something done he probably didn't want to be bothered with the details. Similarly, the military leaders, fearing for their own lives at any hint of failure, were only too happy to keep their leader in the dark about any embarrassing consequences.

Mike Wooldridge was BBC radio's East Africa correspondent at the time, based in Nairobi. Although the world would forever associate the name Michael Buerk with breaking the Ethiopian Famine story, Buerk was a relative newcomer to it when he famously reported from Korem in 1984. By that time Mike Wooldridge had been tracking the story for about eighteen months. Wooldridge, a BBC and Africa veteran and a highly experienced journalist of thirty or more years standing, came into Gem TV one morning to speak to the filmmakers about his work and pass on some interviewing techniques and tips of the trade. He told me that the Relief and Rehabilitation Commission (RRC), the relief arm of the Mengistu government, had not only known about the growing crisis but had been lobbying abroad for international aid since early 1983. Also, aid agencies had been trying to ring the alarm bell, especially Save The Children and Oxfam.

As he said, "Save The Children had pioneered nutrition monitoring and a system of tracking movements of local foods in markets, a systematic early warning system. Even as early as '83, it was nudging the red zone."

So while the military created the problem, the RRC tried to do something about it. It seemed that one part of the *Derg* was not talking to the other. This was evidenced in Mengistu's May Day speech of 1983 when he said: "Compatriots, there is a drought in some regions of our country. This has brought famine among some of our people in the villages. This situation tests our goal. We started off saying that we will at least satisfy our food needs. It is unacceptable that we cannot at least satisfy our food needs. It is a mystery that we are starving when we have enough land that can even produce surplus for other countries, and sufficient manpower. We need to get out of this shameful situation."

By February of 1983, according to figures released by the RRC, ten thousand people were dying in makeshift camps and shelters every week. A horrific figure, but at the time only a dribble that would later swell to a flood. Wooldridge knew about it and tried desperately to get access to the story to check its veracity and bring it to the world's attention. Finally, together with the cameraman and photographer Mohammed "Mo" Amin, Wooldridge was granted access to the north to report on the growing humanitarian disaster. He wasn't alone. An ATV reporter, David Smith, and his film crew were also granted access. Mike remembers, "So we decided to travel in opposite directions. Mo and I went clockwise reporting on the region, and David went anticlockwise." The full hurricane force of the famine had yet to be unleashed, even so Wooldridge could see that the situation was already desperate and widespread.

Wooldridge returned in March 1984, and April and May saw him in the Ogaden in the south, where another famine was breaking out.

"I think it was in Korem," Wooldridge recalled, "where Mo, who always had an eye for a great photo, took a still of a priest outside a church dropping individual kernels of grain into outstretched people's hands."

Back in Nairobi, Wooldridge fought to keep the story alive but editors back in London were more concerned with other unfolding political events and humanitarian disasters in Africa, a continent that always seems to experience more than its fair share of grief. Meanwhile in Ethiopia the shutters had come down and foreign journalists were banned from visiting the north, the government saying that travelling there was unsafe. Ironically, it was the rebels who helped the *Derg* establish the news blackout. In April 1983, rebels raided the feeding centre at Korem, seized humanitarian supplies and took seven relief workers as hostages, including two Britons who were working with Save The Children. All the hostages were released unharmed some weeks later near the Sudan border. But as a result Save the Children suspended its operation in Tigray.

If Mengistu wanted to prevent the world knowing what was happening in the famine region, this action gave him all the excuses he needed to ban foreign journalists from reporting from the region, claiming it was unsafe.

The year 1984 marked the 10th anniversary of Mengistu's Marxist revolution and he had planned large scale celebrations to take place in Addis Ababa. Triumphal arches were built over the roads leading into Revolution Square, now Meskel Square. The Great Hall of the People, a state of the art conference centre with seating for over three thousand delegates, was constructed. It would be filled with Mengistu's guests, high-ranking dignitaries from all over the communist world. Ten storey high posters of Marx, Lenin, and Mengistu were draped over buildings proclaiming the glorious achievements of the revolution.

The event was also designed to showcase the success of Mengistu's economic policies. Nothing was going to rain on his military parade, and that included the desperate plight of eight million Ethiopians. Meanwhile, in Tigray and Wollo, the people continued to die in ever increasing numbers. Within a month the number of people dying had risen to sixteen thousand every week. Mengistu sealed off the area. The first that people living in Addis Ababa knew about the unfolding crisis was when the ghostly figures of starving peasants started appearing on the outskirts of the city. Mengistu promptly had them rounded up by the army, piled into trucks and driven off to die out of sight of the dignitaries flying into the city. It's estimated that Mengistu spent $150 million on these lavish celebrations. Ironically, the same sort of figure the Live Aid concerts would later raise.

Despite Mike Woodridge's one man effort to keep the story alive, another factor that would contribute to the mounting death toll was the West's slowness to react. Western governments tended to play down the rumours that began to emerge about an impending humanitarian disaster because they weren't officially sanctioned by the Ethiopian government. They were also concerned that any financial aid would be swallowed up by Mengistu's tenth anniversary celebrations, or be diverted to feed his voracious military machine. Furthermore, under the *Derg* Ethiopia was firmly placed in the communist bloc's sphere of influence. The West didn't necessarily see Ethiopia as their responsibility. That said, at the time of the famine the West was supplying Ethiopia with ninety per cent of its annual aid.

The role the media played was also crucial. The media can sometimes have a strange relationship with humanitarian disasters, which have to compete with elections, wars, terrorist attacks, sporting victories, celebrity gossip and all the other items that regularly fill our television screens, newspaper pages and tweets. Competition affects things too. Sometimes news organisations will compete with one another over a story, and at other times they won't, thinking that by coming to it late they'll come off second best. Even within a single news organisation internal competition takes place. Journalists and camera people compete with each other to get their stories pushed higher up the running order. This is how media careers are built.

The RRC's earlier efforts to ring the warning bell had been heard in some quarters, and the problem had been on the radar of some British aid agencies working in Ethiopia as far back as 1982. In 1983, a filmmaker, Roger Briottet, brought footage of the Wollo famine to the BBC, but it was turned down for not being broadcast quality. A vital opportunity to raise awareness of the famine a lot earlier was missed. Who knows how many lives could have been saved had the film been broadcast. This is hard to imagine today now that we regularly see news footage on our

TV screens from all over the world, shot by citizen journalists on their mobile phones. Nothing like that existed at the time.

Eventually, articles started appearing in the press in the UK. Later, a UNICEF representative in Addis Ababa went public with an eerie premonition of the immediate future saying, "We have been asking for help since early 1983. It seems you have to have thousands of corpses before people will sit up and take notice." Many years later, the sociologist Anthony Giddens, commenting on climate change, would lend his name to this particular paradox saying that the dangers posed by climate change aren't tangible, immediate or visible in everyday life, so most people will sit on their hands and do very little of a concrete nature. Yet waiting until the dangers become visible and acute before we are stirred to serious action will, by definition, be too late. In 1984, as fears of the impending famine became more concrete, it was already too late for a million Ethiopians who were about to suffer long, agonizing, protracted deaths. However, action did save the lives of many others, but for a vast multitude it was already too late, their death warrants had already been sealed.

It was only when the story broke on television in the UK that things began to move. The catalyst was a documentary called Seeds of Despair, made by Charles Stewart, a film-maker who was working for Central Television.

The BBC got wind of it and a healthy dose of media competition kicked in. They thought they could be missing out on a big story and sent Michael Buerk, their Africa correspondent based in Johannesburg, to cover it. Buerk flew into southern Ethiopia, which was the only area the Derg granted him access to, and covered the Oromo region famine. He never got anywhere near Tigray and Wollo where the main famine had been brewing for close on a couple of years. Buerk's first report aired on the BBC on July 17th, the same day as Seeds of Despair was broadcast.

It appeared half way through the news programme sandwiched between a story about the French prime minister's resignation and Israel's latest incursion in the Lebanon. Even so, between them Seeds of Despair and Buerk's report struck a chord with the British public, who donated £9 million. Then the story died, despite the frantic efforts of Mo Amin and Mike Wooldridge in Nairobi to keep it alive.

Wooldridge was sent back to Ethiopia in 1984 to cover the 10th anniversary celebrations, but as he put it, "I saw it as an opportunity to try and get into the north and report on what was happening there." Fed by conversations with NGO workers who were getting feedback from the handful of remaining aid workers still on the ground in Tigray and Wollo, he knew how desperate the situation was.

As Wooldridge kicked his heels in Addis covering military parades and opulent state dinners, the real story lay tantalizingly out of reach to the north. "I was desperate to try and get a travel permit for Wollo," said Wooldridge, "we besieged people's offices for days." His colleague was the larger than life figure of Mo Amin, the legendary news cameraman. Actually, the term cameraman is never used in the trade. The true term is camera operator, and I suspect it applied to Mo Amin in more ways than one, brilliant though his camera work obviously was. It was Mo Amin who would shortly shoot the famous footage of the starving and dying masses on the plain outside Korem that would touch the conscience of the world. Tragically, it seems that Mo Amin's fate was destined to be inextricably linked with Ethiopia. Some years later Mo Amin died when the Ethiopian Airlines jet he was travelling on was hijacked and crashed into the sea off the coast of East Africa. In remembering him Michael Buerk said, "He was a strange man. He looked and sounded tough. A bit of a swagger, lots of bravura. Brisk, brusque, sometimes downright rude. But he had a wonderful sense of humour, a boyish sense of mischief – he was such fun to be with, especially when the going got tough. When Mo got involved, he did not just lend his name, you got the full force of his personality. Things got fixed. Things got done."

According to Mike Wooldridge, the person who was about to be exposed to the full force of Mo Amin's unique personality was an unsuspecting press secretary at the Ministry of Information. He issued travel permits for both Wooldridge and Mo Amin to travel to the north thinking that there was no way they could get there. He wasn't the first, or the last, to underestimate Mo Amin. It was also about this time that the BBC in London got in touch with Wooldridge to see if he could get their TV news man, Michael Buerk, included on the trip. Once again, Mo Amin went to work and the necessary permits were granted. They managed to hitch a lift on an airplane leased by World Vision and flew to Mekele, the capital of Tigrey province.

Despite Mengistu's best efforts to keep Tigray and Wollo off limits to aid agencies, a number of small groups of aid workers had managed to slip through the net, and were doing their best to cope with an impossible situation. Exhausted aid workers walked amongst the hordes of dying lying on the ground, holding the fleeting power of life and death in their hands. One of them was to become for many the face of the famine. Claire Bertschinger was a young nurse from Hertfordshire working for the Red Cross at a feeding centre near Korem. Many years later she recalled the events she lived through for a discussion programme on BBC Radio 4.

*"It was horrendous. We were surrounded by hundreds of thousands of starving and we had one plane with food arriving every six weeks. And I can remember the selection days. We used to take in sixty or seventy, and we had lines and lines of children, all were just skin and bones, the skin just dripping off their bones because they had no fat left, and out of them I could count ten, twenty lines, with a hundred people in each. And I could take in sixty or seventy for that week. I knew the rest would die within a week, ten days, and there was nothing I could do about it. They were all starving hungry. They all needed to come in. And we decided, amongst the local Red Cross workers, that I would sit them down and walk up and down the lines and give everyone a chance. And I chose the ones, not the worst ones because I knew they would die within the night, but I chose the ones that sort of had a spark of life in their eyes. And that's how I chose them.*

*The other thing about the feeding centre was it was only for the children. So everybody else didn't get food – the adults didn't get food. If they had a sister who was nine or ten, supposedly I wasn't allowed to bring them in. So they would die. Every morning we used to hear – they used an old horn from a cow – we used to hear the horn playing and the parade of people carrying the dead to be buried ... every morning."*

As Buerk, Wooldridge and Mo Amin lifted off from Bole airport in Addis Ababa, huddled in the cramped confines of the twin engine Otter, the three seasoned, seen it all, journalists had no idea of the scale of the horror that awaited them, or that the next few days would impact on their lives forever. On the drive into Mekele from the airport they passed long lines of walking skeletons. Mothers placed their babies in front of their vehicle and hobbled away, hoping that they would stop and take the children. In this way they slowly slalomed around these pitiful bundles of rags, skin and bones all the way into town.

As a grim portent of what lay ahead in Korem, Buerk recalled coming across a group of women picking their way through a pile of donkey shit looking for any undigested grains they could eat. The drive made a haunting impression on Michael Buerk. "It was extraordinary, it was just on such a huge scale. At Korem there were forty to forty five thousand people, and in Makele there were another eighty to ninety thousand. They tended to congregate along the spinal road that led north from Addis where they thought relief would get to them."

But it was in Korem that television history was about to be made. Mo Amin's unflinching footage and Michael Buerk's spare, opening commentary was only 103 words long. It remains one of the most influential news reports in the history of broadcast journalism.

*Dawn, and as the sun breaks through the piercing chill of night on the plain outside Korem it lights up a Biblical famine, now in the twentieth century. This place, say workers here, is the closest thing to hell on earth. Thousands of wasted people are coming here for help. Many find death. They flood in every day from villages hundreds of miles away, dulled by hunger, driven beyond the point of desperation … fifteen thousand children here now – suffering, confused, lost. Death is all around. A child or an adult dies every twenty minutes. Korem, an insignificant town, has become a place of grief.*

The report aired on the BBC Six o'clock news on October 24th. At the time Buerk was under instructions to record a short piece, but having witnessed what was happening himself and seen the horror with his own eyes, he had other ideas. "It's difficult to express the inadequacy I felt. You take refuge in the technicalities of filming, finding sequences, working out the logistics and so on. There were two films, two pieces that finally aired. I knew they wanted about three minutes, but I cut eight and thought, fuck 'em. In those days as a foreign correspondent, communications being what they were, I tended to work on the basis that they got what they were given. I knew it was a very powerful film."

Thousands of miles away in London Bob Geldof saw the Six o'clock news. Watching Buerk's report would change Geldof's life forever as well, and in doing so touch and inspire an entire generation. Searing though those images were, even Mo Amin's fearless camerawork could not detail the full extent of the horror. When a body is severely malnourished it begins to eat itself, digesting its own organs and prioritizing what to consume next, saving the more key organs like the heart and brain till last. However, most of the famine victims didn't actually starve to death. Starvation only served to weaken their frail constitutions so that they were vulnerable to diseases which carried them off.

Many of them, especially children, finally succumbed to measles, pneumonia, typhus, whooping cough, chicken pox, dysentery, diarrhoea, and cholera. The camps became breeding grounds for deadly diseases. Countless others dragged themselves to a bridge over a nearby gorge and threw themselves off. Eyewitness accounts talked about engorged vultures that struggled to get off the ground when they were disturbed because they were too full of human flesh, and packs of hyenas prowled the fringes of the camp at night, gnawing at the emaciated bodies of small children too weak to fight them off; their feeble cries barely audible above the crack of their splintering bones in the vice like grip of powerful jaws. The hyenas grew fat at Korem.

The report was soon taken up by 425 news organisations around the world, reaching an estimated 470 million people. It galvanized them to put pressure on their governments to respond. Back in Ethiopia, Claire Bertshinger's only link with the outside world was a short wave radio with a patchy reception. She was unaware of the effect Buerk's report from Korem was having worldwide. But, however late, help was on its way. As she recalled:

*"Within weeks the first RAF plane arrived, and I remember being asked to go out, and I went at dawn as the sun was rising and I passed these check-points, and the control tower was completely run down and battered, and I climbed onto the roof and just looked around. It was very peaceful and the sun was shining and I could hear this hum in the distance and far away over the mountains I could see this black spot appear, and it grew larger, and larger, and larger, and this enormous Hercules plane landed in this hail of stones and dust and everything. And they opened the back doors and it was full of tons of food, and it was amazing."*

That RAF flight opened the floodgates. Within days the Soviets were flying in supplies, quickly followed by the Poles and the Italians and many more countries besides. The famine citadel had been breached and Mengistu was left with no option but to officially acknowledge the crisis. The scale of it was now too colossal to be hidden. Bob Geldof released a single, *Do They Know It's Christmas*, to raise money, and together with Midge Ure started planning the Live Aid concerts. It would take many months for the relief efforts to reach the starving. For hundreds of thousands of men, women and children help would arrive too late.

It's estimated that one million people died in the famine, making it one of the most terrible human catastrophes of the twentieth century. Some would say one of the worst ever crimes against humanity. Even with international relief efforts flooding into the country, Mengistu was still able to give the knife he had plunged into the heart of the Ethiopian people one final, vicious twist. It would result in tens of thousands of more deaths. The idea was to remove one and a half million people from the famine-struck north, and resettle them in southern parts of the country. On the face of it this sounded like a sensible policy.

However, the policy concealed a far more sinister agenda. Mengistu's true aim was to depopulate and scatter the population of the rebel stronghold, and it quickly became a pogram of forced resettlement. Famine victims were rounded up at the point of a gun and loaded onto trucks and air transports in scenes the likes of which hadn't been witnessed since Auschwitz. Those who refused to go, or who tried to escape, were shot. Husbands were separated from wives, children from mothers and brothers from sisters. Food, some of it possibly paid for by people who watched the Live Aid concerts, became a weapon of war. The *Derg* used feeding centres as magnets to attract local populations so that they could then forcibly resettle them. Victims of resettlement were interviewed for the Africa Watch report.

*There was an announcement from the government that everyone from Sekota should come to get cards to receive food rations. When we arrived there we were surrounded by armed soldiers, who beat and killed us. Everyone, big and small, with or without families, were being forced into the trucks. Those who refused were immediately shot. A lot of people died.*

The aid agencies and NGOs didn't have free rein to carry out their relief work, they had to work under the auspices of the government. In Korem many aid workers who worked in the camps and feeding centres saw what this meant. The *Derg* deliberately withheld grain supplies, blankets and tents for shelter in the bitterly cold highlands. By deliberately restricting available food relief supplies the Derg forced famine victims to accept resettlement.

If the aid agencies reported these practices they would in all likelihood have been expelled from the country. The Derg placed them in a terrible dilemma. Many opted to stay silent believing that by remaining they could still help many more victims. The same story was being repeated at relief centres throughout Tigray and Wollo. Aid workers were forced to leave the camps at night. When doctors and nurses returned in the mornings they were dismayed to discover that many of the people they had been caring for the day before had simply disappeared, taken for resettlement. It was a selective process. The soldiers took the young and left the old to die.

Many died on the journey too. And many more died after being resettled in poor areas where they had little to survive on, or faced violence and intimidation from the local populations who were already struggling to survive on scant resources. Many famine victims brought camp borne diseases with them which infected and killed local native populations. Many tried to escape and make it back to their homelands, or went in search of their families, expeditions which were fraught with danger. They had to avoid roaming bands of government soldiers with orders to shoot on sight, wild animals and flooded rivers. Disease and hunger carried off many on the road.

For those people who were resettled to the west close on the border with Sudan there was an added danger, the Sudan People's Liberation Army (SPLA), a rebel militia that had been fighting against the Sudanese government for any years, and which enjoyed the tacit support of the Mengistu regime. The SPLA enslaved any escapees they caught subjecting them to forced labour, or worse if you were a woman. One woman who survived being held captive by the SLPA told her story after escaping from a large resettlement camp near Gambella.

*My husband and I escaped from that place with a large group of over one thousand people and we fled into the forest. When we reached Sudan we met people who at first gave us food. Then they gave us money and led us to the next village. That is when they took the children away. After that they took us, the women. I don't know why they took the children, for workers maybe, for slaves. These men had uniforms. The people who gave us food did not wear uniforms. When they tried to take us there was a battle. Our husbands tried to fight with them, but it was sticks against guns. Some husbands were killed, some wounded. The army was victorious. The remaining husbands fled into the forest. The army took us to their camp. We stayed there six nights, then the fighters divided us amongst themselves, choosing the most beautiful there were. We were sent to the huts of each fighter and were always guarded, even when we went to the toilet. This is because they wanted to mate with us, they wanted children by us. Other than this we did not understand them because we did not speak their language. During the day we pounded maize for them. There were other wives, women previously captured. When we protested they beat us. I lived in a hut with three fighters. At night they exchanged me among themselves. This went on for two months.*

Forced resettlement lasted into 1986 and was part funded by NGOs, although the evils of it didn't come to light until much later.

The true story of what really happened in the run up to and during the Ethiopia famine will probably never be known. Its history remains shrouded in a fog of rumour, accusation, claim and counter claim. The one thing we can be sure of though is that it was totally avoidable. Perhaps Michael Buerk put it best when he described the scenes he witnessed for the first time at Korem. "Daylight pulled the curtain back on the biggest human tragedy of the late twentieth century. The darkness evaporated and, in the pearly half-light, we began to see what a vengeful God, cruel leaders and an indifferent world could do to the toughest and most stoical flesh and blood."

As well as the commitment and dedication of men like Mike Wooldridge, Mo Amin, Michael Buerk and others who strove tirelessly to bring the famine to the attention of the world, another person who was there and can look back on the terrible events of 1984/85 with her head held high is Claire Bertschinger. Although judging by the remarks she made much later, she had a tough job convincing herself of the value of her efforts.

*"When I came back (to the UK) people started telling me what a marvellous job they thought I had done, and I was trying to explain to them about*

*the situation, and that I hadn't done a good job, and I was trying to explain to them that the majority of people I'd tried to help had actually died. And so within a week or ten days I stopped talking about my experiences because people weren't listening. And I didn't talk about my experiences for over twenty years, until the BBC contacted me to go back. At first, I was horrified, there was no way I was going back because I thought I'd be hated by the Ethiopian people for not helping everybody. And yes I was greeted with open arms. It was wonderful actually. And the children who had been at the feeding centre were now grown people, had got businesses and children of their own. It was fantastic."*

By early 1991 communism was melting away in the former Soviet Union and across Eastern Europe as Mikhail Gorbachev's reforms took hold and the Berlin Wall came tumbling down. Stripped of its number 1 international supporter, the *Derg's* fortunes were also on the wane. At the same time the rebels in the north were growing stronger and had taken the cities of Gondar, Bahar Dar and Dessie. The province of Eritrea, soon to become an independent state in its own right, had all but completely been taken over by rebel forces. It wasn't long before the tanks of the coalition rebel forces under the leadership of Meles Zenawi's TPLF trundled into Addis Ababa where they were met with little to no resistance. Earlier, claiming that he intended to inspect troop bases in the south, Mengistu secretly fled the country.

In December 2006, a court in Addis Ababa found seventy two officials of the Derg guilty of genocide. Thirty-four of them were in court to hear the verdict, fourteen others having died during the lengthy process of bringing their cases to trial, and twenty five, including Mengistu, were tried in absentia. At the time of writing Mengistu continues to live in Zimbabwe under the protection of the Mugabe regime.

The roaring fire threw out as much heat as light as a small crowd of us huddled round it on the ground. It was well past midnight and a light breeze was blowing off the lake at Langano, where we had decamped from Addis for the weekend.

I had hitched a ride with some of Chris Purdy's friends, who had a four-wheel-drive, and a spare room in one of the houses that had been built by the Derg on the edge of the lake. They had all retired early, but I was restless and had gone for a walk along the lake shore. As I passed one of the larger villas a couple of Ethiopians, who were heading to the villa from the opposite direction invited me to join them. This was typical of weekend life at the lake. Langano became one big social occasion where whatever you were doing, everyone was welcome, especially if you were a lone *ferenji*.

The villa was surrounded by a wall of corrugated iron sheets that had been hammered into the earth. Two doors, which were made from the same corrugated sheeting which were framed with bare wood poles, stood open like outstretched hands in a gesture of welcome. There must have been anything up to forty people inside the compound, a mixture of young *ferenjis* and Ethiopians. Normally, walking by the lake late at night, you couldn't hear yourself think for the cacophony made by the cicadas, and other creepy-crawlies, that turned the surrounding acacia forest into a nocturnal orchestra pit of insect nightlife. But tonight, they stood no chance next to the deep throbbing reggae beats that came from the villa.

Someone thrust a cold bottle of beer into my hand and I joined a group who had gravitated to the fire. Dried out acacia logs crackled in an old oil drum that had been sliced down the middle to make an impromptu grate that looked like a trough, propped up on stones. A glowing ember was spat up into the air as the fierce heat of the flames split one of the logs. It rose up into the air in front of me, lifted by a thermal of searing heat. My eyes followed it and were pulled steadily heavenwards to where a starscape of twinkling light filled the entire night sky, before disappearing into infinity, where the stars merged into a far flung pale blue wash in the deepest reaches where the naked eye could no longer fathom.

"Aid is what's killing Africa," said a young Ethiopian, pulling me back to earth with a jolt. "It breeds dependency. Every time I see another rock star doing another mercy trip to some war torn or devastated country in Africa it makes me want to throw up. These jerks are only making the problem worse."

The guy who was speaking was Ethiopian, but judging by his accent he had clearly spent his formative years in the United States. Chances were he was either a returnee, one of the young professionals whose parents had left in fear of their lives when the Derg came to power, or an NGO worker. Or more than likely both.

A young blond woman in her mid twenties rose to the challenge. She wore a sweatshirt which bore the words Stanford University, and she sat with her arms wrapped round her knees which were tucked up to her chest.

"So are we just supposed to ignore famine and death," she asked, "especially if we come from rich countries and can do something about it."

"Look," the man said, "the more foreign rock stars look like they're the ones taking Africa's problems on their shoulders, the less Africans will face up to their own problems themselves. And if we're going to have long term, sustainable development, it has to come from inside, not outside."

"Everyone recognises that," she replied, "but until African governments are corruption free, and people are educated and democracy can take root, and all that is going to take time, there are going to be problems that aren't going to go away for a long while, like AIDS, women's rights, economic development..."

"But foreign aid isn't solving these problems," her adversary interrupted her, "don't you see, it's only making them worse. By plugging the gap it takes away the need for Africa to be more self-reliant. It breeds a dependency culture, not one of self-sufficiency."

Arguments like this were not uncommon when NGO workers got together, especially when they included Ethiopians and other Africans, and they all touched on Live Aid at some point. It didn't take long for this discussion to do so either.

"So Live Aid was a bad idea then," the girl countered with, "and Bob Geldof has been bad for Ethiopia."

"Yes and No," he replied. "You ask a *ferenji* about Live Aid and they get all proud that they did something for starving Ethiopians. And that's true, Live Aid saved a lot of lives. But you ask an Ethiopian what he thinks of Live Aid and he will say that it has created a problem Ethiopia has been living with for years."

"How do you mean?" she said.

"If Ethiopia is going to make its way in the world, we will have to do it by our own efforts. That means economic growth, foreign investment to help develop our resources, we need trade not aid. But you say Ethiopia to anyone in the West and the only image they have of my country is starving people and children with match stick limbs. Live Aid continues to define my country in the eyes of the world as a sort of basket case country," he said shaking his head, "and who's going to invest in that?"

"But that's not Live Aid's fault. Live Aid didn't create the famine, and anyway since then there have been a lot of positive initiatives as a result of Live Aid that are helping to build the capacity to deliver the self-sufficiency you're talking about."

The argument was heated but never boiled over into being confrontational. It was as if each one of them knew deep down that the other one had a point and that they were really approaching the same problem from two different perspectives.

For the next half hour their argument ranged over most of the entire aid and development landscape and took in good governance, microfinance, remittances, even digital technology, because Africa had been fast to adopt new developments like mobile phones. Omar, one day, had summed it up best for me when he said, "Look at the taxi drivers in Addis, the one who is always busy has a mobile phone, and the one who sits by the side of the road all day doesn't." He was right, technology was playing just as important a role in transforming peoples' fortunes in the African Rift Valley as it was in the Silicone one. But sitting by the camp fire, listening to the complex arguments swirl over around my head, I felt like the little girl in the white dress I gave a few coins to every morning on my walk to Gem TV.

As they continued to debate the rights and wrongs of aid and development as they saw it, my mind wandered back to a summer's day in 1985 when, like millions all over the world, I tuned into Live Aid.

Live Aid was pioneering. Nothing even remotely like it had ever been attempted before. It broke new ground in all sorts of ways and like any new initiative there wasn't a rule book to follow. But while the rest of the world's important institutions sat on their respective hands, a bunch of hairy-arsed rock stars got off theirs and did something about what they saw as being a terrible injustice. And make no mistake, Live Aid saved hundreds of thousands of lives. For me, despite having solely fallen in love with this most beguiling of countries, I also looked at the Live Aid legacy in a broader context than just Ethiopia.

For many like me, Live Aid was a defining moment for an entire generation. Before Live Aid there was protest. After Live Aid there was activism. Before Live Aid there was government intervention. After Live Aid people power began to hold politicians to account. In shifting the dynamic of the relationship between people and the establishment, Live Aid changed the way people saw the problems of poverty and the developing world. Live Aid also changed the face of campaigning. There isn't a social movement post 1985, be it HIV/AIDS, climate change or human rights that doesn't owe some sort of debt to Live Aid. Live Aid showed the way. It created an explosion of worthy imitators all over the world. In the UK they include Comic Relief, Red Nose Day, Children in Need, Sport Aid, Red, One, the list goes on, and it's hard to imagine any of them existing without Live Aid. Live Aid created a new culture in our society, one of caring and giving, and of mutual responsibility on a global scale. And it spread all the way from the stage to the boardroom via the playground and more latterly, the blog and the tweet. Live Aid has also made us look at the politics of aid and development more closely than ever before, and perhaps this will be one of Live Aid's most enduring legacies.

To this day Live Aid continues to provoke arguments and discussions, and not just around camp fires but in the marble halls of the United Nations and the World Bank. Live Aid has always had its fair share of critics, and I don't know enough to answer these criticisms. But I do have a belief. And it's one that was defined by Theodore Roosevelt in 1920. "It is not the critic who counts, not the man who points out how the strong man stumbles, or where the doer of deeds could have done them better. The credit belongs to the man who is actually in the arena, whose face is marred by dust and sweat and blood, who strives valiantly, who errs and comes short again and again, because there is not effort without error and shortcomings, but who does actually strive to do the deed, who knows the great enthusiasm, the great devotion, who spends himself in a worthy cause, who at the best knows in the triumph of high achievement, and who at the worst, if he fails, at least he fails by doing greatly. So that his place shall never be with those cold and timid souls who know neither victory or defeat."

On August 13th, 1985, while the politicians and the establishment sat on their hands a couple of rock stars called Bob Geldof and Midge Ure got off their backsides and tried to do something about famine and poverty. For one glorious summer's day at Wembley Stadium they, together, actually became *the man in the arena*.

# SIXTEEN

# Cutaway to Sister Mulu

Sister Mulu was another subject of our Gemini film, but unlike the others she wasn't a beneficiary, she was the nurse who ran Gemini's health centre. A pleasant looking woman in a spotlessly clean white coat, we interviewed her on camera in the main Gemini compound. It occupied an area of slightly under half an acre on a ridge next to a sprawling market. The rooms and offices were shipping containers placed on top of one another which made the compound look like it had been made from giant versions of children's building blocks.

Adanech showed me round the compound stopping frequently to be greeted by various women who recognised her and kissed her on both cheeks, or took both of her hands in theirs. Slowly we made our way from shipping container to shipping container. Each one had been cleaned and painted inside. The first group of containers Adanech took me to were the offices. Inside desks had been crammed into the tight spaces and people were sitting working at rudimentary computers. Another container housed the nursery. Here a group of Gemini mothers, all identically dressed in blue house coats, played with or nursed infants, many of which were twins. The walls had been painted in bright colours and were covered with hand painted renditions of giraffes, lions and monkeys, and other animals just like any nursery you would find anywhere. The women smiled shyly and nodded their heads in greeting at us as their charges giggled and crawled across the floor, or played with the toys that had been donated.

Across the compound from the nursery, Adaench led me to another rusting container. Inside a dozen or more Gemini mothers sat weaving long strands of straw, which their nimble fingers fashioned into intricate colourful patterns. In the corner a small pile of finished baskets stood testimony to their skill and artisanship. Outside a lean-to had been erected onto the side of the container, and here a group of three women pounded away with long pieces of wood at a pot at their feet grinding spices, which were sold at various *ferenji* supermarkets dotted around Addis Ababa, under the Gemini label. In another container three women were bent over old fashioned sewing machines repairing clothes and fashioning new outfits to sell. As well as being a feeding, health and education centre, the Gemini compound was a hive of small scale, income generating activity.

The medical centre, if you could call it that, was another pair of shipping containers. One served as a waiting room and a dozen women sat with young children wriggling on their laps patiently waiting their turn. Just then the door to the connecting container opened and a woman in a spotlessly clean, starched white coat, and with a stethoscope draped round her shoulders, emerged.

She exchanged "Selams" with Adanech before she turned to me and appraised me with calm, kind eyes that I imagined had seen more than their fair share of sickness and grief. Sister Mulu then led us into her consulting room and told us her story.

## Sister Mulu's story

My name is Mulunesh Aga. I am a nurse and I run the Health and Nutrition clinic. I have worked here for fifteen years. I came here soon after my husband died. I used to work at the Black Lion Hospital. But it was difficult to raise my children on my own with the money that the government used to pay me. Some friends of mine knew about Gemini and that they needed a nurse. So I put in my application. I knew Dr Carmela and she knew that I'd worked as a paediatric nurse so I was hired.

In my second or third year here a one year old weighing only three kilos came into the clinic. I was shocked. In fourteen years working in paediatrics at the Black Lion Hospital I had never seen such a thing. I never expected the child to survive. I tried to refer the child to Black Lion Hospital but the mother refused to go there. So I prepared a plastic pipe, inserted it into the child's nose and fed him egg and milk mixed together. The child didn't die and he is now in fourth or fifth grade in elementary school. I am delighted to have been involved in such a task. But treating a three kilogrammes child is unbelievable and I am amazed that the child survived.

One day a six year old child came to the medical centre on his own and told me that he couldn't come with his mother because she had to go to her job making injera. To receive medical service at a hospital or health centre a child has to be accompanied by a parent. At first, I didn't accept a child if he or she was not accompanied by a parent, because sometimes the child can't explain the problem clearly. But after I under-stood that the parents have to work and cannot come with the children, so now we help them without their parents. But we check if the child has provided correct information otherwise we cannot give them medication. Anyway, I asked him what is the problem? He said that his throat aches. When I examined his throat I realised his tonsils were infected, which meant I had to give him a penicillin injection. This is bad on an empty stomach so I asked him if he had eaten breakfast, and he asked me back, "What is breakfast?" So you can guess how poor his family was. So I had to give him one birr to go and get something to eat, just so he could have the injection and get well.

Then came HIV/AIDS. So I talked with Dr. Carmela and suggested that we should do something. The awareness of the people was low. There were cultural hurdles too. And if people found out they had the disease they would be at risk of losing their jobs and their homes. So we eventually started this program, but we have lost many of the first ones. But even though this program was a small one, many lives have been saved.

I remember just as antiretroviral drugs came into use, a mother came to me from Sebeta, which is on the outskirts of Addis Ababa. She was so weak she couldn't sit and when she came into my office she collapsed. I took her to hospital where she tested positive for HIV. She needed to start ARV therapy straight away. But coming from Sebeta she couldn't get the drugs from Addis Ababa, she had to go back. I was told to take her to Debre Zeit, a town about forty kilometres from Addis. But how could I? She was so weak. I had a big argument with the hospital and told them she is very small and too weak and she will probably die if I try and take her to Debre Zeit. Finally, the staff gave in and she started the ARV drugs there. Now she is in the Credit and Saving scheme of Gemini and her life has changed dramatically. She is very happy now. There are many similar examples. But the survival of the three kilogrammes boy, and the woman from Sebata, these are the best moments of my life here.

# SEVENTEEN

# Belafiga

The plane came into land on a bare earth runway. My hands gripped the armrest as we bounced to a halt. The pilot cut the engines and the propellers slowed to grey spinning discs. I looked out of my window at a dilapidated shack. It doubled as both the arrivals and departures terminal.

Tafari Kajela, Oxfam's Regional Manager in Asossa, was there to meet us. Adanech, Teddy and I clambered into his four-wheel-drive and ten minutes later we arrived in the town.

My time working with Gem TV was drawing to a close. They didn't need trainers any more, they were now highly competent film-makers. But before I left there was one job still to do which gave me the opportunity to see a very different way of life. Gem TV had been asked by Oxfam to make a documentary about their work supporting alternative basic education in the region. We were on a recce to research the subject and look at possible locations. Before we left Addis Ababa I looked up Asossa, or at least tried to. There were three guide books in the guest house but only one of them mentioned the place, which was surprising given it's the state capital of the vast Beneshangul region, which lies on Ethiopia's western border with Sudan. It was a short entry, just four words: No hotel. No hospital.

By leaving Addis Ababa we had dropped a couple of thousand metres and the heat was sweltering. Asossa, at first glance, was run-down and dirty. It looked like it wasn't just the children's education that had been forgotten about in this part of the world. The whole place seemed to have been largely written off by all concerned. But not quite, Oxfam was one of a small number of NGOs trying to do something about the region's development. Not much seemed to be happening in town. People wandered aimlessly or sat under the shade of mango trees. The only people in Asossa who seemed to be working were a few women selling mouldy fruit and vegetables from blankets spread on the dirt, and men driving donkeys loaded with firewood. Once again, there was no escaping the unmistakable aroma of the open sewer.

Despite what the guide book said there was a hotel though, of sorts. My room consisted of a bed with a dirty mattress and a couple of blankets. The only other furniture was a wooden table and a stool. The mosquito mesh over the window had holes in it I could put my fist through, and the broken tiled floor was covered in a red, earthy dust that drifted in through the gap under the door. As I sat on the bed, which creaked under my weight, I gazed down and there staring back up at me was a cockroach the size of a small rodent. Its twin antennae twirled slowly in the fetid air.

The bathroom was a trough in the compound which was fed by a large barrel of water above it. The *shintabet*, or toilet, was a hole-in-the-ground squat job that everyone used. It was housed out the back and stood cheek by jowl next to the hut that was the kitchen. The *shintabet* was a tin shack that you could hear buckle and ping as it expanded in the blistering heat of the sun, and the buzz of flies that echoed from it was a constant hum. Inside, great clods of cobwebs hung down from the roof like Miss Haversham's drapes. It was dark inside so you had no idea what else was sharing it with you. One of the most frightening moments I've ever experienced was in the middle of the night, squatting on my haunches, jeans around my ankles, one hand gingerly pressed against the wall to retain my balance, the other clamped over my nose and mouth, when I heard a slithering behind me. This is the stuff they don't tell you at aid worker school. The Dashen Hotel was to be home for a week. It was the shithole at the arse end of the world.

Next morning, thankfully, there wasn't a queue for the *shintabet*. Like a swimmer preparing to do a width underwater, I took a couple of deep breaths, held my breath and pushed the creaking metal door open. A minute later I emerged red-faced and gasping for air. Then I stood in line for the bathroom. The water trough stood in the middle of the compound surrounded by mango trees and at that hour in the morning the air was fresh and cool. I joined a line of half a dozen others holding plastic bowls and clutching slivers of soap that were bright blue and had a gritty feel when you scrubbed up a lather. We took it in turns to fill our bowls and wash ourselves from head to toe as best we could with the small amount of water available. I created something of a stir when I produced a toothbrush. The others cleaned their teeth with *mafagya*, twigs that had been stripped of their bark at one end and the wood pulped to make a natural toothbrush. People in the countryside cut them from bushes growing wild, and I had often seen *mafagya* being sold on street corners in Addis Ababa.

"Did you sleep well?" asked Adanech.

"Fine thanks," I lied. "Have you seen Teddy?"

"He is waiting for us outside."

Teddy was sitting on a pile of old tyres outside the hotel sucking the last vestiges of life out of a cigarette.

"There are only two places to have breakfast," he said.

He led the way across the street. There wasn't much to choose between them. They were both run-down and crowded with men. I never saw a single woman in either of these places all the time we were there, apart from Adanech, and I suspect she only entered them to look after me. This was good of her because being a young woman from Addis Ababa, she attracted a great deal of unwanted attention. We chose one and the owner, a fat man who wore a heavily stained blue housecoat, decided we were important enough to look after us personally. The only thing on the menu was *fool*, an eggy, milky porridge spiked with hot spices and running in melted butter, served with a bread roll. One dunk was enough for me and I passed it over to Teddy who greedily demolished a second bowlful. The saving grace of the place was the owner's pride and joy, an old Gaggia coffee-making machine that hissed and belched in the corner and bravely struggled to keep up with the early morning demand. The one thing the Beneshangul region did produce that I could eat was mangoes. It looked like I was going to have to live off them for lunch and dinner as well. A few minutes later Tafari appeared with his driver to take us to the village.

"We are working with twelve communities here," Tafari told us as we drove out of Asossa. Tafari was tall and big and quietly spoken. He had an air of calm about him that matched his quiet authority. He was Oromo and his English was excellent. Some years earlier Oxfam had sent him to do a management course at Bradford University. It felt strange to share reminiscences with this tall, dark Oromo who chatted happily about Malham Tarn and Gordale Scar as we drove across a dry, flat, scrubby landscape dotted with mango trees and stands of bamboo. We soon got down to business.

"One of the Millennium Development Goals is that every child has a right to quality education," Tafari explained. "But in Ethiopia there are six million children who do not go to school. And over sixty per cent of them are girls."

The problem was the state run education system didn't have the resources to cover the whole country, and it was the people on the most extreme fringes that lost out. It was hard to imagine anywhere in Ethiopia that was more isolated than Beneshangul.

"So where does Oxfam fit in?" I asked him.

"We help provide alternative basic education. This gives children the basics up to grade five."

We headed further west towards the Sudan border, and it wasn't long before we drove through the first of the refugee camps.

"They are Christians who have fled the Muslims in Sudan," said Tafari. "It's strange, because here in Beneshangul the people are Muslim, but there isn't a problem."

As we drove through the camp I spotted the sign boards of different aid agencies: UNHCR (United Nations High Commission for Refugees), Save the Children, USAID and the rest. We drove on until the road simply disappeared. Mohammed, our driver, negotiated our way along tracks that had been made by children herding goats. We crossed dried up riverbeds and each time the land cruiser would plunge into steep, rocky V-shaped clefts, before Mohammed would coax it up the other side; the engine howling in protest as the tyres fought for grip and the land cruiser bucked and bounced over jagged rocks and slid into powdery soft sand. Parched plains gave way to seas of tall grass that rose as high as the land cruiser's roof. Somehow Mohammed steered a course through the swaying wall of pale yellow grass until the curtain parted to reveal a village of twenty or so stick and mud huts. Women watched us with deadpan eyes as they stood outside their huts pounding maize with logs that they lifted with both hands.

"The village we are visiting is called Belafiga," Tafari had to shout to be heard above the roaring of the four-wheel-drive as Mohammed crunched it into in low gear to tackle another steep rise. "The people are Berta," he continued, "they are farmers who have lived here for hundreds of years. They are Muslim, so in many ways they are more like Sudanese people than Ethiopians."

"How did you find them in all this?" I asked as the four-wheel-drive was swallowed up by another sea of tall, willowy grass that engulfed the vehicle like a fog and reduced our speed to walking pace.

"We didn't. It was their idea to build a school and they came to us for help."

"What exactly did you do?" I asked him.

"We gave them some money for building materials, but the men of the village did all the work building the school. We also help by paying part of the teacher's salary and help plan the curriculum."

"Who pays for the rest of the teacher's salary?" I asked.

"The community again, everyone in the village donates some of their maize to be sold at market, and that money goes to help the running of the school. It's a big sacrifice for them."

Circular huts stood on the outskirts of the village, which was bigger than other ones we had passed. Their walls were made of sticks, lashed together with tree bark and plastered with mud and dung. Entire families lived in these one-room dwellings, together with their few goats and chickens, and there was no electricity. The earth was baked hard and fissured with cracks. There were no oxen to pull ploughs, so to grow crops the men had to break the ground with tools that had remained largely unchanged since Cain murdered Abel with one.

As we drove further into the village it was eerily quiet. Mohammed parked the land cruiser and we got out and stretched aching limbs. Dogs snoozed in the shade. A distant sound began to build. A high-pitched, banshee wailing filled the air as hundreds of villagers appeared. In a matter of seconds we were completely engulfed. The women were striking in shawls of dazzling designs and colours. Young men played flutes, their deep, woody notes counter-pointing the women's shrill ululations. Swept up by this wave, we were escorted into the village in a singing, clapping procession.

"Does this happen every time you come here?" I asked Tafari.

"No," he replied with a hint of a smile, "you are the first white person ever to come to this village. Many of these people have never seen a white man before."

I was stunned. I didn't think that places like this still existed in Africa in this day and age. It wasn't as if these people were that remote looking, like the lip plate wearing Mursi people of the Omo valley in southern Ethiopia, but then the Mursi were on the tourist map. Nobody ever came to Beneshangul because there was nothing here except for desperately poor farmers and refugees.

It was easy to spot the school. Unlike the round huts that surrounded it, the school was square and it had a corrugated iron roof. We were ushered inside where a teacher stood in front of a class of about fifty children of mixed ages. The only source of light was the sunlight that streamed in from the windows that had been cut into the walls. There were no desks; the children sat on wooden benches or on the floor. The only other item in the room was a blackboard. Tafari greeted the teacher, a young man, and introduced me to him. The sight of a *ferenji* in their midst had made the class go completely silent.

"They want you to speak," said Tafari, "say something please so they can hear your voice, I will translate for the teacher and he will tell them."

"You mean you don't speak their language," I replied.

"No, they have their own language, but the teacher speaks Orominya so he can translate."

"I am from England," I said, but this was completely lost in translation for the simple reason that they had never heard of England and had no idea where or what it was. The school didn't have a map of the world so I drew my own version on the blackboard and showed them where I came from. The looks on their faces told me they didn't have any notion of what I was talking about. I could have been from another planet. All they knew was that I was a strange man from outside, but they had no idea of what outside was, where it was, how big it was or how different it was. Having failed completely to make any connection whatsoever, the teacher rescued me by getting them to show me their writing skills.

One by one he called some of the elder children, who ranged from about five to fifteen, up to the front of the class to write their names on the blackboard. Each time one of them wrote their name and stepped back the room burst into rounds of applause, and no one clapped louder than me. A little girl, who must have been one of the youngest, sat in the front row. She had a chubby face and her hair was tied in two clumps at the side of her head with a couple of faded red ribbons. Even though she wore a torn dress, her parents took great pride in sending her to school looking her best. Throughout the name writing session she was desperate to show what she could do. Every time the teacher scanned the class for another volunteer she stretched her arm above her head as high as she could and her eyes bore into the teacher like twin lasers. But being so small the tips of her fingers didn't even reach the shoulders of her class-mates. Every time the teacher selected another one to come forward she would whip round and stare daggers at them as they walked up to the blackboard.

When the teacher decided the class had demonstrated enough name writing, big wet tears welled up in big brown eyes. I gestured for her to come forward. At first, she looked away, but the rest of the class had seen me and they started calling out to her. She shot a nervous look at the teacher but he smiled back and said something, encouraging enough to make her take a few hesitant steps forward. I leant down and held out the piece of chalk which she took from my hand the way a wild cub takes food for the first time from a trainer. But disaster – the blackboard was half way up the wall and the only blank space that the other children had left was right at the top, out of her reach. She looked up at me and the tears that had welled up in her eyes lost their grip and trickled down her face leaving wet tracks in grimy cheeks.

Without giving it a second thought I bent down and scooped her up and lifted her so that she could reach the top of the blackboard. She ig-nored the burst of laughter that rang out around the classroom, and with a look of fierce concentration on her face, the pink point of her tongue sticking out between her lips, she slowly wrote out her name, letter by careful letter. When she finished she turned her face, looked me fearlessly in the eye from a matter of a few inches, and her stern features broke into a beautiful smile. I put her down and joined in the applause that accom-panied her back to her seat.

"She is the only one in her family who can spell her name," Tafari told me. "In three years time, if she keeps coming to school, she will get a certificate. It will be the proudest day of her parents' lives."

Next we played a game. Tafari had a torch in the land cruiser and Mohammed was sent to fetch it. Meanwhile, I asked for the shutters over the windows to be closed, pitching the classroom into darkness. I had remembered a famous advertising campaign from the early 1980s for an insurance company called the Prudential. It featured people played by actors talking about what they wanted out of life, and it ended with a slogan that said something like, "Whatever you want to be, you'll want to be with Prudential". With Tafari and the teacher doing the two-stage translating, I flicked the torch on and shone it at a face in the back of the classroom and said, "Doctor". Then I picked out another face with the torch and said "Hotel manager". One by one I went round the class, favouring the girls, saying, "Mechanic", "Pilot", "Footballer", "Musician", "Teacher". They quickly got the gist of it and very soon the whole class was shouting out suggestions each time the beam of my torch lit up a laughing face. Then at the end I told them that whatever they wanted to be, they would need an education and should work very hard at school. But before I brought the game to a close, the last face I lit up was of a little girl in the front row with twin tear tracks on her cheeks. I pointed the torch at her and said, "Writer".

I was curious to know what the benefits of having an education were in a place like this. It wasn't as if having an education would secure you a good job, because there weren't any to be had.

"You can't have sustainable development without education," said Tafari, "and you can't teach new ways of doing things without it. This applies especially to health education and sanitation, and training people in improved farming techniques. Without education these initiatives simply won't take root."

I suspected there was also another, more fundamental reason and I had seen it in close-up a few moments earlier etched into the face of a little girl. With an education behind you, you can look the world square in the eye and say I'm not ignorant. It's a simple matter of human dignity.

"Now, let us show you the well," said Tafari as we filed outside, "it's just as important as the school". Ahead of us women carried earthenware water pots on their heads or plastic jerry cans.

"Water is very scarce," said Tafari, "before the well was built, it took three or four hours to walk to the nearest stream or water hole, and even longer to carry the water back."

He explained that fetching water is a job for young girls, and if they are spending all day fetching and carrying water then they can't go to school. So there was no point in building a school if the village didn't have a well nearby. So Oxfam had been working hand-in-hand with Water Aid who helped the village build a well. And there were other considerations. Fetching water was dangerous for young girls. Many of them became victims of rape, or were abducted by the men of other villages and forced into marriage. Then there was the sanitation issue. Rivers and water holes are shared with animals that pollute the water with urine and defecate nearby, which leaks into the water causing serious health risks.

"Thousands of children die in Ethiopia every day because of unsafe drinking water," said Tafari as we approached the well, "cholera and diarrhoea are the biggest killers."

The well was a simple affair. A borehole had been drilled to a depth of ten metres into an aquifer and capped with a concrete plinth. The pump was worked by a long metal arm that the women lifted up and down. They chatted and laughed as fresh, clean, burbling water gushed out of a large standpipe. Then, with full water pots mounted on their heads, they ambled back to the village like a waddling line of gaudily coloured ducklings, still jabbering and laughing. What had just taken them fifteen minutes used to take their daughters the best part of a day, and one that was fraught with danger. They also knew that the precious water they were bringing into their homes wouldn't make their families sick or kill their children.

For people who had next to nothing their hospitality was without equal. We were invited to lunch. Once again we found ourselves being swept along in another human current of clapping, singing people. They led us to the village meeting place. It had no walls, just a patchy roof of thatch supported by wood poles, but it created an oasis of shade beneath the blistering sun. If I reached up above my head I could have touched the roof of dried grass without having to fully extend my arm. The whole village had gathered, and those who weren't deemed important enough to sit on the floor in the shade crowded outside. They stood in rows like soldiers on parade, oblivious to the heat that hammered down. Goats roamed unattended, ploughing tools lay idle, and even the thump, thump, thump of the women grinding grain, the rhythmic heartbeat of African village life, had fallen silent.

Our small party was afforded pride of place next to the village elders. I was dreading this because if Asossa couldn't serve up an edible meal what chance had Belafiga? First we were served a drink made from the crushed leaves of a local plant. It was dark red in colour and tasted like a sweet version of redcurrant and was delicious and thirst quenching. Then the main meal arrived, chunks of coarse baked bread accompanied by a bowl of brown, runny slops. There was no way I was going to offend these people by not eating their food. I tore off a piece of bread, dunked it into the slops, and put it in my mouth. Much to my surprise it tasted delicious.

"You like the *shiro*, Bob?" asked Tafari.

"It's very good. What is it?"

"It's made from lentils, which are crushed and cooked into a porridge with some herbs and a little spices."

"It's very good. Can I get it in Asossa?" I asked hopefully.

"No," said Tafari shaking his head, "this is something only the country people make."

Just then an old man slowly rose to his feet. He was dressed like all the other men in the village in western hand-me-down clothes. He wore a dark pin-striped jacket that could have had accompanied its original owner into the City every day, from Surrey or Hertfordshire or some other commuter belt enclave, before it had been retired to a High Street charity shop in Cheam or Tring. It hung ill-fitting and loose on his meagre frame, and only the tips of his fingers extended beyond the end of the sleeves. The trousers didn't match and were tied around his waist with string. They flapped around spindly legs like sails in a stiff breeze. Beneath the jacket he wore a white shirt that had faded to grey with age and over washing, and on his feet a pair of dusty leather sandals. Tufts of frizzled, white hair poked out from under a Muslim cap, and underneath it his features were sharp, chiselled from a life of unrelenting hard work; scraping a meagre existence out of the cracked and barren earth that stretched all the way to the Sudan border that shimmered in the heat haze on the horizon. When he opened his mouth to speak his teeth were yellow and gapped. Everyone fell silent.

His voice was strong and clear, belying his age and physical frailty, and as he continued his words were punctuated with murmurs of agreement. He was talking about the school.

Tafari leaned across. "Bob, they want to know what will happen when you return to make the film. Will you say a few words?"

"I'll be gone by then," I said. "Adanech will be coming back with the crew, so she should speak."

I turned to Adanech beside me and spoke quietly so as not to distract attention from the old man. "Adi, the people want to know what will happen when you come back to shoot the film, so you need to explain to them."

Adanech shifted uneasily. The prospect of addressing all the assembled villagers clearly terrified her. She touched me lightly on the arm and her dark brown eyes filled with a mixture of fear and pleading. "Bobbi-eh," she said, using the familiar form that I had eventually earned, and which she well knew would normally wrap me round her little finger, "I think it is better if you talk to them."

"But Adi, I won't be coming back. You will be directing the film with these people, so you have to speak."

She nodded her head in agreement. I knew that if Adanech spoke now it would establish her authority when she returned for the shoot. I also had another reason I wanted her to speak. I had been in Ethiopia long enough to know that people had seen more than their fair share of pale-faced westerners telling them what to do. Here was an opportunity for an Ethiopian to take the lead role for once, and if she just so happened to be a young woman, so much the better.

"What should I say?" Adanech asked nervously.

"Tell them what the film is about. Explain that by making the film, they'll be helping people all over the country just like them to educate their children."

The old man finished speaking and hundreds of pairs of eyes swivelled in our direction. Adanech was a figure of curiosity for the villagers. A city girl, dressed in tight blue jeans and wearing a black, figure-hugging knitted top, her hair was cut short and styled. These people had never seen an Ethiopian like her. Adanech looked almost as foreign to them as I did. She reached into her bag and pulled out a plum coloured scarf, and arranged it so that it covered her head and her bare arms, out of respect for their Muslim tradition. Ironically, it made her look like an African Madonna. Tafari translated her Amharic into Orominya and the teacher again translated Tafari's Orominya into the local language. In this three stage form of translation, Adanech explained that in a few weeks time she would return to the village and make a film about how the people had built a school for their children. She explained to them that the film would be shown to the Ethiopian government, and to other remote communities in the hope of inspiring education for all children in Ethiopia. As I listened, the telltale fire of her passion began to flare in her voice, which strengthened as she warmed to her subject.

Adanech was supposed to have spent her life selling *kolo* on the streets of Mercato. Instead, here she was addressing an entire village that lived on the remotest fringe of Ethiopia; telling them how the film she was going to make would help thousands of other people just like them. Watching her grow in confidence before my eyes, I thought of Andrew who had first had the idea of Gem TV and had battled so valiantly to get it off the ground. I thought of Carmela, who took the fledgling film school under the wing of Gemini and of her unwavering belief in Ethiopian youth. I thought of Bill Locke, who had recruited the Gem TV film-makers by getting them to tell him their stories. I thought of Wonde telling Bill how he had first come to Addis Ababa, hitching a ride in the back of a truck full of wounded soldiers. I thought of all the volunteer trainers who had come out over the years: the camera operators, sound recordists, video editors, script-writers and directors who had given of their time and energy to pass on their film-making skills. And I wondered if any of them had been as lucky as I was at that moment, witnessing the fruits of all that hard work, as Adanech held an entire village spellbound, sharing with them the vision of the film she was going to make.

Adanech waited for Tafari's and the teacher's translations to finish, and then with a respectful bow to her audience she sat down. Her relief was palpable.

"Adi-eh, you spoke very well," I said.

"Thank you," she said with a smile.

We left Belafiga the same way as we had arrived, the whole village singing and clapping as they accompanied us in procession to Mohammed's four-wheel-drive. We were subdued on the drive back to Asossa, each one of us content to enjoy the silence and our own thoughts. We had just spent a day amongst some of the poorest people on earth. I have never met more generous and more cultured people in my life. The faces I had seen in the school reminded me of the faces that stared through the window of the cafe at me when we made the first DKT commercial. Only this time their faces registered hope. I turned to look at Adanech sitting across from me in the land cruiser. Her face was half-turned to the window and she too was lost in thought. A few hours earlier I had looked across at her in the classroom. Then, her eyes had darted with quick-fire intelligence, working out sequences, looking for set-ups and camera angles, and noticing where the light fell through the windows. While I had been entertaining the children, the girl from Mercato had quietly taken control. When she returned in a few weeks time with the other Gem TV film-makers, together they would make a film that would inspire communities all over the country. I wouldn't be there to witness the making of the film, but I knew it would go well. And I knew that it would all begin when Adanech said … "Jemuru".

# EIGHTEEN

# Ethiopia Reflection

Gibbon, in *The Decline and Fall of the Roman Empire*, wrote, "*Encompassed on all sides by the enemies of its religion, the Aethiopians slept near a thousand years, forgetful of the world by whom they were forgotten.*" It is only relatively recently that Ethiopia has roused itself from its self-imposed slumber, and emerged blinking into the harsh light of a globalized world.

Today, Ethiopia finds itself standing at a crossroads as it struggles to redefine itself in the modern era. Its many diverse peoples speak eighty different languages and live very different ways of life. The Oromo are the most populous ethnic group and hail from the south as well as the central highlands where they are farmers and pastoralists. On the Kenya borderlands the Borena people herd their cattle as they have for generations, shifting their small villages of huts whenever the search for new grazing demands. The Borena people see the universe as a chain, the five links being the Sky, Rain for water, Earth for pasture, Animals for livestock and *Geda*, the strict social system under which the Borena live and which regulates disputes and promotes living in harmony with the natural environment. The Konso people number less than a quarter of a million and farm the slopes of the Rift Valley south of Lake Chamo in banks of terraces, and commemorate their dead with striking stelae sculptures. The Lower Omo Valley is home to the most striking of ethnic peoples. Here the Mursi, Karo, Hamar and Desanech, amongst others, live ways of life herding livestock that have remained untouched by time for centuries. Their culture and traditions belong to a forgotten world. The Karo paint their bodies in chalky white, and young Hamar women scar their bodies and wear goatskin skirts elaborately decorated with cowrie shells, while watching their young men jump over the backs of oxen to prove their worthiness as husbands. In the far north, Mekele, the capital of the region of Tigray, is a busy and thriving city. Even so, in the spice market, the camel trains of the warlike Afar people continue to arrive bearing blocks of salt, hewn from the vast geological cauldron that is the Danakil Depression. As well as being home to the Tigrayans, the north, as well as the central highlands, are home to the Amhara, the once rulers of Ethiopia. In stark contrast, Illubabor, which lies to the west and borders Sudan, is a tropical region of lush vegetation fed by the Baro River and the rain which falls for eight months of the year, and where the flora explodes with colourful blooms and flowering shrubs. Traditionally, the Anuak people live by fishing while the Nuer raise cattle, their women resplendent in bright beaded necklaces, bone and ivory bangles, and with spike that pierces their bottom lips and stick out over their chins. To the east lies the medieval walled city of Harar, the fourth most holy city in the Muslim world. And in Addis Ababa, delegates from all over the continent, and beyond, descend on the African Union building in their shiny four-wheel-drives, confirming the city as the diplomatic capital of Africa. Lip plate wearers and mobile phone carriers, Ethiopia is a country of diverse people and dramatic contrasts, where a Harvard educated returnee still believes that a priest can cure you of an illness by drenching you in holy water and beating "the devil's sickness" out of you with a wooden crucifix. Ethiopia is like no other country on earth. Long may it remain so.

# Acknowledgements

**I** joined Gem TV five years after it was started. Having set up the film school, Andrew Coggins then went about recruiting numerous volunteer TV professionals who, over the years, generously gave of their time and experience to train the Gem TV film-makers. Those that went before me did all the hard work and made things very easy for me. In all my time working with Gem TV I was acutely aware that I was standing on giants' shoulders. The other group of people who made such a considerable contribution are all those volunteers who followed afterwards. The heroes now have a song. They include Bill Locke, Deborah Kingsland, Tracy Pallant, Harris Watts, Mike Andrews, Len Lurcuck, Dominique Chadwick, John Dower, Eli Bo, Ben Cole and Liz De Planta, James and Anne Marie, Sara Jolly, Diarmid Scrimshaw, Catherine Williams, Tim Arrowsmith, Sue Manning, Venus Easwaran and Eleni Mekuria. Plus the many others whose names I don't know to mention and to whom I offer my apologies. We owe each and every one of them a huge debt of gratitude, and the Gem TV film-makers have asked me to pass on their heartfelt thanks to every one of them.

I would like to thank BBC News and Current Affairs for allowing me to quote Michael Buerk's historic broadcast from the plain outside Korem, which appeared on the Six O'clock News, October 24th, 1985, and to quote Claire Bertshinger's remarks made on the Radio 4 programme Reunion, broadcast on 30th September, 2009. I am also greatly indebted to Mike Wooldridge of the BBC who shared with me not only his first-hand accounts of reporting the famine but also gave me invaluable insight into the events that led up to it. I would also like to thank Mike for his guidance and encouragement, Ethiopia also holds a special place in his heart. I also acknowledge my debt of gratitude to the authors of the Africa Watch Report, Evil Days: 30 Years of Famine and War in Ethiopia, published in 1991.

Thanks also go to Sarah Monaghan who gave me generous editorial advice in the early stages of writing *Jemuru*, together with my first readers Andie Gaul, Melanie Haslam and Natalie Walsh for their invaluable feedback. I'm also indebted to Boyd Raison, Julia Berg and Chris Moore who proof read the manuscript with great attention to detail and useful advice. Any mistakes are not theirs but mine.

Finally, I would like to say *Amasegnallo* to Selam, Adanech, Wonde, Habtamu, Fikirte, Kebebush, Sintayehu, Misrak, Saba, Wubit, Mehbratie, Tewedros and Shewaddy for rising to the challenge of becoming Ethiopia's first community film-makers, and for allowing me to play a small part in their remarkable achievement.

48192712R00153

Printed in Poland
by Amazon Fulfillment
Poland Sp. z o.o., Wrocław